VOLUME 634   MARCH 2011

THE ANNALS

of The American Academy of Political
and Social Science

PHYLLIS KANISS, *Executive Editor*

Race, Racial Attitudes, and Stratification Beliefs: Evolving Directions for Research and Policy

Special Editors:

MATTHEW O. HUNT
Northeastern University

GEORGE WILSON
University of Miami

Los Angeles | London | New Delhi
Singapore | Washington DC

THE ANNALS

Editorial Office: 202 S. 36th Street, Philadelphia, PA 19104-3806
For information about membership* (individuals only) and subscriptions (institutions), address:
SAGE Publications
2455 Teller Road
Thousand Oaks, CA 91320

For SAGE Publications: Allison Leung (Production) and Lori Hart (Marketing)

From India and South Asia,
write to:
SAGE PUBLICATIONS INDIA Pvt Ltd
B-42 Panchsheel Enclave, P.O. Box 4109
New Delhi 110 017
INDIA

From Europe, the Middle East,
and Africa, write to:
SAGE PUBLICATIONS LTD
1 Oliver's Yard, 55 City Road
London EC1Y 1SP
UNITED KINGDOM

*Please note that members of the Academy receive THE ANNALS with their membership.
International Standard Serial Number ISSN 0002-7162
International Standard Book Number ISBN 978-1-4129-9907-6 (Vol. 634, 2011) paper
International Standard Book Number ISBN 978-1-4129-9906-9 (Vol. 634, 2011) cloth
Manufactured in the United States of America. First printing, March 2011.

Please visit http://ann.sagepub.com and under the "More about this journal" menu on the right-hand side, click on the Abstracting/Indexing link to view a full list of databases in which this journal is indexed.

THE ANNALS

OF THE AMERICAN ACADEMY OF POLITICAL AND SOCIAL SCIENCE

Volume 634 March 2011

IN THIS ISSUE:

Race, Racial Attitudes, and Stratification Beliefs: Evolving Directions for Research and Policy

Special Editors: MATTHEW O. HUNT
GEORGE WILSON

FORKCOMING

Young Disadvantaged Men: Fathers, Families, Poverty, and Policy
Special Editors: TIMOTHY M. SMEEDING, IRWIN GARFINKEL,
and RONALD B. MINCY

The Power of Kinship: Patrimonial States in Global Perspective
Special Editors: JULIA ADAMS and MOUNIRA MAYA CHARRAD

Keywords: race; inequality; ideology; stratification beliefs; racial attitudes; policy

Introduction

By
MATTHEW O. HUNT
and
GEORGE WILSON

Despite Barack Obama's generally "race-neutral" campaign strategy and subsequent policy agenda, his election as the forty-fourth president of the United States has reinvigorated discussions of the meaning of race and the roles of racial discrimination and inequality in shaping the life chances of African Americans and other ethno-racial minorities (Ford 2009; Smith and King 2009). Some observers—particularly political conservatives and various proponents of a "color-blind" perspective and agenda—see Obama's election as further evidence of the country's transition to a "postracial" age (Schorr 2008; Williams 2008). Others are less sanguine, lamenting the Obama presidency's potential to divert public attention from the stark racial disparities still characterizing American society (Bonilla-Silva and Dietrich, this volume).

This debate over the implications of the Obama presidency occurs in an era when scholarly attention to the intersections of race, ideology, and inequality has been expanding in concert with the growing racial and ethnic diversity of American society. During the past several decades, sociologists, political scientists, and psychologists have led the way in addressing a wide range of issues

Matthew O. Hunt is an associate professor of sociology at Northeastern University. His primary research interests involve intersections of race/ethnicity, social psychology, and inequality in the United States. His work has appeared in the American Sociological Review, Social Forces, Social Psychology Quarterly, Social Science Quarterly, Du Bois Review, *and other publications.*

George Wilson is an associate professor of sociology at the University of Miami. His research interests focus on the institutional production of racial and ethnic inequality in the workplace and the social structural determinants of beliefs about the causes and consequences of racial and stratification ideology.

DOI: 10.1177/0002716210386161

ANNALS, *AAPSS*, 634, March 2011

concerning the roles of race, and its perceived importance, in the workings of the American stratification system. Examples of such work include (but are not limited to) analyses of intergroup prejudice (Bobo and Hutchings 1996; Oliver and Wong 2003) and various manifestations of a so-called "new racism" (Kinder and Sanders 1996; Sears, Sidanius, and Bobo 2000; Krysan 2000), beliefs about the availability of opportunity (Kluegel and Smith 1986) and lay explanations of socioeconomic and racial inequalities (Kluegel 1990; Hunt 2007), and the proliferation of a "color-blind" discourse in American society regarding opportunity and the causes of inequalities (Krysan and Lewis 2006; Bonilla-Silva 2006).

Such work stems from two primary, and sometimes overlapping, scholarly domains: racial attitudes and stratification beliefs. *Racial attitudes* research focuses on the antecedents and consequences of beliefs about race, racial prejudice, and racial policy support (Krysan 2000; Schuman et al. 1997). *Stratification beliefs* research focuses on beliefs about the causes of social and economic inequalities (including patterns by race) and the implications of such for relevant public policies (Kluegel and Smith 1980, 1986). Scholarship in these two areas has incorporated "race" in two primary ways: as a *predictor*, focusing on how race/ethnic group membership shapes patterns of adherence to various ideological beliefs and worldviews; and as part of the *content* of ideologies, beliefs, and worldviews. And while important in its own right, research on racial attitudes and stratification beliefs has enormous practical implications because perceptions of the role of race in the operation of the stratification system affect patterns of intergroup relations (e.g., trust and inclusiveness) and shape levels of support for policies designed to ameliorate racial and socioeconomic inequality in American society.

The current volume of *The Annals of the American Academy of Political and Social Science* continues in this tradition by showcasing the research of a set of leading scholars using a diverse mix of methodological and theoretical approaches to broaden our understanding of the complex intersections of race, ideology, and inequality. These are timely issues both because of the nascent Obama "era" and because the last seminal volumes on racial attitudes (Schuman et al. 1997; Tuch and Martin 1997; Sears, Sidanius, and Bobo 2000) and stratification beliefs (Kluegel and Smith 1986) are at least one and two decades old, respectively.[1] Thus, the current volume stands on the shoulders of giants while updating our knowledge with a set of cutting-edge research articles speaking to key issues of the day.

Race, Inequality, and Ideology in Specific Institutional Domains

The first several articles in this volume explore the dynamics of race, inequality, and ideology in relation to specific institutional domains or issues of national concern: crime, religion, work, and immigration/national inclusion.

Thompson and Bobo offer a much-needed study that moves attitudes about crime—a well-documented source of tension between blacks and whites in the United States (Weitzer and Tuch 2005; Hagan, Shedd, and Payne 2005)—more squarely into the purview of the social science literature on stratification beliefs. Specifically, these authors use data from the 2001 Race, Crime, and Public Opinion project to explore the nature, determinants, and policy-related consequences of causal attributions for crime involvement. Their efforts bear significant fruit: race clearly shapes beliefs about crime causation, with whites more likely than blacks to adopt "individualist" attributions, and blacks more likely to hold "structuralist" ones (though whites and blacks show fairly similar levels of support for "mixed" explanations that combine individualist and structuralist attributions). Furthermore, whites' beliefs appear more firmly rooted in political ideology, while blacks' views appear more closely tied to exposure to, and fear of, crime. Finally, these attributions play a role in explaining the race difference in crime policy attitudes, with structuralists more likely than individualists to stress nonpunitive responses to crime and to advocate crime control solutions emphasizing educational opportunities and jobs rather than police and prisons. As with analyses of attitudes toward a range of socioeconomic redistributive policies (Bobo and Kluegel 1993; Hunt 2007), causal attributions prove to be an important tool in shedding light on the causes and consequences of race-specific worldviews around the issue of crime in America. Overall, Thompson and Bobo teach us that there is much to be gained by extending the tools of stratification beliefs research to the dynamics of social cognition around the issue of crime.

In the next article, Light, Roscigno, and Kalev shift our attention to the world of work via an analysis of employers' and employees' interpretations of minority employees' unfavorable work outcomes (e.g., firings and denials of promotion), including how racial stereotypes and "color-blind" ideologies shape employers' decisions and interpretations. Using data from 250 randomly selected racial discrimination cases, filed with and verified by the Ohio Civil Rights Commission (OCRC) between 1988 and 2003, these authors offer a nuanced account of stratification processes and ideologies in the context of a neglected topic in the workplace literature: processes by which racially discriminatory outcomes are generated (see Reskin 2003; Wilson 2007; Roscigno 2007). In particular, the authors situate a set of beliefs associated with the tenets of color-blind racism (see Bonilla-Silva and Dietrich, this volume) as a key element in a complex relational dynamic that includes employee perceptions and specific forms of discrimination behavior. A particularly unique contribution of this study is the empirical demonstration of the intersections of employer and employee beliefs in the context of workplace discrimination events. Contextualizing stratification ideology in this manner is no small feat and operates as a component of relational discrimination "encounters," which the authors convincingly argue is the appropriate unit of analysis (rather than particular human actors—the typical focus when employee and employer attitudes are analyzed) if we are to understand processes of unfolding discrimination. This relational approach emerges as an important new direction and should be utilized to chart configurations of discrimination linking attitudes and behavior.

Next, the Taylor and Merino article focuses our attention on the issue of religion as an important and neglected factor shaping stratification ideology. Specifically, these authors use data from the 1996 through 2006 General Social Surveys (GSS) to explore black-white differences in the relationship between religious affiliation and (1) beliefs about the causes of racial inequality and (2) support for race-targeted policies. In so doing, they bring valuable evidence to bear on a literature that has often neglected "religious factors" (but see Emerson and Smith 2000) and that has privileged the study of whites over examination of the views of important racial minority populations (Hunt 2002; Hunt et al. 2000). Using a typology of twelve "race by religion" categories, Taylor and Merino demonstrate—in contrast to common assumptions based on selected prior work—that the racial stratification beliefs of white conservative Protestants (e.g., Evangelicals) are not uniquely conservative relative to other white Christian groups once background characteristics are controlled. Instead, white Christians of all stripes share a heightened racial conservatism relative to white non-Christians (e.g., Jews and nonaffiliates). In addition, compared with black groups, white Christians are less structuralist in orientation, slightly more individualistic, and clearly less supportive of policies designed to aid African Americans. And finally, this research shows that blacks are not as internally differentiated on the basis of religious affiliation as one might expect based on past work.

Next, in a thought-provoking article, Hochschild and Lang bring an important comparative (i.e., cross-national) perspective to this volume through an examination of attitudes toward immigration and national inclusion. Using data from ten wealthy democracies captured in the 2003 International Social Survey Programme (ISSP), these authors explore how social structural and identity factors (e.g., race, religion, and citizenship) are associated with perceptions of "self-inclusiveness" and support for the "inclusion of others" both within and between nations. Their findings are compelling and should serve to spur significant research into their underpinnings. These authors show, for instance, that countries where residents feel most included are also generally those in which there is greatest resistance to outsiders—an issue having implications for employers of nonnative workers and government policies regarding immigrant incorporation. In addition, countries in which public opinion is most extreme are not necessarily those in which questions of inclusion have generated the most political controversy—pointing to the need for fine-grained analyses of the conditions under which public opinion shapes policy disputes and of ways in which surveys reflect genuine public sentiment. Furthermore, within the countries examined, noncitizens and members of religious minorities and racial/ethnic minorities generally feel less included and believe more strongly in incorporating outsiders than do majority-group members, though this generalization does not always hold. For example, in the United States, blacks and whites have similarly low scores on the goal of including outsiders. All told, this study's findings demonstrate why questions of racial stratification, religious tolerance, and immigrant incorporation prove so difficult to resolve in democratic polities. They also demonstrate the utility of cross-national/comparative analysis in opening new vistas for academic endeavors and political coalition-building.

The remaining articles in the current volume all deal, in one way or another, with racial policy attitudes or the changing nature of racism in twenty-first-century America.

On the Meaning, Measurement, and Implications of Racial Resentment

Three articles in this volume deal directly with current debates over the nature of modern racial prejudice, focusing on the measurement and the implications of a specific topic in the "new racism" literature: racial resentment (Kinder and Sanders 1996). The conceptualization and meaning of contemporary racial prejudice is a fundamental issue in the social sciences; indeed, the nature of a newer, more subtle kind of anti-black sentiment (to replace traditional, more overt, "Jim Crow" prejudice) has been the subject of much scholarly work and controversy in recent years (Sears, Sidanius, and Bobo 2000). As others have noted, identifying the nature of racial resentment is difficult and represents an attempt to specify the nature of modern anti-black sentiment in a way uncontaminated by simultaneously evolving attitudes toward social stratification and politics.

In the first of these articles, Carmines, Sniderman, and Easter take issue with Kinder and Sanders's (1996) measurement of racial prejudice (an index of racial stereotypes) and their corresponding argument that racial resentment and racial prejudice are largely overlapping and generally comparable predictors of whites' attitudes about racial policy. Through a critique and alternative specification of racial prejudice—using the same items from the 1992 American National Election Study (ANES) that Kinder and Sanders used—Carmines and colleagues suggest that the association between racial resentment and racial prejudice is substantially weaker than heretofore claimed. They go on to question whether racial resentment and racial policy attitudes are, in fact, empirically and conceptually distinct phenomena. Based on their results, Carmines, Sniderman, and Easter conclude that racial resentment, as traditionally operationalized, is not a valid measure of racism, thus raising foundational questions about the "new racism" concept and about the conclusion that such racism dominates the political reasoning of white Americans.

In the next article, Wilson and Davis also raise questions about Kinder and Sanders's (1996) approach to the issue of racial resentment and propose a new measurement strategy designed to capture what the authors call "explicit racial resentment" (EXR). While Wilson and Davis accept key tenets of existing definitions of racial resentment, they object to how it has been operationalized. Specifically, Wilson and Davis contend that the survey items commonly used to measure racial resentment (Kinder and Sanders 1996; Carmines, Sniderman, and Easter, this volume) are contaminated by explicit references to government programs and attempts to assess anti-black sentiment relative to sentiment toward other groups, as well as having substantial conceptual and empirical overlap with the related construct of "symbolic racism." With this backdrop, the authors introduce four new EXR survey items via two convenience samples of college undergraduates. Their analyses reveal that their EXR index has statistically sound measurement properties and is meaningfully related to other established correlates of racial attitudes. Such findings suggest substantial promise for the EXR items as an alternative or supplementary measure of racial resentment. As white Americans' racial attitudes continue to evolve in the face of significant events such as the election of President Obama (Welch and Sigelman, this volume), it is useful to have a range of survey indicators to aid researchers in developing valid and mature conceptions of the complex racial dynamics characterizing the new millennium. Wilson and Davis take a meaningful step in moving us in this direction.

Finally, Tuch and Hughes, in a piece that nicely encompasses the major themes of the current volume, use data from the ANES and GSS to explore how racial resentment and a host of other attitudinal and demographic predictors shape white Americans' views of racial policies. The ANES and GSS share several "racial principle" and "racial policy" items in common, but each also contains important explanatory variables that the other lacks. This approach offers a more robust analysis of racial policy outlooks than is typically employed and allows for exploration of the replicability of key findings across these two major social surveys. Interestingly, in light of prevailing rhetoric regarding an increasingly postracial society in the United States, Tuch and Hughes find no evidence that whites' views of racial policy have meaningfully shifted in the past three decades. Furthermore, racial resentment clearly emerges as the strongest determinant of whites' attitudes about racial policy (compared to factors such as traditional prejudice, economic individualism, egalitarianism, and political ideology) in both the GSS and ANES, suggesting that ongoing debates regarding the meaning and measurement of racial resentment (see Carmines, Sniderman, and Easter, this volume; and Wilson and Davis, this volume) are critically important if we are truly to understand whites' racial attitudes in twenty-first-century America.

Social Context, Stereotypes, and Racial (and Nonracial) Policy Support

Two additional articles address issues of long-standing concern to scholars interested in the social and psychological bases of whites' policy attitudes: the impact of social context on racial policy outlooks (Oliver and Wong 2003; Taylor 1998; Welch et al. 2001) and the role of racial prejudice in shaping support for (ostensibly) nonracial policy matters (Gilens 1999; Krysan 2000).

In the first of these articles, McDermott uses data from the 1992 to 1994 Multi-city Study of Urban Inequality (MCSUI) to expand the scope of research on context effects by incorporating and simultaneously examining measures of social class (e.g., education, occupation, and income) and racial composition at three distinct levels of analysis: the metropolitan area ("city"), the census block group ("neighborhood"), and the interview situation itself. In addition, McDermott explores how such factors interact across levels of analysis to shape racial attitudes and policy outlooks. The author's efforts pay off via a rich and nuanced set of results. Social class factors at the neighborhood level and the racial context of the interview situation—when they do affect the modeled outcomes—tend to do so directly. In contrast, the racial composition of cities and neighborhoods tends to matter via cross-level interaction effects. For instance, the percentage of a neighborhood that is black moderates the individual-level effect of being African American such that blacks' support for affirmative action programs is weakened as the proportion of black residents at the neighborhood level increases. Such findings highlight an important message of this study: the contextual sources of individual racial attitudes are more complex than has been previously documented. As such, future research should incorporate additional measures of context and examine their additive and interactive effects, on a broader range of outcomes.

Next, Wilson and Nielsen shift our attention to the so-called "color-coding" phenomenon via an exploration of how whites' racial prejudice affects support for ostensibly nonracial social welfare matters (Gilens 1999). Specifically, using data from the 1996 to 2002 GSS, these authors examine how whites' racial stereotypes shape "social problem spending" to elucidate whether and how whites "racially code" a range of contemporary social issues such as urban problems, crime control, and drug addiction. The authors also model support for spending on "welfare" and "aid to blacks"—two issues known to invoke racial stereotypes—as an empirical and comparative baseline for examining the other spending outcomes. The authors find that color-coding does not extend appreciably beyond established parameters; rather, it appears to operate along a continuum with welfare and spending on "blacks" at one end (heavily influenced by prejudice), spending on urban problems and drug addiction at the other end (not influenced by prejudice), and crime spending in the middle (moderately influenced by prejudice). In addition to shedding light on its breadth, the authors also identify emerging aspects of the color-coding phenomenon, including possible bidirectional effects across policies, and its subordination to political party affiliation in explanatory value.

Race, Racism, and Stratification Ideology in the Obama Era

The two final articles in this volume both deal with issues of racial prejudice or stratification ideology in the context of the election of Barack Obama to the presidency of the United States.

In the first of these, Bonilla-Silva and Dietrich offer a compelling account of the Obama phenomenon from the standpoint of Bonilla-Silva's well-known "color-blind racism" formulation (2006). Their success in this effort highlights the perspective's applicability to some of the most important and cutting-edge political developments of our time. Briefly, Bonilla-Silva's formulation seeks to analyze new forms of racism in advanced capitalist societies that are governed by ostensibly liberal, open, and inclusive race-based principles. As such, color-blind racism is seen as part and parcel of a new racial regime that ensures the perpetuation of deeply rooted racial inequities via subtle, institutional, and ostensibly nonracial dynamics (e.g., ideologies rationalizing inequalities on the basis of nonracial or postracial principles). Along these lines, the authors see President Obama as a potent cultural symbol, given what they see as his postracial persona and presentation of self and his tendency to distance himself from traditional civil rights leaders. In addition, Obama's stances on political matters—including those of race and inequality—are seen as consistent with a color-blind logic. Examples cited include what the authors see as Obama's postracial "self-help" strategy for the disadvantaged and his view of American society as an increasingly unified entity—both of which fail to confront the deep-rooted sources of racial inequity still characterizing American society.

Welch and Sigelman provide the final contribution to this volume. Their thoughtful piece assesses the historic election of Barack Obama in the context of a seminal issue in the racial attitudes literature: identifying the sources of change in whites' racial attitudes. Their study provides valuable new evidence regarding how such change may occur. Using data for non-Hispanic whites from the 1992 to 2008 ANES, these authors measure stereotypes about blacks as "hardworking" (vs. "lazy") and "intelligent" (vs. "stupid")—two established measures of modern prejudice—across a nearly two-decade period. Change across the most recent (2004–2008) period gets special scrutiny in highlighting the apparent "Obama effect" on racial attitudes. These authors' findings indicate that whites—when Obama was running for office and subsequently elected—moved notably in a more racially tolerant direction. The authors view this as evidence that one of the well-established causes of changes in racial attitudes—"dramatic events"—can moderate negative stereotypes (demographic change, specifically cohort replacement, is the other demonstrated cause). In addition, the authors suggest that, since the examined negative stereotypes are least pronounced among younger whites, such anti-black sentiment will likely continue to decline as the current century unfolds. All told, Welch and Sigelman make a strong case for the notion that Obama's election has shaped the observed attitudinal changes, though its precise role—the authors remind us—will require additional study, ideally employing longitudinal data and alternative methodologies.

We reserve the final spot in the Introduction to say a few words about Professor Lee Sigelman, who lost his two-year battle with cancer just weeks after submitting the final draft of the article appearing in this volume (and the last article that he would write with his longtime collaborator, Susan Welch). Sigelman leaves a towering intellectual and scholarly legacy. As the former editor of *American Political Science Review* and *American Politics Quarterly* and as director of the political science program at the National Science Foundation, Sigelman had vital leadership roles in his field. Within that field, Sigelman's research focused most centrally on issues of public opinion, mass communication, and electoral behavior but also "extended in several directions, including American national government, research methods, comparative political analysis, and popular culture" (see Department of Political Science, George Washington University n.d.). Sigelman wrote seven books, including *Black Americans' Views of Racial Inequality* (1991, with Susan Welch), a truly canonical work within the domains of racial attitude and stratification ideology research. Sigelman also regularly published in leading peer-reviewed journals, including *American Political Science Review*, *American Journal of Political Science*, and *Journal of Politics*. Given the importance and centrality of Sigelman's contributions to the research areas highlighted in this issue of *The Annals of the American Academy of Political and Social Science*, we respectfully dedicate this volume to his memory. As guest coeditors, we hope that we have helped to produce a product worthy of his legacy.

Note

1. Schuman et al. (1997) provide a comprehensive overview of the theory and history of racial attitudes, with primary focus on over-time trends among whites. Tuch and Martin's (1997) edited volume focuses primarily on whites' racial attitudes and their sociodemographic determinants, though they also devote three chapters to blacks' attitudes. Most recent is Sears, Sidanius, and Bobo's (2000) edited volume, focusing on contemporary debates over the roles of race and racism in American politics. The seminal (and only book-length) volume on stratification beliefs is more than 20 years old (Kluegel and Smith 1986). These authors develop a theoretical framework for understanding Americans' beliefs about inequality and proceed to examine empirically beliefs about opportunity, economic outcomes, distributive justice, redistributive policies, and selected personal and political consequences of stratification ideology.

References

Bobo, Lawrence, and Vincent L. Hutchings. 1996. Perceptions of racial group competition: Extending Blumer's theory of group position to a multiracial context. *American Sociological Review* 61:951–72.

Bobo, Lawrence, and James R. Kluegel. 1993. Opposition to race-targeting: Self-interest, stratification ideology, or racial attitudes? *American Sociological Review* 58:442–64.

Bonilla-Silva, Eduardo. 2006. *Racism without racists—Color-blind racism and the persistence of racial inequality in the United States* (2nd ed.). Lanham, MD: Rowman & Littlefield.

Department of Political Science, George Washington University. n.d. Lee Sigelman. Available from www.gwu.edu/~psc/people/fac_sigelmanl.htm (accessed 7 January 2010).

Emerson, Michael O., and Christian Smith. 2000. *Divided by faith: Evangelical religion and the problem of race*. Oxford: Oxford University Press.

Ford, Richard Thompson. 2009. Barack is the new black: Obama and the promise/threat of the post–civil rights era. *Du Bois Review* 6:37–48.

Gilens, Martin. 1999. *Why Americans hate welfare: Race, media, and the politics of antipoverty policy*. Chicago, IL: University of Chicago Press.

Hagan, John, Carla Shedd, and Monique Payne. 2005. Race, ethnicity, and youth perceptions of criminal justice. *American Sociological Review* 70:381–407.

Hunt, Matthew O. 2002. Religion, race/ethnicity, and beliefs about poverty. *Social Science Quarterly* 83:810–31.

Hunt, Matthew O. 2007. African-American, Hispanic, and white beliefs about black/white inequality, 1977–2004. *American Sociological Review* 72:390–415.

Hunt, Matthew O., Brian Powell, Lala Carr Steelman, and Pamela B. Jackson. 2000. Color-blind: The treatment of race and ethnicity in social psychology. *Social Psychology Quarterly* 63:352–64.

Kinder, Donald R., and Lynn M. Sanders. 1996. *Divided by color: Racial politics and democratic ideals.* Chicago, IL: University of Chicago Press.

Kluegel, James R. 1990. Trends in whites' explanations of the black-white gap in socioeconomic status, 1977–1989. *American Sociological Review* 55:512–25.

Kluegel, James R., and Eliot R. Smith. 1980. Beliefs about stratification. *Annual Review of Sociology* 7:29–56.

Kluegel, James R., and Eliot R. Smith. 1986. *Beliefs about inequality: Americans' views about what is and what ought to be.* Hawthorne, NY: Aldine de Gruyter.

Krysan, Maria. 2000. Prejudice, politics, and public opinion: Understanding the sources of racial policy attitudes. *Annual Review of Sociology* 26:135–68.

Krysan, Maria, and Amanda Lewis, eds. 2006. *The changing terrain of race and ethnicity.* New York, NY: Russell Sage Foundation.

Oliver, J. Eric, and Janelle Wong. 2003. Intergroup prejudice in multiethnic settings. *American Journal of Political Science* 47:567–82.

Reskin, Barbara. 2003. Including mechanisms in our models of ascriptive inequality. *American Sociological Review* 68:1–21.

Roscigno, Vincent. 2007. *The face of discrimination.* Lanham, MD: Rowman & Littlefield.

Schorr, Daniel. 28 January 2008. A new "post-racial" political era in America. *All Things Considered,* National Public Radio.

Schuman, Howard, Charlotte Steeh, Lawrence Bobo, and Maria Krysan. 1997. *Racial attitudes in America: Trends and interpretations.* Cambridge, MA: Harvard University Press.

Sears, David O., Jim Sidanius, and Lawrence Bobo. 2000. *Racialized politics: The debate about racism in America.* Chicago, IL: University of Chicago Press.

Sigelman, Lee, and Susan Welch. 1991. *Black Americans' views of racial inequality: The dream deferred.* New York, NY: Cambridge University Press.

Smith, Rogers M., and Desmond S. King. 2009. Barack Obama and the future of American racial politics. *Du Bois Review* 6:25–36.

Taylor, Marylee C. 1998. How white attitudes vary with the racial composition of local populations. *American Sociological Review* 63:512–35.

Tuch, Steven A., and Jack K. Martin. 1997. *Racial attitudes in the 1990s: Continuity and change.* Westport, CT: Praeger.

Weitzer, Ronald, and Steven Tuch. 2005. Racially biased policing: Determinants of citizens' perceptions. *Social Forces* 83:1009–30.

Welch, Susan, Lee Sigelman, Timothy Bledsoe, and Michael Combs. 2001. *Race and place: Race relations in an American city.* Cambridge: Cambridge University Press.

Williams, Juan. 30 November 2008. Obama's color line. *New York Times.* Available from www.nytimes .com/2007/11/30/opinion/30williams.html.

Wilson, George. 2007. Racialized life-chance opportunities across the class structure: The case of African Americans. *The Annals of the American Academy of Political and Social Science* 609:215–32.

Thinking about Crime: Race and Lay Accounts of Lawbreaking Behavior

By
VICTOR R. THOMPSON
and
LAWRENCE D. BOBO

Lay or commonsense accounts of the origins of criminal behavior may play a key role in sustaining a strong public appetite for harsh criminal justice policies and undergird large black-white differences in opinion in this domain. Using data from the nationally representative Race, Crime, and Public Opinion project's 2001 survey, the authors develop an explanatory mode typology for accounts of involvement in criminal behavior. These include both individualistic and structural accounts of behavior in addition to a mixed-mode category. The authors identify key differences in the demographic and sociopolitical bases of the attributional types and find significant race differences in these attributional types. Attributions strongly affect how individuals wish to see public policy respond to the problem of crime and explain a small but significant fraction of the black-white difference in crime policy views.

Keywords: crime attribution; race; racial attitudes; crime policy; mode of explanation

Victor R. Thompson received his PhD from Stanford University in 2010 and is now an assistant professor of sociology at Rider University in Lawrenceville, New Jersey. He was a fellow at the Center for Comparative Studies in Race and Ethnicity from 2005 to 2007 and has written on race, crime, and public opinion, in addition to racial classification. His dissertation, "Learning from Multiracial Identity: Theorizing Racial Identities from Response Variability on Questions about Race," explores response variability to questions about race using census data and large-sample surveys.

Lawrence D. Bobo is the W. E. B. Du Bois Professor of the Social Sciences at Harvard University. He is coauthor of Racial Attitudes in America: Trends and Interpretations *(Harvard University Press 1997); senior editor of* Prismatic Metropolis: Inequality in Los Angeles *(Russell Sage Foundation 2000); and coeditor of* Racialized Politics: The Debate on Racism in America *(University of Chicago Press 2000). His most recent book is* Prejudice in Politics: Public Opinion, Group Position, and the Wisconsin Treaty Rights Dispute *(Harvard University Press 2006). He is currently writing a book titled* Unfair by Design: Race, Public Opinion, and the New Law and Order Regime.

NOTE: An earlier version of this article was presented at the Annual American Association for Public Opinion Research conference in Hollywood, Florida, May 17, 2009. We wish to thank Alicia Simmons for her comments on an earlier draft of this article. The authors are responsible for any remaining errors or shortcomings.

DOI: 10.1177/0002716210387057

ANNALS, *AAPSS*, 634, March 2011

Matters of law enforcement and criminal justice remain sources of deep racial tension in the United States. Newsworthy flare-ups over police shootings, accusations of racial profiling, and the War on Drugs—the latter regarded by many as both excessive and unsuccessful—highlight a pointedly race-inflected divide regarding the problem of crime in the United States and appropriate policy responses to crime (Wacquant 2001; Kennedy 2003; Roberts 2003; Western 2006; Tonry and Melewski 2008). In this research we focus on one possible source of this racial polarization: namely, whether there are significant differences in how white and black Americans understand the problem of crime.

High-profile events and some key crime response policies (e.g., the sentencing differential for crack versus powder cocaine) may elicit sharply polarized reactions from blacks and whites, primarily because these groups have very different basic understandings of the sources of criminal behavior. For example, those who generally understand criminal behavior as being rooted in personal dispositions and irresponsible individual choices may be inclined to endorse aggressive and punitive responses to crime in policing and in social policy. Alternatively, those who generally understand criminal behavior as having systematic social roots in poverty, unemployment, and so on may recoil against such punishment-centered responses to crime. If distinctive ways of thinking about the sources of criminal behavior vary systematically by race, then blacks and whites may, in sum, be worlds apart in the basic social meanings that they attach to criminal behavior.

We seek to shed light on this possibility using data from the Race, Crime, and Public Opinion (RCPO) project, which allows us to assess the extent, sources, and effects of black-white differences in attributions for criminal behavior (Bobo and Johnson 2001).[1] The RCPO survey involves large national samples of white and black Americans and includes measures of beliefs about the causes of criminal behavior. The RCPO survey also contains measures of other factors relevant to judgments about crime such as an individual's prior victimization, fear of crime, general sociopolitical identities and ideology, as well as policy views on crime. In addition, we are able to append to these data key contextual information about actual levels of serious crime in the respondent's community.

Background

The attribution process. Social psychologists have long maintained that the meaning social phenomena have for us turns crucially on how we explain or account for the observation of them (Heider 1958). For example, individuals who believe that the unemployed are jobless because they have a poor work ethic—a dispositional attribution according to Heider (1958)—are more likely to see the jobless as personally responsible for their lack of employment. However, individuals who believe that unemployment is rooted in poor economic conditions— a situational attribution (Heider 1958)—are less likely to hold individuals responsible for their unemployment, instead focusing on broad structural conditions. In the 1970s, Weiner (1974) expanded on Heider's typology to include both a locus of causality (internal/external) dimension and a stability dimension (stable/ unstable) that further specify key features of the attribution process.

A great deal of experimental social psychological research on attribution processes, however, focuses on judgments about the sources of individual task performance or direct interpersonal interactions. Sociologists and political scientists have extended these insights to attributions about larger matters of observable supraindividual processes and social conditions. Thus, for example, previous research has measured distinct patterns of popular belief about the causes of social inequality more generally (Kluegel and Smith 1986; Wilson 1996) and with regard to racial inequality in particular (Schuman 1971; Apostle et al. 1983; Sniderman and Hagen 1985; Kluegel 1990; Hunt 2004, 2007).

Sociological attribution. Previous sociological research provides grounds to expect a strong tendency toward individualistic thinking when it comes to attributions about crime. Work on beliefs about general economic inequality has pointed to a dominant individualistic ethos or ideology in U.S. public opinion (Mann 1970; Huber and Form 1973; Kluegel and Smith 1986). Kluegel and Smith (1986, 5) summarize this tendency via what they term the "logic of opportunity syllogism." The major premise holds that there are many opportunities for economic advancement in American society. Next, the logic proceeds, hard work and talent are rewarded in American society. Therefore, any resulting economic inequality is largely seen as the fair and legitimate result of differences in individual effort and ability. While there are significant race, class, and ideological differences in these attitudes (Kluegel and Smith 1986; Bobo 1991), it seems reasonable to expect that a similar strong general individualistic tilt may also exist when the focus shifts from economic inequality in general to the sources of involvement in crime in particular.

The research on how Americans perceive and explain racial inequality has stressed the existence of distinct modes of explanation for race inequality (Apostle et al. 1983; Sniderman and Hagen 1985; Kluegel 1990; Sigelman and Welch 1991; Hunt 2007). These modes reflect the fact that few people express unicausal accounts of racial inequality, with many individuals recognizing the influence of both individual-level factors and external or structural factors. As might be expected, these "modes of explanation" vary considerably by race (Hunt 2007; Kluegel and Smith 1986; Sniderman and Hagen 1985). African Americans are far more likely to attribute racial inequality to structural factors, such as discrimination or inadequate educational opportunities, compared with whites, who exhibit a clearer tendency to accept various dispositional or individualistic accounts (Kluegel 1990).

These modes of explanation help to explain the steady lack of support for race-targeted policies among whites (Kluegel 1990) and reflect the large gap in perceptions of inequality among blacks and whites (Kluegel and Smith 1986; Hunt 2007). For example, whites who adopt individualist explanations for inequality are much less likely to support policies that seek government spending or aid to address racial inequality in the United States than are whites who have a more structurally oriented explanation for inequality (Kluegel 1990). The sizable gap in black and white explanations for inequality remained largely unchanged throughout the 1970s and 1980s (Kluegel and Smith 1986), though recent work suggests that it became slightly less polarized in the 1990s and early 2000s (Hunt 2007).

Still, there is a dearth of research on modes of explanation in the context of public response to crime and crime-related policy. Most of the available research tends to focus on perceptions of the criminal justice system's response to particular types of behavior (Carroll and Payne 1976; Carroll 1978), rather than on how people understand the origins of criminal behavior. There is little, if any, research on how individualist and structuralist accounts of behavior help to explain black and white differences in the evaluation of the criminal justice system and crime policy. In addition, the existing information on racial differences in causal accounts of criminogenic behavior remains largely descriptive in nature and incomplete for recent years (see Erskine 1974). Given the polarization of attitudes between blacks and whites toward the criminal justice system in general (Shaw et al. 1998; Hagan, Shedd, and Payne 2005; Hurwitz and Peffley 2005) and toward such issues as the War on Drugs in particular (Bobo and Thompson 2006), it is possible that racial differences in causal accounts of criminal behavior could help to explain differential support for punitive crime policies.

Race and attributions. There are four important reasons to expect differences in causal explanations for crime between blacks and whites. First, despite enormous change and progress over the past several decades, African Americans remain socio-economically disadvantaged relative to whites and sharply segregated from whites in terms of residential location (Massey 2007). Such profound structural differences in social location are likely to influence thinking about a socially defined and constructed problem such as crime. Second, and more specifically, blacks and whites have historically encountered (Higginbotham 1996; Kennedy 1997) and certainly perceive in the present (Weitzer and Tuch 2006) very different experiences when it comes to their interactions with police and other institutions of the criminal justice system (Tonry 1995; Cole 1999; Mauer 1999; Western 2006). Given these sharply different statuses, histories, and contemporary experiences, we believe that whites and blacks are likely to have polarized views of the causes of crime.

Third, the perception by some that there is a racially biased system of social control (Quinney 1970; Chambliss and Seidman 1971; Hurwitz and Peffley 2005) that reproduces inequality, leading many to question the very legitimacy of the system (Hagan, Shedd, and Payne 2005; Bobo and Thompson 2006), may also act to polarize beliefs about the origins of crime that lead to these disparities in the first place. Fourth, real differences in criminal victimization among blacks and whites (Bobo and Thompson 2010) suggest a pervasive experiential gap in exposure to crime that may lead to very different beliefs about criminogenic behavior (Pettit and Western 2004). For example, Bobo and Thompson (2010) found that blacks were much more likely than white respondents to have a friend or relative incarcerated, regardless of income level or education. Indeed, even among those with a college education earning more than $60,000 a year, nearly one in three blacks had a friend or relative incarcerated, compared with only one in twenty whites. Exposure to the American criminal justice system is far more common in the black community than it is in the white community.

Ideology and attributions. Beyond race itself, value-based and ideological differences among individuals might also be a determining factor for how people understand the causes of crime and the type of crime policies that they support (Tyler and Weber 1982; Tyler and Boeckmann 1997; Bobo and Johnson 2004; Gottschalk 2008). For example, we know that political conservatism is highly correlated with support for such things as the death penalty, three-strike laws, and truth-in-sentencing laws (Soss, Langbein, and Metelko 2003; Barkan and Cohen 2005; Unnever and Cullen 2007; Matsueda and Drakulich 2009). Therefore, it seems likely that a logic of personal responsibility is one of the factors that links value-based and ideological conservatism on one hand to support for punitive policies on the other. The attribution process may be a key piece of this logic. Accordingly, individuals with traditional and conservative outlooks should be more likely than those with more liberal outlooks to make individualistic attributions about criminal behavior.

Crime salience and attributions. Actual exposure to serious crime may also shape attributions. For example, individuals who live in high-crime areas, who have been victimized, and who are highly fearful of crime may be motivated to see crime as more often a matter of individual responsibility than of social structural causation. A more individualistic view of criminal behavior would be consistent with an agentic and, therefore, potentially more rationally controllable and manageable view of the crime problem. Such a view would also be a way of imposing a greater sense of right and wrong, or a moral order, on one's social surroundings and life circumstances. A personal or individual account of criminal behavior would also be a cognitively simple inference from the more general American cultural tendency toward individualism. That is, it is reasonable to expect those for whom crime is a highly salient personal matter to lean in the direction of more individualistic accounts, as doing so should be more psychologically parsimonious and comforting at several levels.

We suspect that all of these factors may determine support for crime policy and causal accounts of criminogenic behavior. However, we seek to understand how causal accounts of criminogenic behavior help to explain the polarized views that blacks and whites have of the criminal justice system, especially their support for crime policies, independent of these other factors. That is, does mode of explanation elucidate the racial gap in support for particular crime policies even after these other factors are controlled? Are the opinions of blacks and whites largely the product of fundamental differences in opinion about the sources of crime? If so, how much of these groups' support for particular crime policies can we explain by these differences?

Analysis and Results

Lay accounts of involvement in crime

To ascertain popular or lay accounts of criminal behavior, the RCPO survey posed a series of four questions to respondents, in an agree/disagree format, specifying different potential root causes of criminal behavior. The four statements and respective response distributions are shown in Table 1. Of the four questions, the most widely endorsed lay account of crime involvement is that "people become criminals because they do not care about the rights of others or their responsibility to society"—88.2 percent of whites and 73.8 percent of blacks endorse this explanation. The next most commonly accepted statement involves the structurally oriented belief that "poverty and low income in our society are responsible for much of [the] crime," with 61.7 percent of whites and 67.4 percent of blacks endorsing this position. Finally, a smaller number of respondents believed that "people turn to crime because they are lazy" (whites = 51.4 percent; blacks = 37.0 percent) or because "our society does not guarantee that everyone has regular employment" (whites = 24.8 percent; blacks = 49.5 percent).

The distributions in Table 1 immediately suggest that most respondents affirm personal or individualistic responsibility for criminal behavior and situational or social structural accounts. Similar tendencies toward a multicausal view of race-based inequality led Apostle and colleagues (1983), Sniderman and Hagen (1985), Kluegel (1990), and Hunt (2007) to identify distinctive modes of explanation of race inequality reflecting the intersection of the degree of acceptance of particular structural and individual accounts. We follow this analytic approach. Specifically, we employ a set of criteria for determining different modes of explanation for involvement with crime similar to those that Kluegel (1990) and Hunt (2007) used. These scholars constructed modes of explanation for how respondents explained the black-white socioeconomic gap using questions that tapped four possible reasons for black-white inequality, two of which were person-centered/individualist in nature (inborn ability and motivation)[2] and two of which were structural in nature (discrimination and education). Our own set of questions measure similar dispositions toward crime involvement. We base our modes of explanation on the joint configuration of responses that people used to explain involvement in crime.

Respondents endorsed any number of explanations for why people commit crimes, and the categories are by no means mutually exclusive. For example, 91.7 percent of those who agree that laziness explains why people commit crimes also agree that people turn to crime because they "do not care about the rights of others" (whites = 95.9 percent; blacks = 86.0 percent). Likewise, 82.3 percent of respondents who agree that the primary reason people turn to crime is because "society does not guarantee that everyone has regular employment" also agree that "poverty and low income" are causes for crime involvement (whites = 85.3 percent; blacks 80.8 percent). Similarly, there is overlap between individualist and structuralist modes of explanation. For example, 35 percent of respondents

TABLE 1
Reasons Some People Turn to Crime

	White	Black
Individual attributions		
People turn to crime because they are lazy.		
Strongly/mostly agree	51.4%	37.0%
Strongly/mostly disagree	48.6%	63.0%
N	965	994
People become criminals because they don't care about the rights of others or their responsibility to society.		
Strongly/mostly agree	88.2%	73.8%
Strongly/mostly disagree	11.8%	26.2%
N	969	997
Structural attributions		
People turn to crime because our society does not guarantee that everyone has regular employment.		
Strongly/mostly agree	24.8%	49.5%
Strongly/mostly disagree	75.2%	50.5%
N	966	994
Poverty and low income in our society are responsible for much of crime.		
Strongly/mostly agree	61.7%	67.4%
Strongly/mostly disagree	38.3%	32.6%
N	963	999

SOURCE: Race, Crime, and Public Opinion Survey, 2001.

agree that laziness contributes to involvement in crime, while also agreeing that a lack of employment guarantees contributes to criminality. Given this overlap, we found it necessary to construct a mixed category for those who endorsed both structuralist and individualist views equally.

Modes of explaining crime

Table 2 shows the joint configuration of responses used to define different modes of explanation. We sorted respondents who were purely individualist or structuralist in their responses into the corresponding mode of explanation. Individualists include respondents who endorsed either one or both of the individualist attributes and neither of the structuralist attributes; structuralists include people who endorsed one or both of the structuralist items but neither of the individualist items. In addition to these pure individualists and structuralists, we also included people in these categories who straddled the individualist and structuralist divide but were balanced in favor of the mode of assignment. In other words, respondents who endorsed both individualist items or both structuralist items but also affirmed one of the other items were included in the structuralist

TABLE 2
Response Patterns for Mode of Explanation for Involvement with Crime

Mode of Explanation	Response Patterns						
	Individual Attributions			Structural Attributions			
	Lazy		Not Responsible	No Jobs		Poverty
Individualist	Yes	(or)	Yes	No		No
	Yes		Yes	Yes	(or)	Yes
Mixed	Yes	(or)	Yes	Yes	(or)	Yes
	Yes		Yes	Yes		Yes
Structuralist	No		No	Yes	(or)	Yes
	Yes	(or)	Yes	Yes		Yes
None	No		No	No		No

SOURCE: Race, Crime, and Public Opinion Survey, 2001.

or individualist category rather than the mixed category since their explanations for crime were biased in the direction of one of these modes.[3]

In addition to these two polar modes of explanation, we created a "mixed" mode of attribution category for those who equally straddled the individualist/structuralist divide. That is, they were equally individualist and structuralist in their explanations. We treated respondents as mixed if they affirmed one of each of the structuralist/ individualist attributes but denied the other in those categories. For example, a mixed respondent might endorse the belief that people become criminals because they "do not care about the rights of others" (an individualist attribute) but also endorse the idea that "society does not guarantee that everyone has regular employment" (a structuralist attribute). We also treated respondents who affirmed all four items as members of the mixed category. About one in three of all blacks and whites fell in to the mixed category (see Figure 1).

Finally, for whatever reason, a small portion of our sample did not endorse any attribute ($N = 79$). Whether this was because they literally had no views about why people turn to crime or they simply did not like the specific options we offered is difficult to assess. There are enough such individuals, however, to warrant treating them as a separate category. Blacks were significantly more likely to belong to this group than whites. Fifty-one were African American (5.3 percent), and twenty-eight were white (2.9 percent). Within the white population, political Independents and liberals were more likely to fall into this group. Among blacks, liberals and respondents with high incomes were more likely to fall into this category. For both blacks and whites, those who feared crime the least were the most likely to fall into this category.

Figure 1 presents the modes of explanation for criminal behavior by race. Several interesting patterns emerge. First, the majority of white respondents are individualists. Second, both blacks and whites tend to endorse explanations that involve at least some individualist explanations for crime involvement. If we combined the individualist and mixed-mode respondents (recall that the mixed-mode

FIGURE 1
Mode of Explanation by Race

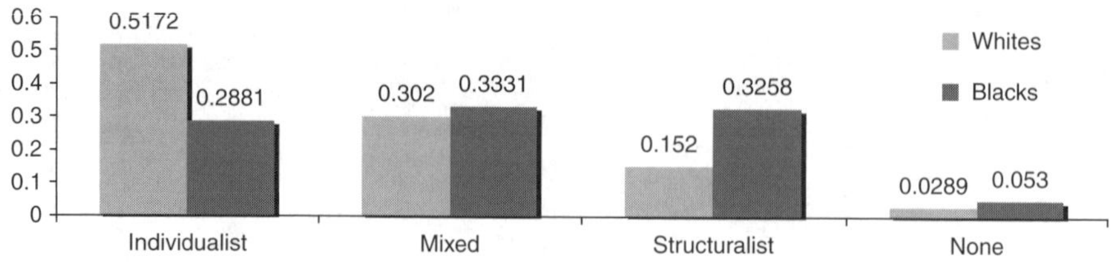

SOURCE: Race, Crime, and Public Opinion Survey, 2001.

responses also contain individualist explanations for crime), nearly eight in ten whites (81.9 percent) and six in ten blacks (62.1 percent) endorse individualist accounts of criminogenic behavior equal to or greater than the level of their endorsement of structuralist accounts. While blacks do lean slightly toward structuralist explanations (32.6 percent are structuralists and 28.8 percent individualists), the combination of individualist and mixed responses reveals the strength of the individualist narrative of crime involvement among both black and white Americans. Finally, when we compare the modes of explanation by race, racial distinctions emerge. This is most apparent when we compare individualists and structuralists to each other—we find that more than half of all whites (51.7 percent) are individualists compared with less than one in three blacks (28.8 percent). Comparatively, 32.6 percent of blacks are structuralists, while only 15.2 percent of whites are structuralists. In short, whites are more individualist in their explanations, while blacks are more evenly distributed across the three groups.

Indeed, nearly two in three individualists in our sample are white (63.9 percent of individualists are white), while the opposite is true for structuralists (68.5 percent of structuralists are black). If individualists are more punitive in their approach to crime policy, and if more of them are white, it may be that a large percentage of the racial gap in support for punitive crime policy is explainable by the fact that individualists tend to be white. That is, modes of explanation may be a key factor in why blacks and whites have very different levels of support for punitive crime policies.

Factors affecting attributions for crime

Table 3 shows means for each of the modes of explanation in addition to the variables we think are important for whether people adopt a particular mode of explanation. The background, value, and ideological variables and crime salience factors point to significant differences between blacks and whites that may shape their causal explanations. For example, blacks are significantly more likely to identify as Democrats and liberals than are whites, implying that blacks might take a more structuralist view of crime causation. However, blacks also report more frequent

TABLE 3
Means and Standard Deviations by Race

	Total	White	Black
Mode of explanation			
Individualist	0.44°	0.55	0.31
	(0.50)	(0.50)	(0.46)
Mixed	0.30°	0.28	0.33
	(0.46)	(0.45)	(0.47)
Structuralist	0.21°	0.13	0.30
	(0.41)	(0.34)	(0.46)
None	0.04°	0.04	0.06
	(0.21)	(0.19)	(0.23)
Demographics			
Female	0.56°	0.54	0.57
	(0.50)	(0.50)	(0.50)
Southern	0.45°	0.35	0.57
	(0.50)	(0.48)	(0.49)
Age (in years)	45.19°	47.47	42.45
	(16.17)	(16.45)	(15.38)
Education (in years)	13.33°	13.63	12.96
	(2.49)	(2.50)	(2.43)
Income	$49,366°	$52,763	$45,287
	($32,943)	($32,426)	($33,119)
Value and ideology			
Democrat	0.50°	0.32	0.73
	(0.50)	(0.47)	(0.45)
Independent	0.31°	0.36	0.25
	(0.46)	(0.48)	(0.43)
Republican	0.19°	0.32	0.02
	(0.39)	(0.47)	(0.15)
Conservatism[a]	2.99°	3.13	2.83
	(0.83)	(0.85)	(0.77)
Church attendance[b]	3.73°	3.46	4.06
	(1.56)	(1.60)	(1.45)
Salience of crime			
Victim of crime	0.06°	0.05	0.07
	(0.23)	(0.22)	(0.25)
Index crime (per 100,000)	4,788.40°	4,145.72	5,560.27
	(2,084)	(1,890)	(2,046)
Murder rate (per 100,000)	9.11°	5.67	13.23
	(10.67)	(7.39)	(12.42)
Fear of crime[c]	2.02°	1.92	2.13
	(0.73)	(0.65)	(0.80)

SOURCE: Race, Crime, and Public Opinion Survey, 2001.

NOTE: For party identification, we asked respondents to identify as a Democrat, Republican, or Independent. Conservatism was measured on a 5-point scale from *very liberal* to *very conservative*, with *moderate* as a midpoint. Church attendance was constructed by creating a 6-point scale based on how often a person attended church over the last year: *never, once a year or less, a few times a year, once or twice a month, once a week,* or *more than once a week.* "Victim of crime" is a dummy variable for respondents who said that their house or apartment had been burglarized in the past year or someone in their household had been a victim of a violent crime. Index crime rates and murder rates are taken from the FBI's Uniform Crime Reports from 2000. Fear of crime is a 5-point scale, ranging from *low fear of crime* to *high fear of crime* based on the responses to two questions that asked how often respondents feared "someone breaking into your house to steal things" and how often they feared "being robbed by someone who has a gun or knife."

°Significant differences between white and black respondents ($p < .05$, two-tailed tests).

church attendance than do whites, which might encourage a more individual-responsibility-focused outlook on crime—though church attendance among blacks may also act in both directions given the black Protestant tradition of emphasizing communal and collectivist orientations and its connections with black political activism (Pattillo-McCoy 1998). Likewise, crime is a more salient experience for blacks than for whites, as blacks are more likely to report criminal victimization, to fear crime, and actually to live in higher-crime areas.

But what do these gaps in social experience and identities mean when it comes to how people explain the sources of criminogenic behavior? We explore these questions by modeling the independent effects of these variables, in addition to race, on support for each mode of explanation separately.

Table 4 presents coefficients for logistic regression models, predicting each mode of explanation category pooled across race and also separately for black and white respondents. Several patterns are worthy of emphasis. First, the results show that the overall effects of race are strong for structuralist and individualist attributions. Blacks were about three times ($e^{1.10}$) more likely than whites to be structuralists and about 0.44 times ($e^{-0.82}$) less likely to be individualists. Second, beyond race, ideological conservatives and Republicans were more likely to be individualists and less likely to be structuralists, all else being equal; though party affiliation does not seem to matter as much for structuralists as it does for individualist and mixed respondents.[4] In addition, among structuralists, southerners and older people were less likely to adopt a structuralist mode of explanation, while those who had a greater fear of crime were much more likely to have a structuralist mode of explanation.

We next asked if whites and blacks take different approaches to explaining crime. Among whites, we find that conservatism is a significant factor in predicting crime attributions for individualists and structuralists, while ideological factors appear to be less influential among black respondents.[5] What matters for blacks and not so much for whites is fear of crime, although the direction of the effect is not what we expected. Blacks who fear crime the most were also the least likely to be individualists and the most likely to have a mixed mode of explanation for understanding criminal behavior.[6] Of interest, among black structuralists, the only variables that proved to be significant were region and age. That is, older southern blacks were less likely than younger nonsouthern blacks to make a structuralist argument about crime origins.[7] In the end, there do appear to be differences between blacks and whites in terms of how they explain crime.

Support for punitive policies

Different modes of explanation may in part help to explain the varying levels of support among blacks and whites for punitive policies toward crime. To test this claim, we explore two points of exposure to the criminal justice system and support for policies that either limit or expand the punitiveness of the American criminal justice system. We first address a policy that seeks to widen the net of punishment and expand the reach of police through increased spending on law

TABLE 4
Logistic Regression Models for Each Mode of Explanation (N = 1,091)

	Dependent Variable (Compared to All Other Categories)											
	Individualist			Mixed			Structuralist			None		
	Total	White	Black	Total	White	Black	Total	White	Black	Total	White	Black
Demographics												
Black	−0.82°°°			−0.15			1.10°°°			0.95		
Female	−0.07	−0.02	−0.16	0.07	0.14	0.00	−0.05	−0.35	0.15	0.26	0.89	0.02
Southern	0.30	0.29	0.44	−0.07	−0.23	0.05	−0.56°°	−0.57°	−0.64°	1.00°	1.35	0.83
Age (in years)	0.44	0.01	1.05	0.22	0.11	0.42	−0.97°	−0.18	−1.54°	−0.06	−0.54	0.30
Education (in years)	0.00	−0.01	0.03	−0.02	−0.02	−0.04	0.05	0.07	0.05	−0.10	−0.08	−0.10
Income	0.23	0.35	0.02	−0.31	−0.51°	−0.16	−0.12	0.10	−0.13	0.98°	0.51	1.39°
Values and ideology												
Independent	0.12	−0.07	0.38	−0.38°	−0.49	−0.29	0.20	0.74°	−0.05	0.48	1.63°	−0.06
Republican	0.50°	0.29	0.74	−0.62°	−0.55	−1.01	−0.27	0.06	−0.13	0.68	1.52	1.32
Conservatism[a]	0.24°	0.41°°	0.01	0.04	−0.04	0.17	−0.26°	−0.57°°°	−0.07	−0.66°°	−0.89°	−0.54°
Church attendance[b]	0.03	0.01	0.04	0.04	−0.01	0.11	−0.07	0.02	−0.10	−0.17	−0.15	−0.18
Salience of crime												
Victim of crime	−0.14	0.02	−0.39	−0.10	0.01	−0.36	0.19	−0.55	0.60	0.67	1.43	−0.29
Index crime (per 100,000)	0.00	0.00	0.00	0.00	0.00°	0.00	0.00	0.00	0.00	0.00	0.00	0.00
Murder rate (per 100,000)	0.01	−0.02	0.02	0.00	0.05°°	−0.01	−0.02	−0.06	−0.01	0.01	−0.13	0.01
Fear of crime[c]	−0.15	0.08	−0.41°°	0.06	−0.17	0.32°	0.24°	0.20	0.23	−0.74°	−0.43	−0.97°
Constant	−5.21°	−5.27	−5.37	1.88	5.76	−2.13	3.61	−2.39	7.29	—	−4.87	—
Wald chi-square (df)	79.82 (14)	29.62 (13)	20.36 (13)	17.08 (14)	29.26 (13)	14.54 (13)	71.83 (14)	29.87 (13)	22.55 (13)	35.16 (14)	61.79 (13)	14.35 (13)
R^2	.07	.01	.09	.02	.05	.04	.08	.07	.06	.12	.17	.12

SOURCE: Race, Crime, and Public Opinion Survey, 2001.
a. Range = 1–5; 1 = *very liberal*; 5 = *very conservative*.
b. Range = 1–6; 1 = *never*; 6 = *more than once a week*.
c. Range = 1–5; 1 = *low fear of crime*; 5 = *high fear of crime*.
°p < .05. °°p < .01. °°°p < .001.

27

TABLE 5
Addressing Crime Problems in the United States by Race

	Whites	Blacks	White to Black Ratio
Question 1: To lower the crime rate in the U.S. some people think more money should be spent on attacking the social and economic problems that lead to crime by improving education and job training programs. Other people think more money should be spent on improving law enforcement and deterring crime by hiring more police and building more prisons. Which comes closer to your view?			
More money for education and job training	35.2%	57.7%	0.6
Both equally	45.2%	35.1%	1.3
More money for police and prisons	10.2%	1.3%	8.0
Neither	9.4%	5.9%	1.6
Total N	781	721	
Question 2: When it comes to granting parole to people in prison, should parole boards be . . .			
More strict	77.7%	65.3%	1.2
Same as they are now/less strict	22.3%	43.7%	0.5
Total N	775	713	

SOURCE: Race, Crime, and Public Opinion Survey, 2001.

enforcement personnel and prisons. Next, we explore support for a policy that encourages parole boards to be stricter, thereby ensuring that those who do become incarcerated remain so for as long as possible.

As Table 5 shows, there are large differences between blacks and whites in their support for these policies. For example, more than half of all whites view spending more money on police and on more prisons as a viable strategy to decrease crime, whether in conjunction with education and job training programs (45.2 percent) or in ways that focus only on police and prisons (10.2 percent). A much smaller percentage of blacks endorsed these same views, believing instead that education and job training programs were better investments when it comes to solving the nation's crime problem. And although the majority of both whites and blacks think that parole boards should be stricter, there is a sizable difference between blacks and whites when it comes to granting parole to people in prison—77.7 percent of whites compared to 65.3 percent of blacks think parole boards should be stricter.

Certainly, one of the causes of this racial polarization is a crisis of legitimacy and lack of trust of the criminal justice system among blacks (Bobo and Thompson 2006). However, a somewhat different explanation for this large gap in support may be that blacks and whites have fundamentally different causal explanations for crime. If people with dispositional attributions for behavior were more likely to blame the individual for his or her failures, then there is good reason to believe that these same people would also be more likely to support punitive crime policies (Carroll 1978). After all, if crime were primarily a product of individual traits, the best way to stop crime may simply be to capture more criminals by placing more police on the streets, building more prisons, and keeping prisoners behind bars longer.

Spending solutions to crime. For the first set of questions addressing solutions to crime, we use multinomial logit models (see Table 6) and find significant evidence for the claim that modes of explanation do indeed influence support for crime policies, net all other variables in our models. When we compare the likelihood of support for each solution to crime relative to the other solutions, we find that mode of explanation is important when comparing support for education and job training spending relative to spending policies that contain an element of support for more police and prisons. This is especially true for individualists, who are much more likely than structuralists to advocate spending for police and prisons over education and job training. While there is support among individualists for education and job training, it is more likely to be in conjunction with spending for police and prisons than exclusively for education and job training. People who have dispositional attributions about the causes of crime are committed to policies that improve law enforcement and expand our capacity to incarcerate and are less concerned with attacking the social and economic conditions that lead to crime in the first place. The same is true for mixed respondents when comparing "both equally" to "education and job training"; however, there are no significant differences between mixed respondents and structuralists when comparing spending for more law enforcement and policies that address the social and economic causes of crime.

As expected, conservatism remains important even after controlling for mode of explanation and race. For each unit increase in conservatism, political conservatives are about twice as likely ($e^{0.75}$) as political liberals to support spending for police and prisons over spending for education and job training programs. In addition, they are more likely to support spending for police and prisons over spending policies that include an element of education and job training, and they are more likely to support police and prison spending in conjunction with education and job training spending over spending on education and job training alone. To be clear, the more conservative people are, the more they view the solution to crime as one that requires the expansion of law enforcement by putting more police on the streets and building more prisons and not *just* addressing social and economic problems. Along the same lines, Republicans were more likely to support spending for law enforcement as a deterrent to crime than spending to address social and economic problems.

Exposure to crime also matters, though it is less consistent across models and, in fact, contradicts our initial expectations about its effects. Namely, the negative effect of fear of crime when comparing support for police or support for education

TABLE 6
Multinomial Logit Models of Support for Education and Job Training, Police and Prisons,[a] or Both Equally (N = 1,088)

	Model 1: Police vs. Education	Model 2: Police vs. Education	Model 3: Police vs. Both Equally	Model 4: Police vs. Both Equally	Model 5: Education vs. Both Equally	Model 6: Education vs. Both Equally
Demographics						
Black	−1.22°°°	−1.05°°	−0.36	−0.32	0.85°°°	0.72°°°
Female	−0.45°	−0.45°	−0.42	−0.41	0.02	0.03
Southern	0.32	0.20	0.12	0.10	−0.20	−0.10
Age (in years)	−0.45	−0.60	−0.05	−0.05	0.40	0.54
Education (in years)	−0.03	−0.03	0.05	0.04	0.08°	0.07°
Income	0.11	0.02	−0.23	−0.29	−0.34	−0.31
Values and ideology						
Independent	0.59	0.57	0.26	0.22	−0.32	−0.36
Republican	0.85°	0.76°	0.40	0.32	−0.45	−0.44
Conservatism[b]	0.80°°°	0.75°°°	0.47°°	0.43°°	−0.32°°	−0.31°°
Church attendance[c]	0.10	0.09	0.09	0.10	0.00	0.01
Salience of crime						
Victim of crime	−0.25	−0.22	0.26	0.29	0.51	0.51
Index crime (per 100,000)	0.00	0.00	0.00	0.00	0.00°	0.00°
Murder rate (per 100,000)	0.02	0.02	0.01	0.02	0.00	0.00
Fear of crime[d]	−0.14	−0.09	−0.32°	−0.32°	−0.18	−0.23°
Mode of explanation						
Individualist[e]		1.12°°°		0.23		−0.89°°°
Mixed[e]		0.09		−0.76		−0.85°°°
None[e]		0.73		−0.45		−1.18°°
Constant	−2.50	−1.49	0.33	1.25	2.83	2.75
Wald chi-square (*df*)	167.15 (28)	208.50 (34)	167.15 (28)	208.50 (34)	167.15 (28)	208.50 (34)
Pseudo R^2	.09	.11	.09	.11	.09	.11

SOURCE: Race, Crime, and Public Opinion Survey, 2001.

a. "More money for police and prisons" and "neither" were combined. We performed a likelihood ratio test to determine whether there were significant differences between models that combined the two categories and concluded there were no significant differences.

b. Range = 1–5; 1 = *very liberal*; 5 = *very conservative*.

c. Range = 1–6; 1 = *never*; 6 = *more than once a week*.

d. Range = 1–5; 1 = *low fear of crime*; 5 = *high fear of crime*.

e. Compared to structuralists.

°p < .05. °°p < .01. °°°p < .001.

and job training versus both equally is in the opposite direction of what we expected. We initially thought fear of crime would lead people to support more spending for law enforcement, but we find instead that it is correlated with more support for a mixed strategy of spending as a solution to crime. We can only speculate that people who have a greater fear of crime are also more likely to live in places where the exposure to crime is greater.[8] Thus, because of the more personal relationship to crime, they may take a more holistic approach to solving crime by supporting spending on law enforcement and prisons while at the same time supporting spending that addresses the social and economic conditions that lead to crime.

We next direct our attention to the possibility that mode of explanation acts as an intervening variable in explaining racially polarized attitudes about the criminal justice system. In each model that contains "education and job training" as a comparison group, race is a strong predictor of support for spending policy before mode of explanation is introduced (see model 1) and continues to be significant even after we introduce mode of explanation. However, the mode of explanation variable does help partially to explain away some of the effects of race. In the end, there is only a 15.6 percent decrease in the overall effects of race when comparing support for spending on police and prisons to more spending on education and job training and a 12.2 percent decrease in the likelihood of support for education and job training compared to both equally (converted to probabilities before calculating percentage decrease). There is no effect of race in our models that compare support for more spending on police and prisons to both equally. Mode of explanation is an important part of the story behind the racial gap in support for crime spending policies, but it is not the entire story.

We can draw two conclusions from these models. First, mode of explanation does have an independent effect on support for spending policies, irrespective of other factors. Similarly, it acts to explain part of the gap between blacks and whites, though—and this is important—*not* the entire gap. Second, mode of explanation, along with race, is significant only when the comparison group is spending on education and job training. That is, the key distinction appears to be between those who support spending policies that focus entirely on education and job training and those who support spending for more law enforcement and prisons, even if it includes an element of education and job training spending.

Support for stricter parole boards. These spending policies address only the entry side of the crime problem in America. In cases where crime prevention fails, we must decide what to do with convicted criminals once we have them and, if we decide to incarcerate them, how long we should keep them locked up. As the number of prisoners in the nation's prisons continues to swell, the answer to the latter question becomes an important matter of public policy and human rights. In the next set of models, we test the effects of mode of explanation on people's support for making parole boards more or less strict and find that mode of explanation does indeed predict support for these policies, independent of other variables.

TABLE 7
Logistic Regression of Support for Making Parole Boards
"More Strict" versus "Less Strict/Leaving Them the Same"[a]

	Model 1	Model 2
Demographics		
Black	−1.01[***]	−0.89[***]
Female	0.37[*]	0.39[*]
Southern	0.18	0.09
Age (in years)	−0.66	−0.81[*]
Education (in years)	−0.10[**]	−0.10[**]
Income	−0.06	−0.10
Values and ideology		
Independent	−0.46[*]	−0.48[*]
Republican	−0.05	−0.14
Conservatism[b]	0.31[**]	0.28[**]
Church attendance[c]	0.08	0.07
Salience of crime		
Victim of crime	−0.14	−0.10
Index crime (per 100,000)	0.00	0.00
Murder rate (per 100,000)	0.00	−0.01
Fear of crime[d]	0.35[**]	0.42[***]
Mode of explanation		
Individualist[e]		0.95[***]
Mixed[e]		0.53[*]
None[e]		0.81
Constant	4.41	4.99
N	1,077	1,077
Wald chi-square (*df*)	70.21 (14)	82.69 (17)
Pseudo R^2	.07	.09

SOURCE: Race, Crime, and Public Opinion Survey, 2001.
a. "Same" and "less strict" were combined. We performed a likelihood ratio test to determine whether there were significant differences between models that combined the two categories and concluded there were no significant differences.
b. Range = 1–5; 1 = *very liberal*; 5 = *very conservative*.
c. Range = 1–6; 1 = *never*; 6 = *more than once a week*.
d. Range = 1–5; 1 = *low fear of crime*; 5 = *high fear of crime*.
e. Compared to structuralists.
[*]$p < .05$. [**]$p < .01$. [***]$p < .001$.

    First, the results from these models, shown in Table 7, reflect some of what we saw in the previous models when it comes to conservatism. Conservatives are more likely to support stricter parole boards than are liberals.[9] The effects of conservatism are almost equally strong before and after the mode of explanation variables are introduced, likely reflecting the strong current of "tough on crime" approaches within the dominant conservative political discourse. When it comes to conservatism, the effects are strong regardless of whether we look at solving the origins of crime or dealing with criminals once they are incarcerated.

Next, there were somewhat mixed results when it comes to exposure to crime and fear of crime. While crime rates have no impact on support for making parole boards stricter, fear of crime is an important part of the story. People who fear crime the most are also more likely to support stricter parole boards, independent of the crime rates and mode of explanation. We also find that fear of crime is in the expected direction when it comes to attitudes about parole, indicating a more direct link between fear of crime and support for crime policies that promise to keep convicted criminals off the street longer. Ensuring that prisoners remain behind bars for as long as possible may act to alleviate some of the fear that people have about crime.

Last, mode of explanation does have an impact on support for making parole boards more or less strict and seems to also have a small effect on race differences in policy outlooks. Individualists are 2.6 times more likely ($e^{0.95}$) to support stricter parole boards than are structuralists, and those in the mixed-mode category are about 1.7 times more likely ($e^{0.53}$) to do so than structuralists. Mode of explanation is one of the most important predictors of support for stricter parole boards. Nevertheless, race remains a strong predictor of support for stricter parole boards, regardless of what we introduce to the model, and the decrease in the likelihood of supporting stricter parole boards is only about 12.2 percent (converted to probabilities before calculating percentage decrease). Once again, we find mode of explanation to be a significant factor in explaining support for more punitive crime policies, yet it stops short of fully explaining the gap between blacks and whites, only marginally acting as an intervening variable.

A visual representation of these models may sum it up best. Figures 2a and 2b show the main effects from both models after controlling for race and mode of explanation. First, individualists and structuralists, regardless of race, are not likely to support spending money *only* on police and prisons. All else being equal, there tends to be more support for policies that include education and job training. Whites, however, are somewhat split, with more white individualists leaning toward support for policies that include some form of spending for police and prisons and white structuralists being slightly more supportive of policies that include spending for education and job training. Blacks, on the other hand, tend to lean toward policies that include spending for education and job training programs, reflecting a more liberal stance on how America should deal with crime. This is true for both types of policies in Figures 2a and 2b.

Perhaps the most striking finding in terms of whether whites and blacks are truly worlds apart when it comes to understanding the problem of crime is the fact that even the most externally oriented group of whites—structuralists—are hardly any different from the most dispositionally oriented group of blacks. Put differently, from a policy viewpoint, black individualists are substantively no different from white structuralists. Blacks and whites, despite the significant differences

FIGURE 2a
Predicted Probability of Support for Crime Solutions
for Individualists and Structuralists by Race

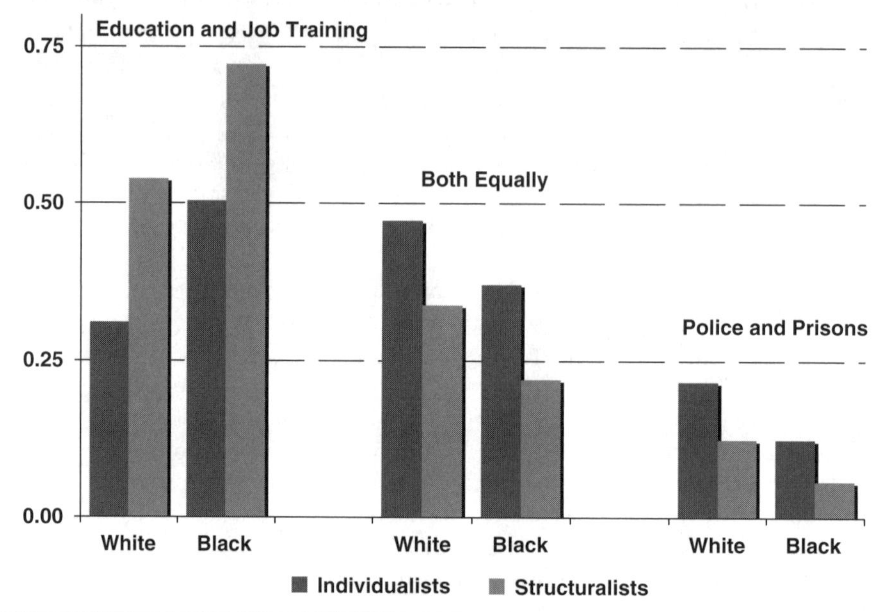

SOURCE: Race, Crime, and Public Opinion Survey, 2001.

FIGURE 2b
Predicted Probabilities of Support for Making Parole
Boards "More Strict" versus "Less Strict/Leaving Them the Same"

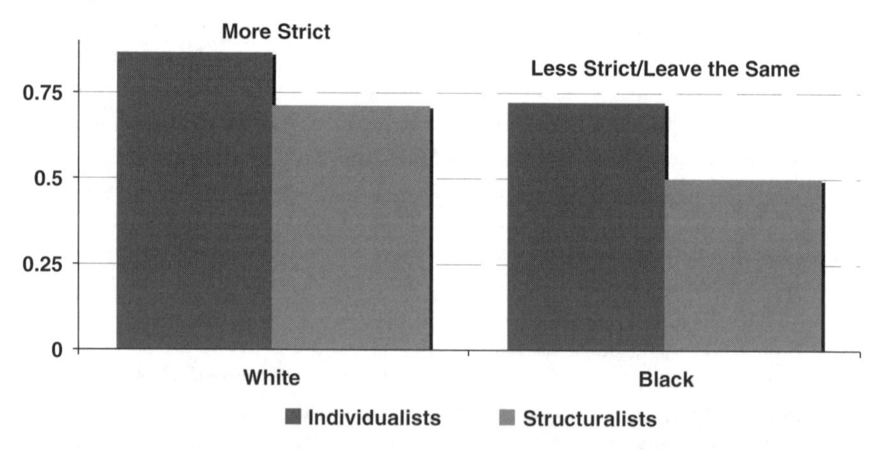

SOURCE: Race, Crime, and Public Opinion Survey, 2001.

between structuralists and individualists within each racial group, remain extremely polarized even when mode of explanation is taken into account.

Discussion and Conclusions

Racial polarization on matters of law enforcement and criminal justice remains a problem. We sought to determine whether one factor underlying this polarization involved sharply different ways of explaining criminal behavior among black and white Americans. Our results point to real differences in the extent to which whites and blacks understand crime as having roots in individuals' choices, dispositions, and failings, on one hand, and situational or structural constraints and limitations, on the other. To be sure, we find that African Americans are substantially more likely than whites to adopt structuralist accounts for criminal behavior and that just the opposite pattern exists with regard to endorsing individualist accounts for crime. Yet blacks and whites are about equally likely to adopt mixed accounts for crime, straddling the line between structuralist and individualist views of criminal behavior. In sum, there are real differences in core attributional tendencies between blacks and whites. These differences, however, do not constitute a sort of gaping polarization in thinking about crime.

Beyond race, we find that values and ideology help to shape crime attributions. In particular, political ideology plays a clear role among whites, though it is less consistently influential among blacks. Among black respondents, exposure to and particularly fear of crime do more to shape attributional modes.

Explanatory modes for crime matter considerably for crime policy outlooks. As expected, structuralists are more likely than individualists or those offering mixed accounts to stress a nonpunitive response to crime. They are more supportive of trying to prevent crime, with an emphasis on educational opportunities and jobs rather than on more police and prisons. They are also more likely to encourage less stringent practices by parole boards. Blacks and whites are significantly different on these policy matters in the expected directions. Race-linked differences in attributional patterns account for a part of the race gap in policy views between blacks and whites. However, most of the gap remains even after we have taken into account black-white differences in explanatory modes.

The latter pattern suggests that other factors beyond the attributional process account for the black-white polarization in the domain of criminal justice. Some of these other factors may include differential personal, family, and community-based experiences with agents and institutions of the criminal justice system. It may also reflect a sort of group cultural identity and outlook. On the former, it seems that direct, personal, negative experiences with agents of the criminal justice system, or knowledge of bad experiences reported by family members and close friends, is sufficiently common in black communities that these experiences create a pervasive cynicism about law enforcement and an expectation of race bias (Wilson and Dunham 2001). On the latter, these ideas are also sufficiently widely shared and long-standing that they may rise to the level of an aspect of group culture and identity, especially among the most politically engaged segments of the black population. To wit, the lion's share of the foundation of polarized policy views and of enormous differences in expectancies for fair treatment may have more to do with direct experience and group culture than with fundamentally different understandings of the nature of crime.

Notes

1. Descriptions of and reports on the surveys (Bobo and Johnson 2004) and focus groups (Bobo 2004; Bobo and Thompson 2006) have appeared elsewhere (see also Johnson 2008; Bobo and Thompson 2010).

2. Hunt's (2007) terminology differs from Kluegel's (1990) in that Hunt uses "person-centered" to describe these traits because the "lack of ability" response to the General Social Survey (GSS) question denotes a deterministic behavior rather than one that reflects individual choice. Unlike Kluegel (1990) and Hunt (2007), our "individualist" responses ("lazy" and "do not care") are presumably choices an individual makes and not the result of biological determinism.

3. We initially considered a more complex nine-category explanatory mode typology. After extensive analysis, we concluded that this complexity was not warranted. Specifically, we treated respondents who chose only individualist attributes or only structuralist attributes as "strong individualists" and "strong structuralists" and those who chose both individualist and one structuralist attribute or both structuralist attributes and one individualist attribute as "weak individualists" and "weak structuralists," respectively. However, there were few differences among several of these more finely grained groupings. The differences that do exist are among white respondents. Southern whites were more likely to be weak individualists, and ideologically conservative whites were more likely to be strong individualists, all else being equal. Older whites were also less likely to be strong structuralists.

4. There are also significant predictors among respondents in the "none" mode of explanation. Among the total sample, higher-income southerners who were less conservative and had low fear of crime were more likely to be in this category. Among whites, less conservative independents were more likely to choose "none." Higher-income blacks who were less conservative and had a lower fear of crime were the most likely blacks to fall into the "none" category. Though we do include them in our models, we elected not to draw too many conclusions about them given space constraints and the small number of persons in this category ($N = 28$).

5. Full interaction models show that black-white differences are slightly significant for ideological conservatism among individualists ($p < .10$) and structuralists ($p < .05$).

6. Full interaction models show significant differences ($p < .05$) between blacks and whites in both cases.

7. Full interaction models suggest only slight differences between blacks and whites for the effects of age ($p < .10$) and no differences for living in the South.

8. That fear of crime is positively correlated with crime rates and negatively correlated with income and education supports this claim.

9. We performed tests to determine whether there were differences between the "leave the same" and "less strict" categories and concluded that statistically speaking, there were no significant differences.

References

Apostle, Richard A., Charles V. Glock, Thomas Piazza, and Marijean Suelzle. 1983. *The anatomy of racial attitudes*. Berkeley, CA: University of California Press.

Barkan, Steven E., and Steven F. Cohen. 2005. Why whites favor spending more money to fight crime: The role of racial prejudice. *Social Problems* 52:300–14.

Bobo, Lawrence D. 1991. Social responsibility, individualism, and redistributive policies. *Sociological Forum* 6:71–92.

Bobo, Lawrence D. 2004. Inequalities that endure? Racial ideology, American politics, and the peculiar role of the social sciences. In *The changing terrain of race and ethnicity*, eds. Maria Krysan and Amanda E. Lewis, 13–42. New York, NY: Russell Sage Foundation.

Bobo, Lawrence D., and Devon Johnson. 2001. *Race, crime, and public opinion survey*. Cambridge, MA: Department of Sociology, Harvard University.

Bobo, Lawrence D., and Devon Johnson. 2004. A taste for punishment: Black and white Americans' views on the death penalty and the war on drugs. *Du Bois Review* 1 (1): 151–80.

Bobo, Lawrence D., and Victor R. Thompson. 2006. Unfair by design: The war on drugs, race, and the legitimacy of the criminal justice system. *Social Research: An International Quarterly of Social Sciences* 73 (2): 445–72.

Bobo, Lawrence D., and Victor R. Thompson. 2010. Racialized mass incarceration: African Americans and the criminal justice system. In *Doing race: 21 essays for the 21st century*, eds. Hazel Markus and Paula M. Moya, 322–55. New York, NY: Norton.

Carroll, John S. 1978. Causal theories of crime and their effect upon expert parole decisions. *Law and Human Behavior* 2 (4): 377–88.

Carroll, John S., and John W. Payne. 1976. The psychology of the parole decision process: A joint application of attribution theory and information processing psychology. In *Cognition and social behavior*, eds. John S. Carroll and John W. Payne, 13–32. Hillsdale, NJ: Lawrence Erlbaum.

Chambliss, William J., and Robert B. Seidman. 1971. *Law, order, and power*. Reading, MA: Addison-Wesley.

Cole, David. 1999. *No equal justice: Race and class in the American criminal justice system*. New York, NY: New Press.

Erskine, Hazel. 1974. The polls: Fear of violence and crime. *Public Opinion Quarterly* 38 (1): 131–45.

Gottschalk, Marie. 2008. Hiding in plain sight: American politics and the carceral state. *Annual Review of Political Science* 11:235–60.

Hagan, John, Carla Shedd, and Monique R. Payne. 2005. Race, ethnicity, and youth perceptions of criminal injustice. *American Sociological Review* 70:381–407.

Heider, Fritz. 1958. *The psychology of interpersonal relations*. New York, NY: Wiley.

Higginbotham, A. Leon. 1996. *Shades of freedom: Racial politics and presumptions of the American legal process*. New York, NY: Oxford University Press.

Huber, Joan, and William H. Form. 1973. *Income and ideology*. New York, NY: Free Press.

Hunt, Matthew O. 2004. Race/ethnicity and beliefs about wealth and poverty. *Social Science Quarterly* 85 (3): 827–53.

Hunt, Matthew O. 2007. African American, Hispanic, and white beliefs about black/white inequality, 1977–2004. *American Sociological Review* 72:390–415.

Hurwitz, Jon, and Mark Peffley. 2005. Explaining the great racial divide: Perceptions of fairness in the U.S. criminal justice system. *Journal of Politics* 67:762–83.

Johnson, Devon. 2008. Crime salience, perceived racial bias, and blacks' punitive attitudes. *Journal of Ethnicity in Criminal Justice* 4 (4): 1–18.

Kennedy, Joseph E. 2003. Drug wars in black and white. *Law and Contemporary Problems* 66:153–82.

Kennedy, Randall. 1997. *Race, crime, and the law*. New York, NY: Vintage.

Kluegel, James R. 1990. Trends in whites' explanations of the black-white gap in socioeconomic status, 1977–1989. *American Sociological Review* 55 (4): 512–25.

Kluegel, James R., and Eliot R. Smith. 1986. *Beliefs about inequality: Americans' views of what is and what ought to be*. New York, NY: Aldine de Gruyter.

Mann, Michael. 1970. The social cohesion of liberal democracy. *American Sociological Review* 35:423–39.

Massey, Douglas. 2007. *Categorically unequal: The American stratification system*. New York, NY: Russell Sage Foundation.

Matsueda, Ross L., and Kevin Drakulich. 2009. Perceptions of criminal injustice, symbolic racism, and racial politics. *The Annals of the American Academy of Political and Social Science* 623 (1): 163–78.

Mauer, Marc. 1999. *Race to incarcerate*. New York, NY: New Press.

Pattillo-McCoy, Mary. 1998. Church culture as a strategy of action in the black community. *American Sociological Review* 63 (6): 767–84.

Pettit, Becky, and Bruce Western. 2004. Mass imprisonment and the life course: Race and class inequality in U.S. incarceration. *American Sociological Review* 69 (2): 151–69.

Quinney, Richard. 1970. *The social reality of crime*. Boston, MA: Little, Brown.

Roberts, Dorothy E. 2003. The social and moral cost of mass incarceration in African American communities. *Stanford Law Review* 56:1271–1305.

Schuman, Howard. 1971. Free will and determinism in public beliefs about race. In *Majority and minority: The dynamics of racial and ethnic relations*, eds. Norman R. Yetman and C. Hoy Steele, 382–90. Boston, MA: Allyn & Bacon.

Shaw, Greg M., Robert Y. Shapiro, Shmuel Lock, and Lawrence R. Jacobs. 1998. The polls—trends: Crime, the police, and civil liberties. *Public Opinion Quarterly* 62 (3): 405–26.

Sigelman, Lee, and Susan Welch. 1991. *Black Americans' views of racial inequality: The dream deferred*. New York, NY: Cambridge University Press.

Sniderman, Paul M., and Michael Gray Hagen. 1985. *Race and inequality: A study in American values*. Chatham, NJ: Chatham House.

Soss, Joe, Laura Langbein, and Alan R. Metelko. 2003. Why do white Americans support the death penalty? *Journal of Politics* 65:397–421.

Tonry, Michael H. 1995. *Malign neglect—Race, crime, and punishment in America*. New York, NY: Oxford University Press.

Tonry, Michael, and Matthew Melewski. 2008. The malign effects of drug and crime control policies on black Americans. *Crime and Justice: A Review of Research* 37:1–44.

Tyler, Tom R., and Renee J. Boeckmann. 1997. Three strikes and you are out, but why?—The psychology of public support for punishing rule breakers. *Law & Society Review* 31 (2): 237–65.

Tyler, Tom R., and Renee Weber. 1982. Support for the death penalty: Instrumental response to crime, or symbolic attitude? *Law & Society Review* 17:21–46.

Unnever, James D., and Francis T. Cullen. 2007. Reassessing the racial divide in support for capital punishment: The continuing significance of race. *Journal of Research in Crime and Delinquency* 44 (1): 124–58.

Wacquant, Loïc. 2001. Deadly symbiosis: When ghetto and prison meet and mesh. *Punishment and Society* 3:95–134.

Weiner, Bernard. 1974. *Achievement motivation and attribution theory*. Morristown, NJ: General Learning Press.

Weitzer, Ronald J., and Stephen A Tuch. 2006. *Race and policing in America: Conflict and reform*. New York, NY: Cambridge University Press.

Western, Bruce. 2006. *Punishment and inequality in America*. New York, NY: Russell Sage Foundation.

Wilson, George. 1996. Toward a revised framework for examining beliefs about the causes of poverty. *Sociological Quarterly* 37 (3): 413–28.

Wilson, George, and Roger Dunham. 2001. Race, class, and attitudes toward crime control. *Criminal Justice Behavior* 28 (3): 259–78.

Racial Discrimination, Interpretation, and Legitimation at Work

Research on race stratification and employment usually implies discrimination as a key mechanism in race stratification, although few if any analyses bring attitudes, employee-employer interpretations, and established discriminatory behavior into a singular analysis. In this article, the authors do so and offer a relational account of how discrimination operates, drawing on a large sample of verified racial discrimination cases. Building on racial stratification literature and theory on "color-blind" racism, the analyses focus on employee and employer interpretations and then use dyadic analyses coupled with qualitative case immersion to shed light on the relational nature of discrimination and how employers justify such conduct. Findings highlight significant interpersonal disjunctures in descriptions of common events as well as the ways in which employers evoke broad organizational and societal ideals of meritocracy— ideals that often fall by the wayside in concrete decision-making pertaining to and in evaluation of minority employees.

Keywords: discrimination; workplace; legitimation; racial inequality; gender inequality; beliefs; relational approach

By
RYAN LIGHT,
VINCENT J. ROSCIGNO,
and
ALEXANDRA KALEV

Race stratification in employment remains problematic. Recent research, relying on industry or firm-level data, describes how labor market variations in opportunity (Cohen 1998; Huffman 2004), job segregation (Tomaskovic-Devey 1993), and social closure more generally (G. Wilson and McBrier 2005) affect race-specific inequalities in hiring, mobility, firing, and wages. Although many conclude that discrimination is playing a role, it is typically only inferred to be a stratifying mechanism. Driven in part by data difficulties, limited empirical attention to discrimination may also be a consequence of the little theoretical attention to relational insights surrounding social closure, gatekeepers' subjective evaluative processes, and tangible discriminatory behaviors (Tilly 1998).

Cultural critics suggest that prominent theories of stratification, grounded in liberal race theory, poorly account for the contemporary prevalence

DOI: 10.1177/0002716210388475

of racial discrimination (Dyson 2004; West 1999). Sociological theorists of race/ethnicity concur with this suggestion, noting that a new, more nuanced racial ideology has developed in the post–civil rights era that makes it difficult to understand why discrimination persists (Bonilla-Silva 2003). Indeed, with the expansion of race-neutral ideology within contemporary American culture, as taught in schools and promoted through various media, whites have increasingly accepted the idea that all should be evaluated and treated on meritocratic grounds (Schuman et al. 1997). And many employers have seemingly followed suit, incorporating bureaucratic structures and procedures that lend themselves, on the face of it, to race-neutral hiring and promotion practices. Both theory and empirical research, however, have recognized the limits of such structures and procedures (Nonet and Selznick 1978; Dobbin, Schrage, and Kalev 2009; Castilla 2008), while others have called for process-centered analyses of stratification and elaboration of mechanisms more generally (Reskin 2003; Gross 2009).

Building on prior work and extending the literature on racism, this article explores issues of interpretation and discriminatory action and their fundamentally relational nature. We first highlight the strengths and limitations of work relying on aggregate statistical analyses or accounts of employer attitudes and biases. We also discuss the relevance of our research to scholarly developments in the realm of antidiscrimination law and the remediation of inequality. We then turn to an integrated theoretical typology of how subjective evaluation by gatekeepers may be playing a role in generating inequality and why the relational nature of the discrimination process, including its embeddedness in power variations, organizational structures, and cultural discourses, warrants attention. Drawing from unique quantitative and qualitative data on discrimination cases, our analyses examine employers' and employees' subjective interpretations of common events. Of particular interest

---

Ryan Light is an assistant professor of sociology at the University of Oregon, where he studies culture, inequality, and social networks. His current work builds on network methods and rich archival data and examines the intersection of history, culture, and power relative to race relations in the antebellum South.

Vincent J. Roscigno is a professor of sociology at Ohio State University, currently analyzing workplace discrimination and bullying using a variety of methods. He is the author of The Face of Discrimination *(Rowman & Littlefield 2007) and has published in* American Sociological Review, American Journal of Sociology, Social Problems, *and* Social Forces.

Alexandra Kalev is a sociologist at the University of Arizona who is currently examining corporate compliance, antidiscrimination law, workplace restructuring, and their implications for women's and minorities' careers and for corporate performance. She has published in the American Sociological Review, American Journal of Sociology, Administrative Science Quarterly, *and* Law and Social Inquiry.

NOTE: The authors are grateful to participants of the Ohio Discrimination Project Research Practicum in the Department of Sociology at Ohio State University for partially funding portions of this research and to the editors, Matthew Hunt and George Wilson, for their helpful suggestions. An earlier version of this article was presented at the annual meeting of the Law and Society Association, May 2009, Denver, Colorado.

is the degree of interpretational disjuncture in the employer-employee dyad and the ways in which often-neutral organizational policies are used to discriminate, legitimate discrimination, or both.

Racial Stratification and Discrimination in Employment

There is much attention within the racial stratification literature on wage disparities as well as variations in upward mobility. Although most concede that human capital deficits may account for some outcome differences, studies have consistently found that income and wage gaps (e.g., Cotter, Hermsen, and Vanneman 1999; Marini and Fan 1997; Tomaskovic-Devey 1993; Tomaskovic-Devey and Skaggs 2002), employment variations (Cohn and Fossett 1995; F. Wilson, Tienda, and Wu 1995), and inequalities in promotion and authority attainment (Smith 2002; G. Wilson 1997; G. Wilson, Sakura-Lemessy, and West 1999) remain despite human capital controls. But why?

Recent analyses suggest that sorting mechanisms, including discretionary decision-making and discrimination by employers and coworkers, may be partially responsible for racial stratification. Research pertaining to hiring and promotion (Reskin and McBrier 2000), downward race and gender mobility (McBrier and Wilson 2004), and employment exits (Reid and Padavic 2005), for instance, suggests that discrimination, and specifically arbitrary and subjective decision-making within firms, may be key. Huffman and Cohen's (2004) and Petersen and Saporta's (2004) analyses of racial and gender wage disparities, although not measuring or analyzing discrimination directly, similarly come to the conclusion that discrimination in worker allocation and exclusion are likely playing a part in the persistent disparities that they find. While the existence of gaps is well documented, the processes that lead to such gaps remain unclear.

Research that locates and observes discriminatory actions, using experimental techniques, partially fills the void. Based on the classic "correspondence test" of Schwartz and Skolnick (1962), some innovative contemporary work has employed audit tests of businesses, centering specifically on the hiring process. By sending two similar candidates to job interviews, for instance, Pager (2003) isolates the effect of having a criminal record. In her analyses, race appears to be an exacerbating factor above and beyond a criminal record; however, criminal records compound the hiring disadvantage that minorities face. Such audit-based research centers attention on gatekeepers' decision-making, thus drawing the employment stratification field closer to the well-established literature on racial attitudes. Yet audit studies continue to suffer from acknowledged generalizability issues (Pager 2003). Moreover, they are limited to hiring, thus leaving relatively unexplored ways in which social closure processes may also be shaping mobility inequalities, discriminatory firing, as well as more general processes of workplace racial harassment.

Race Attitudes, Ideology, and Discrimination

Rather than documenting levels of stratification within particular workplace contexts, attitudinal research takes as its analytic question why inequality persists and the extent to which persistent stereotypes and preferences for social distance play a role. General work in this regard, such as that from Schuman et al. (1997), depicts shifting discrimination trends. Whites are now more likely than ever to report acceptance of neighborhood, workplace, and school diversity, with the caveat that tolerance diminishes as minority representation increases. Moreover, whites, along with Hispanics and blacks, increasingly see inequality as driven by individual motivation rather than structural processes (see Hunt 2007). This by no means suggests that whites are not race-conscious. Rather, whites continue to wrestle with the historical legacy of racism, have difficulty communicating about racial matters, or express outright ambivalence toward race (see Bell and Hartmann 2007; Bonilla-Silva 2003).

Although some attitudinal trends paint an optimistic picture, qualitative work on black experiences indicates that discrimination remains a persistent problem. In his study of racial discrimination in public places, Feagin (1991) highlights the ways in which blacks continue to experience a range of discriminatory actions, from avoidance while walking down the street to physical confrontation based on the color of their skin. Within employment, and according to self-reports, a similar range of experiences persists, from the subtle to more explicit (Feagin and Eckberg 1980; Feagin and McKinney 2003; Pierce 2003; Roscigno 2007).

How do we navigate the divide between the optimistic reports of general attitudes of whites and the evidence that suggests blacks continue to experience racial discrimination? And more important, what do these patterns mean for racial inequality at work? Some scholars have employed methods to tackle these questions that aim at uncovering relations between attitudes and discriminatory actions. Kirschenman and Neckerman (1991) and Moss and Tilly (2001), for instance, make use of in-depth employer interviewing and uncover subtle forms of racial bias and preconceptions. Specifically, they point to the subjective aspects of evaluating employees and potential hirees and locate acts of discrimination in hiring, primarily within the evaluation of "soft skills," such as friendliness, appearance, attitude, and commitment. Complementary research decodes the language used when discussing race and interaction in the workplace (Pierce 2003).

Bonilla-Silva (2003), who also relies primarily on open-ended interviewing techniques, describes the subtle forms of discrimination underlying the way that whites discuss race. Whites continue to struggle with racial identities, he suggests, but this struggle appears to have taken a turn unaccounted for in previous theories of racism. Whites, according to Bonilla-Silva's theory of color-blind racism, often express support for meritocratic ideals—that is, they acknowledge the right of all people to the pursuit of upward mobility, or the "American dream"—yet they remain reticent to acknowledge potential structural and historical impediments that minority groups face. Consequently, meritocracy remains a key cultural justification for inequality (see Lamont 2000), while the effects of continued racial bias often go unacknowledged.

The use of meritocracy as a cultural framework for explaining inequality has institutional manifestations as well. Employers, encouraged by personnel professionals, have increasingly relied on formal performance evaluations to justify the distribution of rewards (Dobbin 2009). These formal performance evaluations have increasingly gained the deference of judges as a justification for inequality (Edelman et al. 2006); and as recent laboratory studies show, managers too tend to trust the firm's merit-based system and invest less cognitive effort in checking their own biases (Castilla and Benard 2009). At the same time, evidence abounds about racial stereotypes affecting formal performance evaluations (McKay and McDaniel 2006; P. Roth, Huffcutt, and Bobko 2003) and merit-based personnel decisions (Castilla 2008; Elvira and Town 2001; L. Roth 2006). The idea of meritocracy is thus more than a matter of individual attitudes. Formal meritocratic procedures and rhetoric can become an institutionalized cloak for ongoing ascriptive bias—a legitimating discourse, where managers, employers, and judges exchange symbols of meritocracy for equality. Bonilla-Silva's (2003) notion of color-blind racism thus manifests in, and is enabled by, organizational and institutional processes. When formal procedures are in place, managers (and judges) are more apt to believe the structure is unbiased and that unequal outcomes therefore reflect differences in merit.

Attitudinal research adds an essential micro-interactional component to our understanding of workplace stratification. The findings of such work correspond with the suggestion of macro-level analyses that discrimination is likely occurring in evaluation, perhaps cloaked in neutral, meritocratic assumptions. Yet gatekeepers' attitudes are seldom, if ever, matched with the experiences of potential victims. As is evident in audit studies (e.g., Pager 2003; Pager and Quillian 2005), the discrimination process is a relational or dyadic one: an interaction that takes place between the employer and employee or between employees (Tilly 1998).[1] Conceiving of discrimination in such a manner, as we suggest below, provides leverage for understanding how social closure occurs, how gatekeepers perpetuate it knowingly or unknowingly, and the ways in which status dynamics and organizational contexts may constrain or enable it.

Interpretational Disjuncture, Legitimation, and Social Closure

Subjective experiences of discriminatory behavior and how they unfold in relation to each party's explanation of relational events must be simultaneously considered to fill the empirical gaps pertaining to the persistence of racial stratification at work (see Pager and Quillian 2005). Social closure as a sociological construct offers an orienting theoretical framework, directing scholars toward an in-depth comprehension of the *processes* through which individuals and social groups both define and maintain stratification hierarchies (Weber 1968/1978; Parkin 1974).

Though social closure can occur through institutional exclusion and dominant group positioning, it may also unfold, consciously and unconsciously, within the context of everyday interaction—interaction that, through language, symbolic acts, or physical control or force, has as its aim status-hierarchy preservation (Ridgeway 1997; Roscigno 2007). To underplay such interactional processes would be misleading insomuch as "social structures exist only in the action and interaction of persons; they exist not as states, but processes" (Young 2001, 13). The benefit, beyond a more in-depth understanding of stratification in particular, also entails more explicit theoretical development concerning mechanisms. Indeed, effective theorizing not only takes as its logical aim the denotation of relations (e.g., How does X affect Y, or What is the magnitude of that relation?), but also the explication of processes (e.g., How does X influence Y, or What processes and mechanisms are involved in that relation?) (Gross 2009; Reskin 2003).

In the first of these sets of questions, research has been quite strong, denoting the empirical relevance of human capital attributes, segregation, and so forth, often concluding that discrimination is occurring. In the second, however, both empirical work and theory are less clear. It is for this reason that we begin by theoretically disentangling dimensions of closure, including discrimination, through a two-by-two classification of types.[2] In Figure 1, the horizontal axis signifies the extent to which discrimination can be observed or is explicit. The vertical axis indicates the level as either macro (structural) or micro (relational). The shading differentiation denotes these forms of discrimination as either "overt" discrimination (non-shaded), as encompassed by traditional liberal race theories, or "color-blind" (shaded), as suggested by both recent theories of discrimination and more nuanced forms of liberal race theory.

Within the United States, state-sanctioned racial discrimination (the macro-explicit box) no longer operates explicitly, though it certainly carries implications into the modern era through lingering structural inequalities (macro-implicit). Contemporary structural arguments suggest that rational market forces, along with the law, prevent broad-based employment discrimination. Here, diverse occupational outcomes largely result from the differing structural impediments among various racial groups. Blacks, for instance, face an uphill battle in employment due to poor educational systems in their neighborhoods, less effective social networks, and so forth. Rather than being due to discrimination, inequality in this conception results largely from structural impediments that minorities face and historical remnants of racial discrimination, captured by contemporary differentials in skills, education, and wealth (e.g., Conley 1999; W. Wilson 1978).

Two theories grounded in liberal race theory—viewing discrimination as the result of overt racism (the micro-explicit box) or statistical discrimination (the micro-implicit box)—suggest that discrimination continues to be consequential and in quite salient relational ways. Proponents of the overt racism perspective assert that discrimination is the result of broad and explicitly racist behaviors, such as the use of derogatory names and the creation of hostile work environments. Statistical discrimination theory posits that perceived differences in productivity or skill generate discriminatory behavior by employers, knowingly or

FIGURE 1

Typology of Social Closure and Discrimination by Level and Explicitness

	Explicit	Implicit
Macro	State-Sanctioned Discrimination (e.g., Jim Crow laws)	Structural-Historical Disadvantage (and Related Inequalities in Human Capital)
Micro	Overt Race-Based Discrimination and Harassment	Covert Discrimination (e.g., Soft Skills Criteria, False Meritocratic Claims, Differential Rule Application, Etc.)

unknowingly, and perpetuate racial stereotyping (Tomaskovic-Devey and Skaggs 1999). Both explicit and implicit forms of racism are likely to be evidenced in our data; however, more recent theoretical arguments suggest that broader ideological justifications that are color-blind in nature (captured by the micro-implicit quadrant of our typology) have come to predominate (see Bonilla-Silva 2003; Sturm 2001).

The theoretical formulations above, while addressing the role of gatekeepers within organizational environments, leave the fundamentally relational nature of discriminatory encounters, status variations, and power dynamics unspecified. Indeed, much extant research is actor-centric, focusing singularly on victim experiences or potential employer biases as the units of their analysis rather than on the *discriminatory encounter*. The first portion of our analyses follows an actor-centric approach in an effort to highlight patterns revealed in prior work. The second portion of our analyses—and the core contribution of this article—offers a relational account, wherein the relational interpretation of the discriminatory encounter (or the dyad between victims' and perpetrators' narratives) is the core unit of analysis. Here we examine dominant patterns of justification for discrimination between the employee and employer; the extent to which race-neutral, meritocratic justifications are used; and the degree to which this varies depending on the form of discrimination and the presence of legal advice. Legitimacy is integral for the maintenance of power (Bendix 1956; Weber 1968/1978), and culturally acceptable justifications (Foucault and Gordon 1980; Mills 1940) are effective means to gain that legitimacy. Justifications are inherently relational (i.e., they are inherently relative to the other's narrative), and they may reflect employers' motives at the time of action or merely rhetorical devices. In either case, the possibility that meritocratic, color-blind rhetoric and personnel procedures are implicated in a wide range of discriminatory actions suggests a powerful cultural schema worthy of attention.

Sociologists have long shown that personnel antidiscrimination structures often remain decoupled from everyday practice (Edelman and Petterson 1999; Kalev, Dobbin, and Kelly 2006), that bias infiltrates many formalized procedures (L. Roth 2006), and that managers and employers actively engage in social closure, despite the presence of antidiscrimination structures (Roscigno 2007). The recent scholarly focus on unconscious bias and structural antidiscrimination measures (Sturm 2001; Reskin 2000; Bielby 2000), while highly valuable, runs the risk of reifying structures and losing sight of the prevalence of bias (conscious and unconscious) within and despite these structures. The evidence presented in this article corroborates these points. Our dyadic analyses highlight key interpretational and interactional disjunctures surrounding narratives of discriminatory events as well as the ways in which the very relations and discrimination experiences specified are embedded in and enabled by power hierarchies, organizational structures, and broader legalistic and cultural discourses.

Data

Our data consist of 250 randomly selected racial discrimination cases filed with and verified by the Ohio Civil Rights Commission (OCRC) between 1988 and 2003. The OCRC is responsible for enforcing state laws against discriminatory practices in employment, housing, public accommodations, credit, and higher education (OCRC 2004). The OCRC is a neutral party and can render a "probable cause" recommendation, in accordance with the U.S. Equal Employment Opportunity Commission (EEOC), federal, and state guidelines, only when the "preponderance of evidence is sufficient to substantiate that discrimination has occurred" (OCRC 2004). The neutral position of the OCRC, its power as an investigative body, and its review process provide strong evaluative evidence of whether discrimination has occurred. Since 1978, the OCRC has had work-share arrangements with the EEOC so that employment charges are dually filed (OCRC 2004). The EEOC, however, often relies on the opinion of the OCRC, unless the case falls into an already-existent EEOC investigation, litigation, or national initiative. These cases are, in effect, both state and federal discrimination cases and from a relatively representative state. In the 2000 census, for example, 11.5 percent of Ohio's population was African American. This is comparable to the 12.4 percent rate for the United States. Employment statistics and industrial concentrations for African Americans in the state are also quite comparable to those of the nation (Mong and Roscigno 2010).

The case data include key variables such as the charging party's race and sex, the basis of the charge, the industry in which the claim occurred, and the outcome of the investigation. We considered only those cases in which the charging party self-identified as African American and in which the basis of the charge is race (N = 15,094). Because it would be inaccurate to assume that every claim that is filed is one in which discrimination actually occurred, we limit our analyses and use of qualitative materials to a random subsample (n = 250) of all verified race cases (N = 9,103). Verified cases include those with either a probable cause finding or a high-level favorable finding for the charging party such as a settlement arbitrated by a neutral third party (OCRC or a district attorney's office). Focusing on verified cases bolsters confidence that the cases discussed indeed represent actual discrimination, rather than alleged, perceived, or unsubstantiated discrimination.[3]

Discrimination is, admittedly, significantly underestimated by virtue of the fact that a case must be reported. Indeed, for a case to be reported, someone discriminated against must (1) understand his or her rights under the law, (2) interpret his or her treatment as discrimination, (3) actively seek out a civil rights commission office, and (4) go through an entire investigative process. There is also a subjective element to the process and to the cases analyzed—one wherein a charging party's subjective interpretation of the discriminatory experience and corresponding filing of a charge align with the law and meet investigative criteria. This interpretation is then juxtaposed with the defendant narrative, which, for a case to be won by a defendant, should align with the law's criteria of nondiscrimination. While these subjective elements could be seen as a weakness of the data, this article builds on these very disjunctures in narratives to gain insight into employers' perceptions of discrimination and what they see, or choose to claim, as legitimate action. Relative to prior work and despite these caveats, these cases reveal notable heterogeneity in discriminatory form, occupational status, and across industry; and the qualitative materials provide a level of detail and richness seldom seen in the stratification, occupational, or race literatures.

Analytic Strategy and Results

The analyses proceed in two steps. First, we examine how employees and employers describe the episode at the center of the discrimination claim of which they were a part. This portion of the analyses, taking an actor-centric approach, follows the steps of previous research on workplace discrimination. When viewed in isolation, each story must be taken somewhat literally. While reading between the lines is sometimes necessary when trying to uncover the more covert forms of discrimination, this process is quite difficult when the opposing side's story is unknown.

The second, core portion of our analyses turns to the dyadic modeling of claims and counterclaims. This analytic step borrows from network analysis to garner insight into how victims' experiences and perpetrators' justifications are relationally patterned. A dyad, after all, consists of two nodes and the possible connections between them (Wasserman and Faust 1994). Here, the nodes represent the narratives of employers and employees. The narratives follow particular themes, such as claims of differential treatment by the victims or claims of meritocracy by managers. The connection between these "nodes" represents the frequency with which a thematic response matches a thematic claim. We observe these patterns by using a bipartite graph. This method preserves the relational conception, outlined previously, and highlights the general patterning of discrimination claims and counterclaims contained within the data. We supplement the dyadic patterns reported with two additional analyses reported in the text. First, we examine whether meritocracy-based employer claims prevail across the board of discriminatory claims, including when racism is relatively explicit. Second, and given the central role of legal professionals in constructing what counts as antidiscrimination compliance (Dobbin 2009; Edelman, Fuller, and Mara-Drita 2001), we analyze whether the presence of legal advice heightens the likelihood of meritocratic justifications.

Interpreting Racial Discrimination

Workplaces and employers accused of discriminating are rarely willing to admit having done so. Taking an actor-centric approach here, we examine the interpretations of employees and employers relative to verified instances of discrimination across a wide array of workplaces. We use evidence from case materials to illustrate the range of discriminatory actions that victims report and employers' responses to these accusations.

What employees say

Employees experiencing workplace racial discrimination most often claim differential treatment (56 percent) relative to white employees. Differential treatment claims range from not receiving a promotion, to being discriminatorily fired for workplace rule infractions, to being asked to undertake job duties that other employees are not asked to do. Take, for instance, the case of Raymond Jackson. In 1989, the Mid City School District decided to diversify the responsibilities of its employees. Due to the summer lull in activities, a number of the district's bus drivers were asked to mow grass. Jackson, an employee of the district for more than 30 years, tried his hand on the tractor. He quickly realized that he was not comfortable with his new duties, owing to his height, which "made it unsafe for [him] to reach the brake or clutch in an emergency." He demonstrated this hazard to several supervisors who agreed with his misgivings. However, by the end of the summer, Jackson was suspended and subsequently fired for refusing to mow grass. Another employee also demonstrated her inability to mow the grass and was allowed to continue her duties as a bus driver. Jackson felt that he was treated differently because of his race; he was black and his colleague was white. In a similar case, Jason Thomas, an African American customer service representative, was fired for failing to follow procedures, while employees who similarly violated procedure retained their jobs. Thomas stated that he "was denied the same privilege of continued employment."

Differential treatment also revolves around subjective judgments of qualifications. For instance, an African American mental health professional's contract was not renewed because, in her words, "high profile, high priority and well-funded projects were assigned to all white employees." The meritocratic difference between this African American professional and her white counterparts is largely due to differential treatment.

Another form of covert discrimination is isolation (reported in 8 percent of cases). Isolation occurs when workplaces are overwhelmingly dominated by a single race, typically nonminority. The employees or hirees experiencing discrimination in these instances often have little evidence of discrimination beyond numerical observations of minority presence or a cursory knowledge of a critical gatekeeper's race. Take, for instance, D. J. Houston, an African American machine operator, who applied for a job at a public utility company. The company had recently adopted a formal procedure for hiring new employees. Unbeknownst to Houston, the employer required the completion of a written application form for all prospective hirees. Multiple people inside the organization neglected to let Houston know of this change in policy despite his numerous inquiries regarding job openings at the company.

While differential treatment and to some extent isolation cases could be cast in race-neutral terms, at least at first glance, cases pertaining to overt racism and racist environments certainly cannot be. Combined, such cases comprise 27 percent of all victim claims and demonstrate the persistence of traditional racism as touched upon earlier (see Figure 1, micro-explicit quadrant). Jim Carson, for instance, employed at an automobile parts company for nearly 16 years, reached a breaking point due to severe racial harassment that compelled him to lodge a discrimination charge:

> For the past year a six-page letter with 114 racial jokes has been circulating throughout [the parts company]. A picture of various types of monkeys has been posted on the bulletin board, which included a picture of myself. It was posted in plain sight for all to view.

Additionally, a "nigger application for employment," a mock letter to a "jungle bunny hunter," and a cartoon of an African American woman giving birth to a child holding a boom box were posted at the company. This hostile climate made it difficult for Jim to perform his duties and influenced his ability to do his job.

Others face similar impediments to successful job performance because of hostile treatment. In one case, a deputy clerk of courts overheard coworkers refer to her as "the nigger." In another case, white supervisors continually forced an African American custodian to walk around the building that he cleaned, while white employees were allowed to take shortcuts through the facility. He was also taunted with racial slurs as he worked. Importantly, within our data, such incidents of overt racism take place across an array of job types and regardless of gender. Although there are clearly negative employment outcomes in such incidents (e.g., termination and worsened job performance), there are also significant emotional and psychological consequences—consequences warranting further research attention.

What employers say

Employers are required by law to respond to discrimination charges, and these responses illustrate a variety of reasons for the actions that led the employee to seek reprisal. The majority of employers (57 percent) claim that their organization is purely meritocratic in terms of workplace decisions, adheres to the equal opportunity employment laws, and respects the tone of such laws. Thus, employment decisions are arguably never made on the basis of race but, rather, are made through concrete and fair evaluations of worker performance.

Examining case narrative materials reveals problematic dynamics associated with evaluations that seem, at first glance, to be meritocratic and neutral. Evaluations based upon skill often take place informally, in a short period of time, or without informing the employee of his or her poor performance. For example, managers made a quick decision in the case of an experienced freight operator who was fired after only a week on the job.

> As Charles Howell's supervisor for the week that he was employed at our company I agreed with the decision to terminate him. I did not feel that his lift skills were at the same level as the other new hires at the same point. . . . As I do with new hires I have to rely on feedback from the people they work with to a certain degree . . . the comments about Charles were that he was still having trouble with the ties of the freight.

This case exemplifies how gatekeepers often use merit to defend the decisions that they make. By describing their decisions as based upon merit, they conform to the post–civil rights ideal of equal opportunity. The onus then rests on the performance of the employee and not on the climate created by, actions of, or differential treatment by management and coworkers.

While less common than meritocratic justifications, some employers perceive that their decisions—decisions deemed discriminatory by civil rights investigators—were made with legitimate organizational concerns in mind (10 percent of cases). For example, in the case of Brenda Smith, an administrative assistant terminated by a historical preservation society, the personnel officer for the organization cited budgetary concerns as the primary reason for her dismissal: "Last September, due to budget cuts from the State of Ohio, we experienced a significant layoff, the result of which prompted the above charge." Notable in her case, however, was the fact that she was laid off while all other employees (all white) were simply reassigned. Such organizational, budgetary, and financial justifications are relatively common in age discrimination cases (Roscigno et al. 2007). They are clearly evident in race discrimination cases as well, although to a smaller extent.

Five percent of the time employers place the responsibility directly on the employee by stating that the adverse employment outcome, typically termination, was the employee's decision. These explanations "blame the victim." Often the employer reacts to charges of discrimination by suggesting that the employee never sought a promotion or that the employee agreed to a transfer. In cases of firing, the employer, citing the employee's decision, makes the claim that an employee "voluntarily terminated" himself or herself.

A similarly small portion of employers (6 percent) deny discrimination strictly on legalistic or procedural grounds, while others simply deny that discrimination ever occurred (13 percent). In one such instance of legalistic denial, a community-based human rights organization addressed the charge that it discriminated against minorities. A statement from the executive committee of the organization stated that the organization "is an independent organization with only one employee. We understand that the commission does not investigate organizations with only one employee." Other claims were that the "statute of limitations" had been reached or, in an extreme case, that a Civil Rights Commission conspired against the employer, violating the employer's civil rights. These legalistic denials do not revert back to the performance of the employee but challenge the legal validity of the discrimination claim. In the case of outright denials, the employer simply states that the alleged discrimination never occurred.

The Dyadic and Relational Nature of Workplace Discrimination

Analyzing employees' and employers' independent interpretations, as we have done above, extends previous, sometimes disconnected, lines of research: employees' interpretations correspond with previous retrospective accounts of minority experiences, while employers' justifications largely align with previous research on white attitudes and color-blind racism or on the unconscious nature of bias. Discrimination, however, does not occur in isolation, but rather dyadically between the individual discriminated against and the discriminator(s) and within an organizational context and structure that may mitigate or enable discriminatory action (Tilly 1998). By connecting the employees' experiences to the employers' justifications, as we do in this section, we gain greater insight into the rift between victims' and offenders' perceptions. This advances our understanding of discrimination by examining the degree of disjuncture in the interpretations of common discrimination episodes, the extent to which meritocratic claims prevail even in the face of explicitly racist treatment and with or without legal representation.

Figure 2 reports the stacked bipartite graph, constructed in UCINET (Borgatti, Everett, and Freeman 2002), of the aggregated dyadic structure of discrimination narratives across our 250 cases. Network analysts have used bipartite graphs for some time because they shift the attention from the groups to the relations between them. We merge the intuitive interpretational value of the bipartite graph with the more traditional stacked bar graph to show the relationship between two categorical variables—in this case, employees' claims of discrimination and

FIGURE 2
Dyadic Structure of Employer and Employee Interpretations

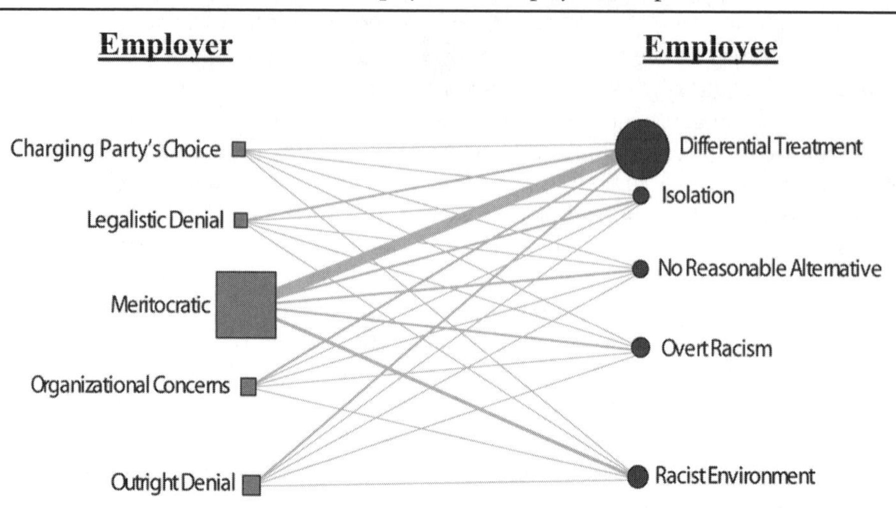

employers' responses to these claims. Stacked bar graphs become cumbersome when comparing variables with more than a handful of attributes. Our construction of the stacked bipartite graph, however, permits the comparison of multiple attributes without losing the information contained within the bar graphs. The lighter square "nodes" represent the coded counterclaims of employers. The darker circle nodes represent the coded narratives of victims. The size of the nodes represents the frequency with which specific parties used each of these themes. The size of the lines connecting the nodes represents the frequency with which employers' counterclaims appear in relation to employees' experiences.

Most notable is the meritocratic-differential treatment dyad, symptomatic of a major interpretational disjuncture that occurs within the discourse of workplace racial discrimination. On one hand, there are minority employees who denote the ways in which they are treated distinctly relative to their white counterparts. Such differential treatment most often invokes a meritocratic counterargument by a supervisor, who has status in the organization—status that allows, the offender access to seemingly race-neutral rules and procedures. The use of such rules and procedures (e.g., soft-skill criteria, workplace conduct, attendance policies, etc.) and their very existence are evoked as evidence of a meritocratic environment by employers, glossing over the fact that such procedures can be enacted with discretion.

Viewing discrimination as a dyadic process allows for the demystification of some workers' experiences. Sometimes, as in the case of overtly racist acts and actors, minority workers are straightforwardly victims of discriminatory treatment. In other cases, poor workplace performance and minority status are confounded.

Here, poor performance provides justification for employers' actions. Legally important, however, is that equally poorly performing white workers are not similarly penalized or sanctioned. Thus, what may seem to be justifiable employer actions surrounding lackluster performance from or commitment by certain minority employees is hardly the point. Discrimination can and does occur to "bad" employees and with seemingly good intentions by employers. This discrimination often occurs in the form of "differential policing" (Roscigno 2007), wherein employers apply rules and penalties for poor conduct differentially based on an employees' race. In these cases, the employee claims differential treatment. The employer, often citing a formal procedure, states that they have made a reasonable and, indeed, meritocratic decision.

The case of David Owens, an African American claims adjuster, serves as a case in point. Owens was having trouble at work. In numerous notes within his personnel file and official evaluations, his bosses chastised him for "a steady decline from a performance standpoint." He lost files and reported insurance claims late. In a handwritten note, a supervisor pleads with Owens and establishes a severe, if vague, consequence: "David, what's going on with this. . . . You don't need the type of trouble this type of flagrant failure to report situations is going to bring you." Within three months of this note, the insurance company terminated Owens's employment. This decision seems, at first glance, reasonable. Owens, however, was aware of several white colleagues who were offered and accepted demotions when the paperwork became too much for them. An EEOC report summarizes Owens's claim: "The Charging Party alleges that Respondent discriminated against him by discharging him and subjecting him to unequal terms and conditions because of his race, black." In simple terms, Owens was not treated similar to the other poorly performing adjusters.

In response to these charges, the insurance company claimed that meritocracy drove their decision-making process. While in previous years company policy supported a more relaxed disciplinary system, current policy relied on a system of "individualized motivation," whereby employees were dealt with on a case-by-case basis. A similarly situated white employee was offered better disciplinary terms because he appeared more receptive to his individualized motivation. The company writes, "Owens told his supervisor 'you're not taking care of me,' while [the white employee] assured his supervisor that he was 'living with' his files." In other words, Owens sought assistance from his supervisor, while, according to the company, the white employee took responsibility for his poor performance. This difference, again, relates to the company's disciplinary policy as outlined by their counsel:

> The company's system of counseling with and disciplining employees is individualized and is not an automatic, clock-work system. To assert that [the white employee] and David Owens were similarly situated and then to expect precisely the same application of a non-existent system of discipline is to simplify and to unrealistically distort reality.

Take as a second example the case of Raymond Jackson, the Mid City bus driver mentioned previously, who was asked to operate a lawnmower. A representative for Mid City school district offered this merit-based justification for Jackson's termination:

> Mr. Jackson was discharged due to the charges of Insubordination and Neglect of Duty being sustained and in consideration of his past record as it related to discipline. Specifically, Mr. Jackson refused a summer assignment mowing grass, after exhausting all other types of leave. He refused to demonstrate his claimed inability to operate the tractor/mower. He refused, on more than one occasion, to demonstrate that he could not operate the equipment by making an attempt.

Jackson was terminated on "meritocratic grounds," yet civil rights investigators found his firing to be discriminatory. As noted earlier, a female at the same workplace similarly refused to work the lawnmower, for a variety of reasons. Rather than being fired like Jackson, however, her request for an alternative assignment was approved, and she was not cited for insubordination or neglect of duty.

Supplementary analyses that we undertook highlight that employers are likely to rationalize discrimination on meritocratic grounds regardless of employees' claims, even when discriminatory actions are overtly racist or pertain to overtly racist environments. Jim Carson, for instance, the employee mentioned previously who suffered severe harassment in the form of racist jokes and offensive visuals, was eventually fired based on merit, specifically "time away from work and long lunches and job performance." This example illustrates the myopic fallacy of meritocratic discourse. Regardless of whether Carson took long lunches, the meritocratic discourse shifts the attention from blatant harassment to race-neutral terms. This shift to race-neutral terms has implications for the legal and sociological focus on unconscious bias and structural approaches to antidiscrimination remediation. As the qualitative materials in this article show, an unreflective focus on antidiscrimination structures (in this case formal performance evaluation) glosses over various forms of discrimination that are folded into the construction of a seemingly race-neutral, performance-based metric. If there is much, if any obvious, difference in employer rationales relative to discriminatory form, it is that employers are more likely to engage in outright denial regarding overtly racist acts or an explicitly racist environment than they are with more subtle forms of discrimination, both of which arguably undermine the credibility of race-neutral, meritocratic claims.

A secondary, though no less important, issue is whether legal representation matters for the discourses in which employers engage. On the one hand is the possibility that legal professionals construct employer responses in ways that courts might find more legitimate. This would be consistent with research on professionals' role in defining civil rights compliance (Edelman, Fuller, and Mara-Drita 2001; Dobbin 2009). On the other hand, if meritocratic rhetoric is prevalent, regardless of legal advice, this would attest to a more general pervasiveness and strength of meritocratic, color-blind frames in our culture and the ways in which they help to justify inequality and differential treatment (Bonilla-Silva 2003). To examine this,

FIGURE 3

Employer Justifications Relative to Legal Representation ($N = 250$)

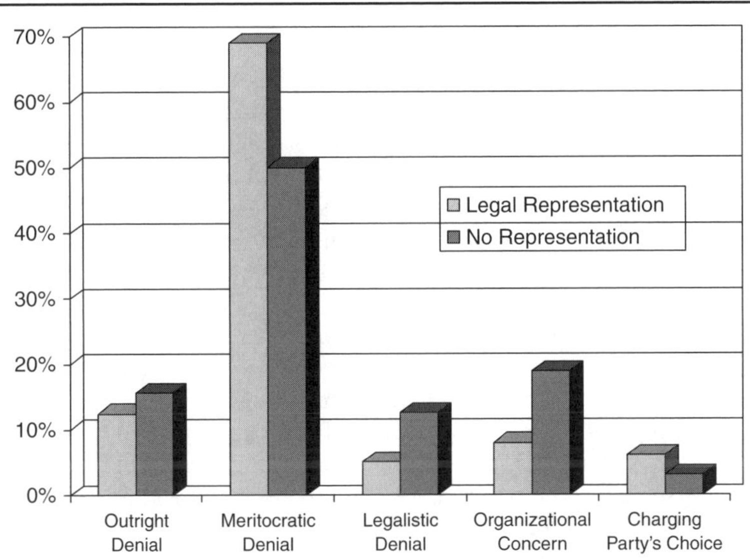

we analyze variation in employers' counterclaims as a function of legal representation and summarize our findings in Figure 3.

What stands out clearly, as in the earlier dyadic representation, is that meritocratic justifications for discriminatory acts predominate, although they are more highly represented among employers using a legal advocate. Of those with legal representation, approximately 68 percent justify their actions in meritocratic terms, compared to about 50 percent of those without such representation. This difference is statistically significant and suggests that legal presence is, to some degree, a filter for the discourses that employers use. Notable, however, is the fact that nearly half of employers who do not have legal representation similarly draw on race-neutral justifications, such as alluding to formal company policies, employee delinquency, and so forth. Although some of this may be a function of prior encounters with the legal system, it may also reflect broader cultural and seemingly legitimate societal discourses—discourses on color-blindness that employers, like much of the population, are attuned to and embedded within.

Conclusion

Employment discrimination is a complex phenomenon, confounded in sociological analyses by significant disjunctures between behaviors, on one hand, and attitudes and interpretations, on the other. This disjuncture renders understanding the mechanisms of discrimination all the more difficult. In this article, we began with an actor-centric approach, confirming what much prior work has suggested, but then turned attention to a dyadic conception—a conception wherein the unit of analysis is not a singular actor (e.g., employer or worker) but, rather, the discriminatory encounter itself.

The unique nature of our data and ability to match discriminators and discriminatees allow us to model dominant dyadic and relational patterns observed within discriminatory encounters. We revealed some important inconsistencies in claims and justifications of race-based employment discrimination. Victims of discrimination, by and large, discuss differential treatment and the use of organizational policies and penalties in differential, unfair ways. Employers, for their part, largely cling to meritocratic rationales and justifications for discriminatory behaviors in which they engage, citing the existence of fair employment policy, supposedly neutral evaluative criteria, or employee deficiencies. This pattern seems to hold even when explicitly racist actions occur. And although the presence of an attorney heightens the likelihood that employers will draw on meritocratic discourse, color-blind rationales dominate employer justifications even when there is no observable legal defense present.

The disjunctures and the patterning of race-neutral, meritocratic rationales that our analyses reveal suggest an understudied dimension and mechanism of inequality at work, namely, the interplay of dominant discourse of race-neutrality and formal meritocratic procedures. This interplay provides a protective shield for employers' discriminatory actions, regardless of whether the discourse is objectively false. The implications for discussions among legal scholars and social psychologists about conscious and unconscious biases are clear. While organizational structures may be effective in reducing both conscious and unconscious bias (Bielby 2000; Reskin 2000), they can also serve as harbors for bias. The integrity of implementation, and not only the presence of structures, should thus be given greater weight. As others (Kalev, Dobbin, and Kelly 2006; Sturm 2001) have shown, implementation of compliance measures without accountability leads to null or negative results. Part of the reason, as indicated by our results, is that bias and meritocratic structures can and often do exist together.

While a dyadic approach is useful for the reasons specified above, it is essential to recognize that the relational aspects specified are embedded in a hierarchical and status system with corresponding differentials in power. Such power allows some actors (i.e., employers and supervisors) the ability to invoke and use seemingly neutral organizational procedures in a discretionary, oftentimes discriminatory, manner. When held accountable, such actors rely on the presence of these procedures to bolster meritocratic claims—claims that are bureaucratically espoused by work organizations and that are consistent with broader cultural and legalistic discourses pertaining to race-neutrality and race-blind ideals. Thus, the "relational" is fundamentally embedded in structure and culture, and its implications and relevance for understanding more completely why and how discrimination persists must be interpreted in this light.

Notes

1. By asserting the relational nature of discrimination, we do not dismiss the effects of institutional discrimination or group harassment; rather, we hope to highlight that these forms of discrimination are most often experienced at the most proximate level. The theoretical typology that we introduce in this article further describes the relationship between the structural and relational dimensions that are influential.

2. Theoretical typologies provide clarity to important dimensions (e.g., micro/macro or covert/overt) of concepts (e.g., discrimination). While typologies cover the preponderance of empirical possibilities in the "real world," we acknowledge that few classificatory schemes can lay claim to all possibilities.

3. We use pseudonyms for persons and places discussed or quoted in the qualitative analysis to protect the privacy of these victims of workplace discrimination.

References

Bell, Joyce M., and Douglas Hartmann. 2007. Diversity in everyday discourse: The cultural ambiguities and consequences of "happy talk." *American Sociological Review* 72:895–914.

Bendix, Reinhard. 1956. *Work and authority in industry: Ideologies of management in the course of industrialization*. New York, NY: John Wiley.

Bielby, William T. 2000. Minimizing workplace gender and racial bias. *Contemporary Sociology: A Journal of Reviews* 29:120–29.

Bonilla-Silva, Eduardo. 2003. *Racism without racists: Color-blind racism and the persistence of racial inequality in the United States*. Lanham, MD: Rowman & Littlefield.

Borgatti, S. P., Martin G. Everett, and Lin C. Freeman. 2002. *UCINET for Windows: Software for social network analysis*. Lexington, KY: Analytic Technologies.

Castilla, Emilio J. 2008. Gender, race, and meritocracy in organizational careers. *American Journal of Sociology* 113:1479–1526.

Castilla, Emilio J., and Stephen Benard. 2009. The paradox of meritocracy: Hidden risks of merit-based performance systems. Paper presented at the annual meeting of the American Sociological Association, 8–11 August, San Francisco, CA.

Cohen, Philip N. 1998. Black concentration effects on black-white and gender inequality: Multilevel analysis for U.S. metropolitan areas. *Social Forces* 77:207–29.

Cohn, Samuel, and Mark Fossett. 1995. Why racial employment inequality is greater in northern labor markets: Regional differences in white-black employment differentials. *Social Forces* 74:511–42.

Conley, Dalton. 1999. *Being black, living in the red: Race, wealth and social policy in America*. Berkeley, CA: University of California Press.

Cotter, David A., Joan M. Hermsen, and Reeve Vanneman. 1999. Systems of gender, race, and class inequality: Multilevel analyses. *Social Forces* 78:433–61.

Dobbin, Frank. 2009. *Inventing equal opportunity*. Princeton, NJ: Princeton University Press.

Dobbin, Frank, Daniel Schrage, and Alexandra Kalev. 2009. Someone to watch over me: Coupling, decoupling, and unintended consequences in corporate equal opportunity. Working Paper, Department of Sociology, Harvard University, Cambridge, MA.

Dyson, Michael Eric. 2004. *The Michael Eric Dyson reader*. New York, NY: Basic Civitas Books.

Edelman, Lauren B., Sally Riggs Fuller, and Iona Mara-Drita. 2001. Diversity rhetoric and the managerialization of the law. *American Journal of Sociology* 106:1589–1641.

Edelman, Lauren, Linda H. Kreiger, Scott R. Eliason, Catherine Albiston, and Virginia A. Mellema. 2006. When organizations rule: Judicial deference to institutionalized employment structures. Presented at Empirical Legal Studies Conference, 27–28 October, Austin, TX.

Edelman, Lauren B., and Stephen M. Petterson. 1999. Symbols and substance in organizational response to civil rights law. *Research in Social Stratification and Mobility* 17:107–35.

Elvira, Marta M., and Robert Town. 2001. The effects of race and worker productivity on performance evaluations. *Industrial Relations* 40:571–90.

Feagin, Joe R. 1991. The continuing significance of race: Antiblack discrimination in public places. *American Sociological Review* 56:101–16.

Feagin, Joe R., and Douglas Lee Eckberg. 1980. Discrimination: Motivation, action, effects, and context. *Annual Review of Sociology* 6:1–20.

Feagin, Joe R., and Karyn D. McKinney. 2003. *The many costs of racism.* Lanham, MD: Rowman & Littlefield.

Foucault, Michel, and Colin Gordon. 1980. *Power/knowledge: Selected interviews and other writings, 1972–1977.* New York, NY: Pantheon.

Gross, Neil. 2009. A pragmatist theory of social mechanisms. *American Sociological Review* 74 (3): 358–79.

Huffman, Matt L. 2004. Gender inequality across local wage hierarchies. *Work and Occupations* 31:323–44.

Huffman, Matt L., and Philip N. Cohen. 2004. Occupational segregation and the gender gap in workplace authority: National versus local labor markets. *Sociological Forum* 19:121–47.

Hunt, Matthew O. 2007. African American, Hispanic, and white beliefs about black/white inequality, 1977–2004. *American Sociological Review* 72:390–415.

Kalev, Alexandra, Frank Dobbin, and Erin Kelly. 2006. Best practices or best guesses? Assessing the efficacy of corporate affirmative action and diversity policies. *American Sociological Review* 71:589–617.

Kirschenman, Joleen, and Kathryn M. Neckerman. 1991. "We'd love to hire them, but . . .": The meaning of race for employers. In *The urban underclass*, eds. Christopher Jencks and Paul E. Peterson. Washington, DC: Brookings Institution.

Lamont, Michelle. 2000. *The dignity of working men: Morality and the boundaries of class, race and immigration.* Cambridge, MA: Harvard University Press.

Marini, Margaret Mooney, and Pi-Ling Fan. 1997. The gender gap in earnings at career entry. *American Sociological Review* 62:588–604.

McBrier, Debra Branch, and George Wilson. 2004. Going down? Race and downward occupational mobility for white-collar workers in the 1990s. *Work and Occupations* 1:283–322.

McKay, Patrick F., and Michael A. McDaniel. 2006. A reexamination of black-white mean differences in work performance: More data, more moderators. *Journal of Applied Psychology* 91:538–54.

Mills, C. Wright. 1940. Situated actions and vocabularies of motive. *American Sociological Review* 5:904–13.

Mong, Sherry N., and Vincent J. Roscigno. 2010. African American men and the experience of employment discrimination. *Qualitative Sociology* 33 (1): 1–21.

Moss, Phillip, and Chris Tilly. 2001. *Stories employers tell: Race, skill, and hiring in America.* New York, NY: Russell Sage Foundation.

Nonet, Philippe, and Philip Selznick. 1978. *Law and society in transition: Toward responsive law.* New York, NY: Octagon Books.

OCRC. 2004. About OCRC. Columbus: Ohio Civil Right Commission. Available from http://crc.ohio.gov/mission.htm (accessed 2 November 2004).

Pager, Devah. 2003. The mark of a criminal record. *American Journal of Sociology* 108:937–75.

Pager, Devah, and Lincoln Quillian. 2005. Walking the talk? What employers say versus what they do. *American Sociological Review* 70:355–80.

Parkin, Frank. 1974. Strategies of social closure in class formation. In *The social analysis of class structure*, ed. Frank Parkin. London: Tavistock.

Petersen, Trond, and Ishak Saporta. 2004. The opportunity structure for discrimination. *American Journal of Sociology* 109:852–901.

Pierce, Jennifer L. 2003. Racing for innocence: Whiteness, corporate culture, and the backlash against affirmative action. *Qualitative Sociology* 26:53–70.

Reid, Lori L., and Irene Padavic. 2005. Employment exits and the race gap in young women's employment. *Social Science Quarterly* 86:1242–60.

Reskin, Barbara F. 2000. The proximate causes of employment discrimination. *Contemporary Sociology: A Journal of Reviews* 29:319–28.

Reskin, Barbara F. 2003. Including mechanisms in our models of ascriptive inequality. *American Sociological Review* 68:1–21.

Reskin, Barbara F., and Debra B. McBrier. 2000. Why not ascription? Organizations' employment of male and female managers. *American Sociological Review* 65:210–33.

Ridgeway, Cecilia. 1997. Interaction and the conservation of gender inequality: Considering employment. *American Sociological Review* 62:218–35.

Roscigno, Vincent J. 2007. *The face of discrimination: How race and sex impact work and home lives*. Lanham, MD: Rowman & Littlefield.

Roscigno, Vincent J., Sherry Mong, Reginald Byron, and Griff Tester. 2007. Age discrimination, social closure and employment. *Social Forces* 86:313–34.

Roth, Louise Marie. 2006. *Selling women short: Gender and money on wall street*. Princeton, NJ: Princeton University Press.

Roth, Philip L., Allen I. Huffcutt, and Philip Bobko. 2003. Ethnic group differences in measures of job performance: A new meta-analysis. *Journal of Applied Psychology* 88:694–706.

Schuman, Howard, Charlotte Steeh, Lawrence Bobo, and Maria Krysan. 1997. *Racial attitudes in America: Trends and interpretations*. Cambridge, MA: Harvard University Press.

Schwartz, Richard D., and Jerome H. Skolnick. 1962. Two studies of legal stigma. *Social Problems* 10:133–42.

Smith, Ryan A. 2002. Race, gender, and authority in the workplace: Theory and research. *Annual Review of Sociology* 28:509–42.

Sturm, Susan. 2001. Second generation employment discrimination: A structural approach. *Columbia Law Review* 101:458–68.

Tilly, Charles. 1998. *Durable inequality*. Berkeley, CA: University of California Press.

Tomaskovic-Devey, Donald. 1993. Labor-process inequality and the gender and race composition of jobs. *Research in Social Stratification and Mobility* 12:215–47.

Tomaskovic-Devey, Donald, and Sheryl Skaggs. 1999. Workplace gender and racial composition and productivity: An establishment level test of the statistical discrimination hypothesis. *Work and Occupations* 26:422–45.

Tomaskovic-Devey, Donald, and Sheryl Skaggs. 2002. Sex segregation, labor process organization, and gender earnings inequality. *American Journal of Sociology* 108:102–28.

Wasserman, Stanley, and Katherine Faust. 1994. *Social network analysis: Methods and applications*. Cambridge: Cambridge University Press.

Weber, Max. 1968/1978. *Economy and society*. Berkeley, CA: University of California Press.

West, Cornel. 1999. *The Cornel West reader*. New York, NY: Basic Civitas Books.

Wilson, Franklin D., Marta Tienda, and Lawrence Wu. 1995. Race and unemployment: Labor market experiences of black and white men, 1968–1988. *Work and Occupations* 22 (3): 245–70.

Wilson, George. 1997. Pathways to power: Racial differences in the determinants of job authority. *Social Problems* 44:38–54.

Wilson, George, and Debra McBrier. 2005. Race and loss of privilege: African American/white differences in the determinants of job layoffs from upper-tier occupations. *Sociological Forum* 20:301–21.

Wilson, George, Ian Sakura-Lemessy, and Jonathan P. West. 1999. Reaching the top: Racial differences in mobility paths to upper-tier occupations. *Work and Occupations* 26:165–86.

Wilson, William Julius. 1978. *The declining significance of race: Blacks and changing American institutions*. Chicago, IL: University of Chicago Press.

Young, Iris Marion. 2001. Equality of whom? Social groups and judgments of justice. *Journal of Political Philosophy* 9:1–18.

Race, Religion, and Beliefs about Racial Inequality

By
MARYLEE C. TAYLOR
and
STEPHEN M. MERINO

This article focuses on stratification beliefs and racial policy opinions among white and black Americans who differ in religious preference. First, it summarizes earlier research on white conservative Protestants and outlines characterizations of Black Protestant church congregants. It then reports patterns of stratification beliefs and racial policy opinions among blacks and whites varying in religious preference who responded to the 1996 through 2006 General Social Surveys. Comparisons across twelve race-by-religion categories did not provide persuasive evidence that white conservative Protestants are uniquely conservative in their stratification beliefs, once background characteristics are controlled, nor was the Black Protestant group distinctive. Compared to blacks, whites were less inclined to structuralist explanations of racial inequality, slightly more inclined to individualist explanations, and consistently more negative about policies and programs to aid blacks. What is more, white Christians were more racially conservative in all these ways than non-Christian whites.

Keywords: racial attitudes; religion; racial conservatism; stratification beliefs

Background

Stratification ideology has been of special interest to race relations scholars and advocates

Marylee C. Taylor is an associate professor of sociology at the Pennsylvania State University. Her research addresses questions about race-related attitudes that white and black Americans hold. Much of her current work entails contextual analysis: using census data linked to General Social Survey responses, she is examining a set of provocative questions about the influence of the local environment on the psychological well-being of black Americans and on the racial and ethnic attitudes of non-Hispanic whites.

Stephen M. Merino is a graduate student in sociology at the Pennsylvania State University. His master's thesis examined Americans' attitudes toward Muslims and Hindus, with particular attention paid to the influences of theological beliefs and interreligious contact. His current research examines the effect of religiosity on volunteering and the receipt of informal social support from a social network perspective.

DOI: 10.1177/0002716210389537

because, as Kluegel and Smith (1986, 211) conclude, "There is clear evidence . . . that beliefs about social stratification do play a major role . . . in shaping white Americans' response to equal opportunity policy" (see also Kluegel 1990). Support for ameliorative programs and policies is encouraged by the belief that racial inequality results from discrimination and other structural impediments; such support is discouraged by the conviction that inequality derives from "individualistic" factors, especially motivation and effort. This article examines stratification beliefs and potentially linked policy attitudes, focusing on variation in the perspectives of black and white Americans who differ in religious preference.

The "dominant ideology"—Emphasis on individualism

Opportunity is widespread and those who work hard will be rewarded with success: these beliefs and the associated acceptance of inequality, dubbed the "dominant ideology" by Huber and Form (1973), have been prevalent in the United States and can be construed more broadly as an element of Western culture (Kluegel and Smith 1986).

Experience and self-interest, as well as socialization, are said to affect the degree of adherence to this perspective. Thus, those who have suffered as the result of limited opportunity or laissez-faire social policies are less likely to wholeheartedly endorse the dominant ideology. However, research has shown that beliefs about stratification are not necessarily internally consistent: logically incompatible elements may be "layered on," individualistic notions coexisting with acknowledgment that the equal opportunity ideal falls short of realization. Structuralism is more variable across groups, individualism more universally espoused (Kluegel and Smith 1986).

Race and stratification ideology

Race has figured in studies of stratification beliefs in two ways: race differences in stratification beliefs have been one focus; second is beliefs specifically about *racial* inequality. Explanations for wealth and poverty were shown by Kluegel and Smith (1986) to differ for black and white respondents, blacks holding more structuralist beliefs than whites, along with less individualistic beliefs about the causes of wealth. These researchers also confirmed that in general, whites are inclined toward individualistic rather than structuralist explanations for racial inequality, tending to "blame the victim" (Ryan 1971). In Kluegel and Smith's research, "Explanations of all kinds show fewer status effects among blacks than among whites, meaning perhaps that blacks view the world in terms of racial group identification; in effect, as if they possessed a uniform status" (1986, 101–2). Matthew Hunt (1996) made a similar point when a Southern California sample revealed a significant race gap in structural beliefs even after controls for sociodemographic variables. Referring to a "group identification model," Hunt concluded that whatever their personal histories, blacks' beliefs may reflect their understanding of the history and status of their racial group. These observations foreshadow findings we report later in this article.

M. Hunt's (1996) Southern California sample was unusual. Along with the customary finding that blacks' beliefs about the causes of poverty were more structuralist than whites' beliefs, individualistic beliefs were also more prevalent among blacks than among whites. Less surprising was the pattern M. Hunt (2007) reported in explanations for racial inequality that white, black, and Hispanic respondents gave in the 1977 through 2004 General Social Surveys (GSS). These data show convergence over time in whites' and blacks' adherence to the central individualistic explanation under debate today: motivation. By the 2000 to 2004 period, whites were more likely than blacks to endorse the motivation explanation for racial inequality by just 5 percentage points. The race gap in structural explanations was considerably larger, whites being less likely to affirm that the lack of a "chance for education" or "discrimination" is important by about 10 and 30 percentage points, respectively. These results resonate with the early (Kluegel and Smith 1986) observation that individualism is relatively universal, while structuralism varies more across groups.

The role of religion in shaping stratification beliefs

Connections between religion and stratification ideology have been of interest in sociology since the writings of Weber (1958) and Durkheim (1951). Modern sociologists picked up the theme. National survey data from 1969 showed individualism to be higher and structuralism lower among white Protestants and Catholics than among Jews and black Protestants (Feagin 1975). Overlapping findings from Kluegel and Smith (1986) show that both conservative and nonconservative Protestants, as well as Catholics, were more inclined to individualistic explanations for poverty than Jews, those of other faiths, and survey respondents claiming no religious affiliation. Similar patterns in a Southern California sample inspired M. Hunt to write of a status hierarchy among religions, with Protestants and Catholics constituting the dominant groups and other faiths and nonaffiliates being "minority" religious traditions (2002, 815). Hunt translated the "underdog thesis" (Robinson and Bell 1978) that dominant ideologies are more likely to be espoused by privileged groups into a "religious underdog" explanation of the lower levels of individualism and antistructuralism that characterize the non-Christian groups.

Focus on white conservative Protestants

As M. Hunt (2002) notes, earlier research on religious differences in stratification beliefs among whites often focused on the Protestant-Catholic split. With the structural assimilation of white Catholics into U.S. society, the Protestant-Catholic difference and related research interests have diminished, and a new focus of social science interest has arisen: white conservative Protestants, a growing group now estimated to comprise nearly one-third of the white U.S. population (see especially Emerson, Smith, and Sikkink 1999; Emerson and Smith 2000). The argument presented in Emerson, Smith, and Sikkink (1999), though relevant for sociologists, is less sociological than theological. The sociopolitical perspective of white conservative Protestants purportedly reflects a subcultural "tool kit" (Swidler 1986), which this group's theology provides; like other such subcultural tool kits, it may be generalized to multiple contexts (Sewell 1992). Three convictions are central to conservative Protestant theology: "accountable freewill individualism," "relationalism," and "antistructuralism." Conservative Protestant churches teach that individuals are responsible for their own behavior and fate. Emphasis on a personal relationship with Christ as a prerequisite to salvation is translated into parishioners' beliefs that the quality of interpersonal relationships has a crucial impact on life outcomes. Finally, this emphasis on individual responsibility and personal relationships is incompatible with structuralist understandings of societal processes (Emerson, Smith, and Sikkink 1999; Emerson and Smith 2000).

The upshot, according to Emerson and his colleagues, is a tendency toward individualistic and antistructuralist attributions among the swelling number of conservative Protestants—attributions that may influence their political views and slow efforts to redress inequality.

Using national data from the 1996 GSS and from their own study, Emerson and his collaborators compare white conservative Protestants to other whites and find the conservative Protestants more likely to attribute racial inequality to differences in motivation and willpower and less likely to blame discrimination and poor schools (Emerson, Smith, and Sikkink 1999; Emerson and Smith 2000). Critics have quarreled with various aspects of these conclusions, but the methodology employed in the opposing studies was typically too different from that of Emerson and his colleagues to provide a direct empirical challenge.

Our recent examination of 1996 to 2000 GSS data (M. Taylor and Merino 2010) indicates that the depiction that Emerson and his colleagues offer is partially accurate for certain white conservative Protestants—the 8 percent of whites who identify themselves as evangelical, fundamentalist, or Pentecostal; believe that the Bible is the literal or inspired word of God; and have faith in an afterlife. Even after equalizing for background characteristics, these self-identified white conservative Protestants are more individualistic than any category except other Protestants, and they ascribe less to structuralist explanations than do other religious categories save Catholics. However, the consequences of their racial stratification beliefs for racial policy opinion are not what Emerson, Smith, and Sikkink (1999) would predict. These white conservative Protestants are not different from other Christian groups or from Jews of similar background in their support for affirmative action or their opinion about whether the government is obliged to help blacks. Only in their high levels of opposition to spending do white conservative Protestants show distinctive racial policy opinions.

The story is different for the larger group of white conservative Protestants so labeled according to the widely used "RELTRAD" (religious tradition) classification of denominations (Steensland et al. 2000). The 30 percent or so of white Americans whose denomination is considered conservative Protestant are especially likely to live in the South, and they are less educated than mainline Protestants. Similar to other white southerners with limited education, they are more individualistic and antistructuralist than average. Also, they are more conservative than mainline Protestants on the three racial policy issues we examined. However, when region, education, and other background characteristics are controlled, these white conservative Protestants are statistically indistinguishable from mainline Protestants and Catholics in their explanations for racial inequality and differ on only one racial policy issue (M. Taylor and Merino 2010).

A pattern of distinctiveness in raw data that dissolves when background characteristics are controlled must be described carefully. RELTRAD white conservative Protestants do differ from other groups, including mainline Protestants. However, the fading of their distinctiveness with the introduction of controls for background characteristics, especially region and education, contradicts claims that conservative Protestant *theology* plays the central role in shaping their racial stratification beliefs. Rather, the telling influences seem to be structural and geographic location.

The clearest difference in stratification beliefs and racial policy opinions that M. Taylor and Merino (2010) found was between Christians and the non-Christian groups that M. Hunt (2002) would call religious minorities—Jews, those of other faiths, and the nonaffiliated. Compared to white Christians, these white non-Christian groups were less individualistic and more structuralist in their explanations for racial inequality, and they were more supportive of intervention on behalf of racial equity.

Focus on black churches

The church has long been a central institution in the lives of black Americans, serving as an important social, economic, cultural, and political resource (Lincoln and Mamiya 1990). Religion and church culture are said to pervade everyday African American life to a far greater extent than they do for most white Christians (Lincoln and Mamiya 1990; Pattillo-McCoy 1998). Black Americans have been reported to exhibit higher levels of public and private religious behavior than do whites and to place greater importance on religion (Roof and McKinney 1987; R. Taylor et al. 1996), although Hunt and Hunt (1999, 2001) outline important qualifications to this generalization.

Because American religion is so deeply segregated along racial lines (Emerson and Kim 2003), most white Americans are unfamiliar with the worship style and content of black Christianity. While theologically and organizationally similar to white evangelical denominations, African American churches typically stress different aspects of scripture and Christian doctrine than their white counterparts. Scholars have noted the communitarian ethos of black churches (Pattillo-McCoy 1998), as well as their theological and cultural emphasis on "the equality of all persons under God" (Paris 1985). Sermons routinely speak of "the structures of oppression which cause black suffering" (Gilkes 1980). As Edgell and Tranby (2007) note, earlier writers remind us not to overdraw the contrast between black churches and other religious groups. Black churches often stress individual responsibility along with the need for collective action to enact structural change.

Nonetheless, these scholars acknowledge that the emphasis in black churches differs from the more starkly individualistic, antistructuralist themes often featured in white churches (Hinojosa and Park 2004; Lincoln and Mamiya 1990).

Though generally conservative on social and moral issues, members of black churches tend to be liberal on economic issues and identify overwhelmingly as Democrats (Wald 2003). Furthermore, the black church has played an important role in racial politics. During the civil rights movement, black churches provided organizational tools and resources; and they emphasized religious themes, such as biblical resistance to oppression, that served as motivation and justification for action (Morris 1984; Harris 1999). Using survey data from the civil rights movement era, Harris (1999) found that black Baptists and Methodists were especially likely to vote and to support protests. Black churches remain more politically active than other churches even today (Chaves 2004). Frequent opportunities for political activism may reinforce black church members' commitment to racial equality and social justice; political messages may alert them to social structural causes of inequality and encourage their support of government intervention.

While a majority of African Americans affiliate with one of the historically black denominations, national surveys document sizable percentages affiliating with predominantly white Protestant denominations and with the Roman Catholic Church (Feagin 1968). However, affiliating with a predominantly white denomination does not mean participating in a predominantly white congregation. As noted earlier, the vast majority of American religious congregations are essentially uniracial (Emerson and Kim 2003). Major predominantly white denominations encompass numerous black congregations, as evidenced by such organizations as the Black Methodists for Church Renewal, the Office of Black Ministries of the Episcopal Church, and the National Black Catholic Congress. President Barack Obama's former predominantly black congregation in Chicago is associated with the United Church of Christ, a predominantly white, liberal, Protestant denomination.

In short, as Pattillo-McCoy (1998) argues, it is safe to conclude that many blacks outside the historically black denominations attend local "mainline" churches with predominantly black congregations that are culturally and politically similar to those of traditionally Black Protestant churches. The affinity of black congregations in mainline Protestant denominations with emphasis of the historically Black Protestant church has been said to extend even to black Catholic congregations (see Cavendish, Welch, and Leege 1998; Cavendish 2000).

We need a better understanding of how religion shapes blacks' beliefs about racial inequality and race policy opinions. The unique cultural and political role of the historically Black Protestant denominations may mean that members more often espouse structuralist explanations and less often individualistic explanations for racial inequality and are more likely than other blacks to support intervention on behalf of racial equity. However, if the ethos of the Black Protestant church holds sway even in black congregations within the Catholic church and predominantly white Protestant denominations, respondents affiliated with Black Protestant denominations may not differ in stratification ideology or policy opinions from other black churchgoers.

Evidence about Stratification Beliefs and Policy Attitudes within White and Black Religious Categories in the United States, 1996–2006

Given the provocative literature reviewed above, the views of white conservative Protestants and members of Black Protestant churches will be of special interest as we examine recent data on stratification ideology and racial policy opinions among blacks and whites of varying religious preferences. However, each religious tradition may have a story to tell. Hinojosa and Park (2004) remind readers of the role played by mainline Protestant churches in the civil rights movement and note the many instances of alliance between Jews and blacks. Edgell and Tranby (2007) join Hinojosa and Park (2004) in noting the distinctiveness of the Catholic tradition, which Edgell and Tranby describe as "a religious subculture that favors communalism and a collective and institutional understanding of the moral responsibility for social action" (2007, 282). The stratification ideology of Catholic respondents may reflect their distinctive "tool kit."

Data for our project come from six GSS that the National Opinion Research Center administered at the University of Chicago in 1996, 1998, 2000, 2002, 2004, and 2006. Face-to-face interviews were conducted with nationally representative samples of U.S. households.

The RELTRAD classification relied on here defines seven religious preference categories: (Evangelical) Conservative Protestant, Mainline Protestant, Black Protestant, Catholic, Jewish, Other Faith, and Non-Affiliated.[1] Note that "Black Protestant" refers to historically African American denominations, not to the race of the survey respondents.

Two categories—white respondents claiming denominational preference for Black Protestant churches and black respondents identifying themselves as Jewish—are too small for reliable analysis. Thus, we discuss here the remaining six categories of whites and six categories of African Americans. The religious preferences of the 12,937 whites who figure in our analyses are as follows:

Conservative Protestant: 29.9 percent
Mainline Protestant: 21.5 percent
Catholic: 24.6 percent
Jewish: 2.7 percent
Other Faith 5.3 percent
Non-Affiliated: 16.0 percent

Among the 2,462 blacks represented in this discussion, the breakdown is as follows:

Black Protestant: 60.1 percent
Conservative Protestant: 12.3 percent
Mainline Protestant: 5.6 percent
Catholic: 6.4 percent
Other Faith: 4.9 percent
Non-Affiliated: 10.7 percent

Fortunately, key survey questions were repeated in multiple years, so that pooling across six surveys yields enough cases to analyze in each of these categories. Overall, race differences exist on many background variables. Blacks in these samples were more likely than whites to live in the South at the time of the survey and at age 16; to have less education and lower income; to be younger, female, and unmarried; and to live in metropolitan and larger communities.

Within their respective racial groups, how are particular religious categories different from others? White conservative Protestants were more likely than other whites to live in the South at the time of the survey and at age 16, to have fewer years of schooling, to be married, and to live outside metropolitan areas or large communities. White Catholics were unlikely to live in the South at the time of the survey or at age 16. Jewish respondents had more education and higher income, and they were more likely to reside in metropolitan areas and larger communities. White nonaffiliates were younger than other whites and less likely to be married. (White mainline Protestants and those of other faiths looked much like other whites.)

Blacks in predominantly white conservative Protestant denominations had higher family incomes than blacks in general and were more likely to be married. Black Catholics were less likely to reside in the South than other African Americans at the time of the survey and at age 16, and they had more years of schooling and lived in larger communities than other African Americans. Blacks of other faiths were less likely to live in the South at the time of the survey or at age 16 and resided in larger communities than blacks in general. Finally, compared with other blacks, nonaffiliates were relatively unlikely to live in the South at the time of the survey or at age 16, and they were younger, more likely to be male, and less likely to be married. (African Americans in Black Protestant and mainline Protestant denominations were similar in background to the overall black sample.)

Stratification beliefs

Our measure of individualism comes from a question asking whether, on average, blacks have worse jobs, income, and housing than white people "because most blacks just don't have the motivation or will power to pull themselves up out of poverty." The antistructuralism scale score is the mean of respondents' opinions on whether white-black inequality is "mainly due to discrimination," and whether that inequality exists "because most blacks don't have the chance for education that it takes to rise out of poverty."

The light gray bars in Figures 1 and 2 portray the average individualism and antistructuralism levels for the six religious categories applicable to whites and the six categories for blacks as those groups actually exist in U.S. society (i.e., unadjusted for background characteristics).

This look at patterns across the twelve race-by-religion groups shows why white conservative Protestants have attracted the attention of researchers. Before introducing controls, white conservative Protestants report greater individualism than any other group. The other white Christian groups come next. Blacks of all

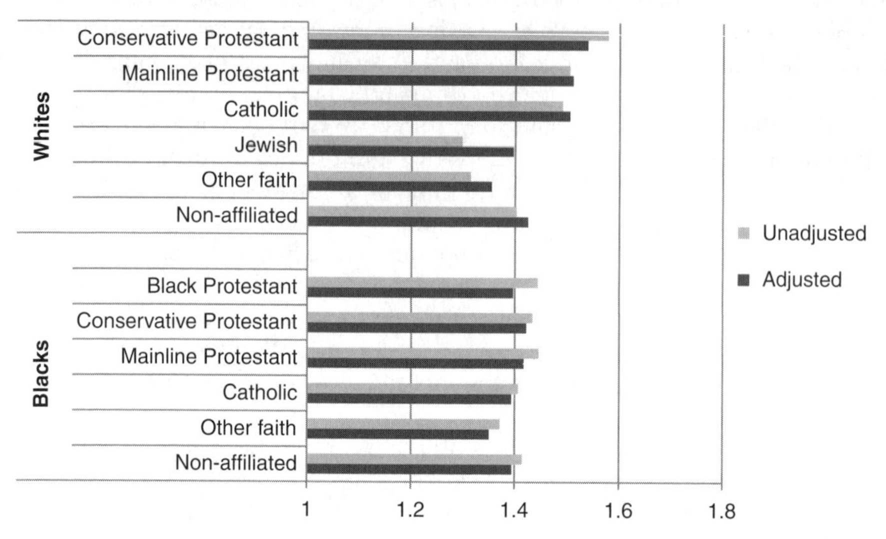

FIGURE 1

Levels of Individualism among Race-by-Religion Subgroups

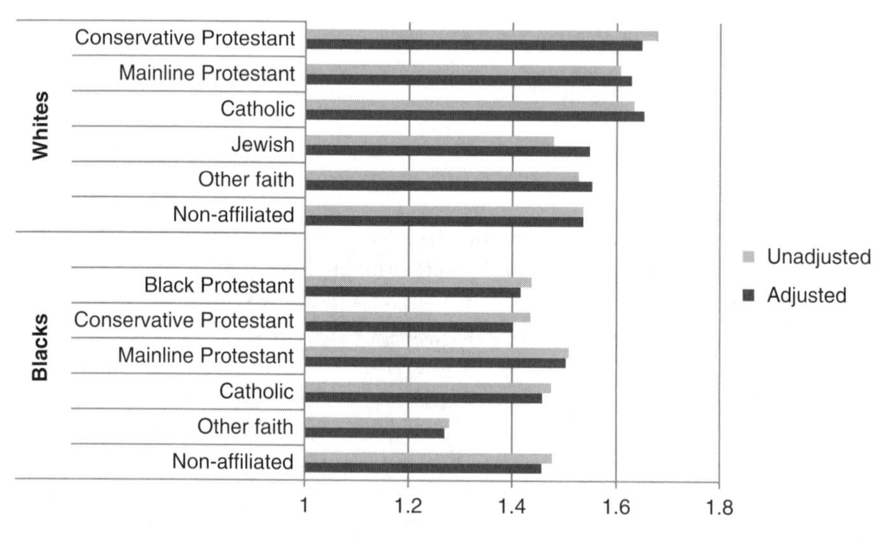

FIGURE 2

Levels of Antistructuralism among Race-by-Religion Subgroups

religious categories report less individualism than the white Christian groups, but non-Christian whites have levels of individualism lower than those of the four black Christian groups.

The unadjusted antistructuralism averages portrayed in Figure 2 bear some similarity to the individualism results, but there are differences as well. White conservative Protestants have the highest average on antistructuralism, and they are not that different from other Christians. Jews are least likely among the white groups to be antistructuralist, as they were least likely to score high on individualism; those of other faiths and the nonaffiliates were not much higher on antistructuralism than Jews. We do see a larger race difference here. The white groups are clearly higher on antistructuralism—there is almost no overlap between the values for white and black religious categories. Among blacks, mainline Protestants are the most antistructuralist and those of other faiths least antistructuralist.

But we should not stop with a look at these raw subgroup averages. Given the interest in effects of religion per se, the more telling information is group standings after statistical controls for background characteristics have been implemented. To learn how groups of respondents compare with those in other religion-by-race categories who are of similar background, we performed an analysis of covariance controlling for region of residence at the time of the survey and at age 16 (South versus non-South), education, family income, age, gender, marital status, metropolitan residence, community population size, and survey year. The dark bars in Figures 1 and 2 represent the adjusted means.[2]

To avoid making too much of unreliable intergroup differences, we performed a series of significance tests to address questions of particular interest. The twelve religious groups permit formulation of eleven questions that are entirely independent of each other, in the sense that one answer has no implications for answers to other questions. The eleven questions we ask are as follows:

1. Are the white religious groups different from the black religious groups overall?

And among whites:

2. Are conservative Protestants different from other Christians?
3. Are mainline Protestants different from Catholics?
4. Do the three Christian groups differ from the three non-Christian groups?
5. Do Jews differ from those of other faiths and the nonaffiliates?
6. Are those of other faiths different from nonaffiliates?

Among blacks:

7. Do members of historically Black Protestant churches differ from the other three black Christian groups?
8. Do blacks affiliated with predominantly white conservative Protestant denominations differ from mainline Protestants and Catholics?
9. Do mainline Protestants differ from Catholics?
10. Do the four Christian groups differ from the two non-Christian groups?
11. Are those of other faiths different from nonaffiliates?

For individualism, statistical significance tests on the adjusted averages indicate that only two of the eleven questions can be confidently answered in the affirmative. First, there is an overall race difference, whites being more individualistic than blacks—an even bigger race difference in the averages adjusted for background characteristics than was seen in the raw data. Also, the three white Christian groups are more individualistic than the three white non-Christian groups. (It is also the case that white conservative Protestants reported greater individualism than other white Christian groups, and that white nonaffiliates were more individualistic than whites of other faiths; however, these patterns only approached the conventional .05 criterion for statistical significance; they did not reach it.[3])

Regarding antistructuralism, group differences specified in four of the questions asked above were statistically significant. The first two mirror the findings for individualism: Whites are more antistructuralist than blacks. Here the race difference after controls was approximately equal to the race gap before controls. And the three white Christian groups are more antistructuralist than the three white non-Christian groups—Jews, those of other faiths, and nonaffiliates. In like fashion, the black Christian groups expressed more antistructuralism than the black non-Christian groups. Also, between the two black non-Christian groups, the nonaffiliates were more antistructuralist than those of other faiths; in fact, as Figure 2 reveals, it is the very low antistructuralism of the other faith category that creates the Christian/non-Christian difference among blacks.

Racial policy opinions

Emerson and his colleagues (Emerson, Smith, and Sikkink 1999; Emerson and Smith 2000) suggest that differences in stratification beliefs among white religious groups will produce predictable differences in race policy opinions. Indeed, as noted in the introduction to this article, much of the interest in stratification ideology has grown from evidence that these beliefs are linked to sociopolitical stance. To paraphrase Kluegel (1985), if racial inequality grows from blacks' lack of motivation, not discrimination or other structural processes, government remedies are inappropriate.

Here we report race-by-religion differences on three race policy questions: opposition to affirmative action, denial of government obligation to help blacks, and calls for decreased national spending on blacks. The light gray bars of Figures 3, 4, and 5 portray the raw (unadjusted) averages on each race policy question for the six white religious categories and the six categories for blacks.

From visual inspection of the light bars in Figure 3, we can see that whites are more opposed to affirmative action than blacks are. The white Christian groups are somewhat more opposed than the non-Christian categories. Blacks of other faiths and black conservative Protestants express more opposition than other black groups do; black Catholics and nonaffiliates are least opposed.

The light gray bars in Figure 4 reveal that whites are more likely to deny government obligation to help blacks, again with some tendency for the white

FIGURE 3
Levels of Opposition to Affirmative Action among Race-by-Religion Subgroups

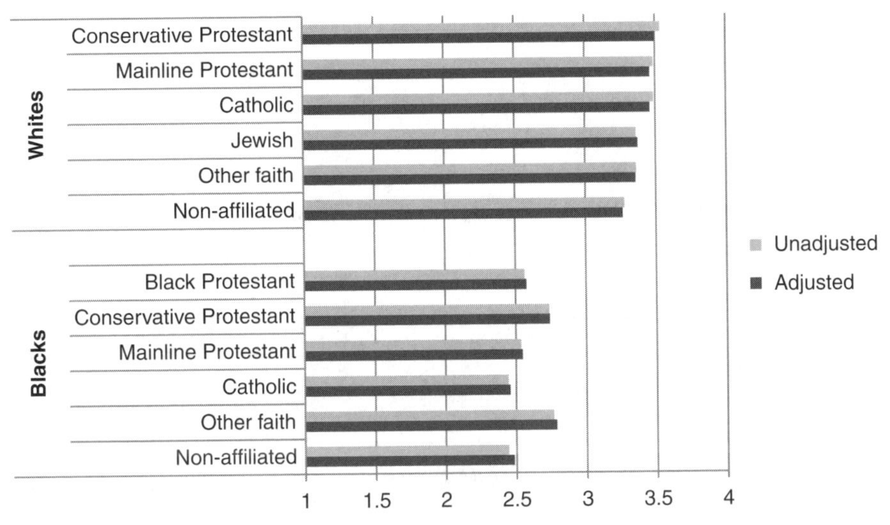

FIGURE 4
Levels of Denial of Government Obligation to
Help Blacks among Race-by-Religion Subgroups

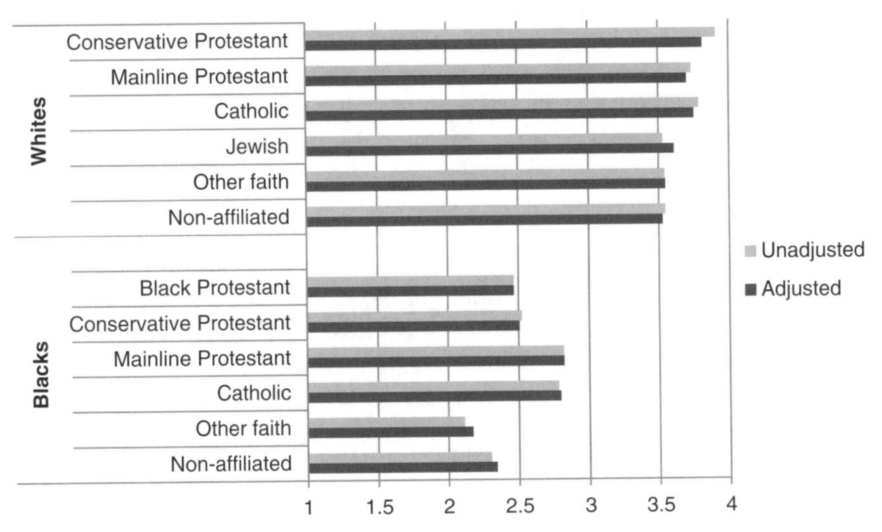

FIGURE 5

Levels of Opposition to Spending for Blacks among Race-by-Religion Subgroups

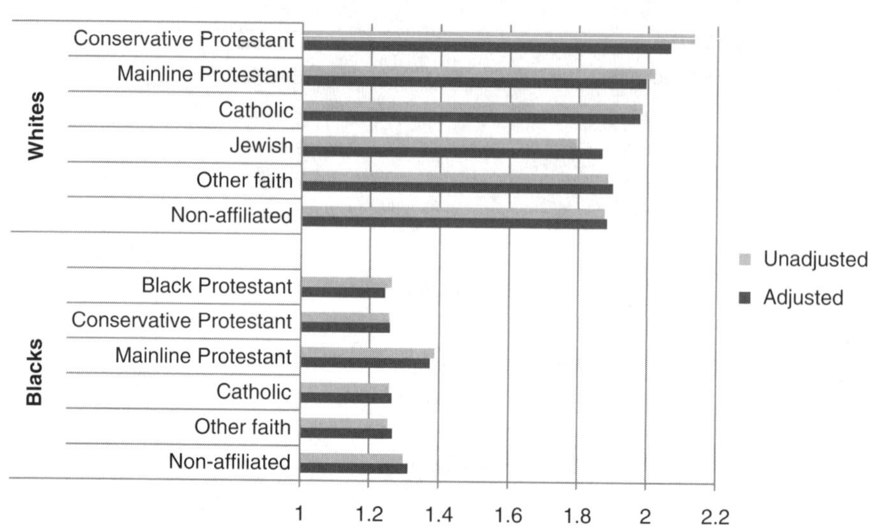

Christian groups to be especially negative. Among the black groups, mainline Protestants and Catholics most often reject the proposition that government is obligated to help blacks; blacks of other faiths most often accept this notion.

The race difference seen for the other two policy variables exists for spending as well. The light gray bars in Figure 5 show that all white religious groups are more opposed to spending for blacks than any of the black religious groups. White conservative Protestants are most opposed.

The dark bars in Figures 3, 4, and 5 portray, for each race-by-religion category, the average levels of racial conservatism on these policy questions after controls have been introduced for background characteristics and survey year. What answers to the eleven questions about explanations for racial inequality are given by the adjusted averages that allow comparisons with others of similar background?

Across all three policy opinions the largest difference, with the most dramatic statistical significance, was the overall gap between whites and blacks, whites being more opposed to these forms of ameliorative intervention. Also, for all race policy measures, the three white Christian groups showed greater opposition than did the three white non-Christian groups. And white conservative Protestants more often than the other Christian groups denied government obligation to help blacks and opposed spending on blacks.

The only other significant differences appeared on the issue of helping blacks. The four black Christian groups were more likely to deny government obligation to help blacks than the two black non-Christian groups. Black Protestants, for their part, were less likely to deny this obligation than the other three black Christian groups.

Is there evidence that individualistic and antistructuralist explanations for racial inequality are driving the group differences in race policy opinion reported here? We included the individualism and antistructuralism variables in multivariate analyses of variance to address this question. If policy opinion differences among groups were entirely a product of stratification beliefs, the race-by-religion differences in policy opinion should have disappeared when the two measures of stratification ideology were introduced into the multivariate analysis. In general, group differences did contract when the stratification ideology measures were included as controls, indicating that stratification beliefs do play a role in race policy opinion. But of the ten significant group differences in policy opinion reported here, seven remained significant net of stratification beliefs. Thus, factors other than stratification beliefs must be driving much of the race-by-religion variation in race policy opinion.[4]

Discussion

In our analyses of the twelve religion-by-race categories, white religious groups in general displayed more racial conservatism than did blacks on measures of stratification ideology and the three policy issues. With one exception, the race gap was pronounced, even after adjustment for background characteristics, supporting the "group identification" proposition (Hunt 1996; Kluegel and Smith 1986) that black Americans' perceptions of their group's history and status shape their thinking, above and beyond their own experiences.

The one exception came on the individualism measure. In the 1996 to 2006 GSS data, the race gap in responses to the motivation question we focus on here was only just statistically significant, and as indicated in Note 3, for an individualism scale built from both the inborn ability and the motivation question, the overall race gap was not statistically significant. Such relatively uniform acceptance of individualistic explanations for inequality has been noted throughout the literature on stratification beliefs (see Kluegel and Smith 1986).

Our other consistent finding was that white Christian groups are generally more racially conservative than non-Christian groups; that is, Christians are more likely than non-Christians to hold individualistic and antistructuralist views and to oppose government action to address racial inequality.

Compared with other individuals of similar backgrounds, white conservative Protestants are not uniquely conservative in their explanations for inequality: a trend approaching significance reflects a tendency for conservative Protestants to be somewhat more individualistic than mainline Protestants and Catholics, but there is no indication they are less structuralist in their stratification beliefs. Their opinions on affirmative action do not set them apart. Conservative Protestants are more likely than the other Christian groups to deny government obligation to help blacks and, by a larger margin, to oppose spending for blacks; however, the distinctiveness of white conservative Protestants relative to other Christian groups is modest and inconsistent compared with the differences between the three white Christian groups and the three non-Christian groups. This suggests that instead of a subcultural tool kit specific to conservative Protestants (Emerson, Smith, and Sikkink 1999; Emerson and Smith 2000), perhaps we should speak of the common tool kit shaping American Christians' views of race and racial inequality or, more broadly, of the dominant ideology said to pervade American thought (Huber and Form 1973).

An important remaining question is how to understand the other side of that comparison, the contrasting perspective of the multifaceted white non-Christian categories whose views are represented here: Jews, adherents of non-Christian faiths, and the nonaffiliates whose numbers in this country are growing.

The progressive posture of American Jews on racial issues has long been noted. Sometimes described as sympathetic identification with the underdog, Jewish attitudes about black-white issues have been seen to derive from Jewish experiences as a disparaged minority (see Glazer 1997). As reported earlier, M. Hunt (2002) has suggested that religious groups outside the Protestant/ Catholic mainstream are minorities of a sort and may share a "religious under-dog" perspective that positively inclines them toward other "out-groups." This proposition is certainly worth exploring.

Another plausible explanation is that non-Christian groups are relatively insu-lated from dominant ideology messages and policy positions deduced from these messages, by virtue of less frequent participation in settings where the dominant ideology is promulgated or assumed. In the case of nonaffiliates, a selection factor may add to the picture: whether the posture of nonaffiliates is a personal or paren-tal choice, adopting a nonnormative religious identity may be part of a broader skepticism that encompasses sociopolitical as well as religious thinking. The other side of that coin was depicted by Edgell and Tranby (2007, 267): "Churchgoers are 'joiners' and tend to have faith in the mainstream social institutions through which they acquire social capital; this could lead to endorsing individualistic explanations for inequality." These researchers note another potentially influential factor: "Racial isolation characterizes the religious experience of most churchgoers, and church going may reinforce racial isolation effects on racial attitudes" (2007, 267).

These ideas provide a few starting points. The differences between white Christians and the non-Christian groups in attributions for racial inequality and racial policy opinions certainly merit further theorizing and research.

As for differences among the black religious groups, there are not consistent patterns. Those affiliated with historically Black Protestant churches were more likely than other black Christian groups to say that the government is obliged to help blacks, but in the other four measures, there was no hint of a distinctive "Black Protestant" perspective. There was a nearly significant trend for black members of predominantly white conservative Protestant denominations to be more opposed to affirmative action than black mainline Protestants and Catholics were, but, otherwise, that group was not distinctive. By and large the four black Christian categories were similar in perspective to each other.

Why do we not see evidence of a uniquely progressive perspective among members of historically Black Protestant churches? As suggested by certain earlier writers, perhaps the image of a uniquely progressive Black Protestant church has been too starkly drawn, partly because the race composition of the local congregation may be more determinative of church culture than denomination. Many blacks participating in conservative Protestant, mainline Protestant, or Catholic congregations are members of predominantly black congregations that may share much of the perspective associated with historically Black Protestant denominations.

But if there were a common black congregation influence on black Christians, encouraging structuralist rather than individualistic beliefs and support for ameliorative intervention, we should find the four black Christian groups to be more progressive than the two non-Christian groups, and they are not. In fact, compared to the black Christian categories, the non-Christian groups hold significantly more structuralist beliefs about the causes of inequality, and they are more inclined to say that the government is obliged to help blacks.

How can the black Christian/non-Christian gap in these two views be explained? Recall Edgell and Tranby's (2007) point about the Christian/non-Christian divide among whites: churchgoers are joiners who tend to have faith in mainstream social institutions.

And as we suggested in relation to the white patterns, nonaffiliates may be nonconformists, skeptical about the dominant sociopolitical ethos just as they are skeptical of religion.

Distinctions among black religious categories should not deflect attention from the sizable overall gap between blacks and whites, whatever their religious preferences. This brings to mind the group identification proposition (M. Hunt 1996; Kluegel and Smith 1986) that black Americans' thinking is shaped by their consciousness of collective history and status, over and above personal experience. Perhaps that common consciousness often eclipses the impact of religion as well.

Do our observations carry messages for advocates and policy-makers? Perhaps this: predominantly white Christian congregations committed to addressing social problems may be in need of intervention—the provision of information and encouragement to base their charitable programs on a more sociologically sophisticated understanding of social life. Many students of racial inequality believe that structural analyses are prerequisite to the development of effective solutions. Meeting the social justice goals of religious institutions must, for example, entail organizing to promote universal health coverage as well as volunteering at walk-in clinics. It must entail lobbying for more vigorous enforcement of fair employment laws and a higher minimum wage as well as staffing soup kitchens. In cultivating this kind of understanding within white churches, we have a long way to go.

Notes

1. Details on classification criteria can be found in Steensland et al. (2000). In this article, we amend the Steensland et al. label for the focal group, using "Conservative Protestant" where they used "Evangelical

Protestant." "Evangelicals" are often discussed as a subset of the category defined by Steensland et al.'s operation; across the relevant literature, "Conservative Protestant" is the most common label for this group.

2. For ease of interpretation, reported results for all dependent measures come from parallel analyses of covariance. However, findings for individualism were confirmed with logistic regression.

3. Following Emerson, Smith, and Sikkink (1999) and Emerson and Smith (2000), our individualism measure focused solely on motivation and willpower, not encompassing an inborn ability explanation ascribed to by few respondents in recent surveys. Contemporary public debate focuses heavily on motivation, and rarely on inborn ability, as a cause of racial inequality. We did examine results for an individualism measure that encompassed the inborn ability explanation. Group differences were muted, presumably because of the minimal variability on the inborn ability question. White Christians held significantly more individualistic beliefs than white non-Christians did, and there was a nonsignificant trend for whites to be more individualistic than blacks. Also, among whites, the religious nonaffiliates were more individualistic than those of other faiths.

4. Across the three policy opinions, stratification beliefs most substantially accounted for opinions about whether past discrimination created an obligation for the government to assist black Americans. Perhaps the closer tie of this opinion to stratification ideology comes because the "government obligation to help" question is a statement of principle, while affirmative action and spending questions refer to practice.

References

Cavendish, James C. 2000. Church-based community activism: A comparison of black and white Catholic congregations. *Journal for the Scientific Study of Religion* 39:371–84.

Cavendish, James C., Michael R. Welch, and David C. Leege. 1998. Social network theory and predictors of religiosity for black and white Catholics: Evidence for a "black sacred cosmos"? *Journal for the Scientific Study of Religion* 37:397–410.

Chaves, Mark. 2004. *Congregations in America*. Cambridge, MA: Harvard University Press.

Durkheim, Emile. 1951. *Suicide*. New York, NY: Free Press.

Edgell, Penny, and Eric Tranby. 2007. Religious influences on understandings of racial inequality in the United States. *Social Problems* 54 (2): 263–88.

Emerson, Michael O., and Karen C. Kim. 2003. Multiracial congregations: An analysis of their development and typology. *Journal for the Scientific Study of Religion* 42 (2): 217–27.

Emerson, Michael O., and Christian Smith. 2000. *Divided by faith: Evangelical religion and the problem of race in America*. New York, NY: Oxford University Press.

Emerson, Michael O., Christian Smith, and David Sikkink. 1999. Equal in Christ, but not in the world: White conservative Protestants and explanations of black-white inequality. *Social Problems* 46: 398–417.

Feagin, Joe R. 1968. Black Catholics in the United States: An exploratory study. *Sociological Analysis* 29:186–92.

Feagin, Joe R. 1975. *Subordinating the poor: Welfare and American beliefs*. Englewood Cliffs, NJ: Prentice Hall.

Gilkes, Cheryl T. 1980. The black church as a therapeutic community: Suggested areas for research into the black religious experience. *Journal of the Interdenominational Theological Center* 8:29–44.

Glazer, James M. 1997. Toward an explanation of the racial liberalism of American Jews. *Political Research Quarterly* 50:437–58.

Harris, Frederick C. 1999. *Something within: Religion in African-American political activism*. New York, NY: Oxford University Press.

Hinojosa, Victor J., and Jerry Z. Park. 2004. Religion and the paradox of racial inequality attitudes. *Journal for the Scientific Study of Religion* 43:229–38.

Huber, Joan, and William H. Form. 1973. *Income and ideology: An analysis of the American political formula*. New York, NY: Free Press.

Hunt, Larry L., and Matthew O. Hunt. 1999. Regional patterns of African American church attendance: Revisiting the semi-involuntary thesis. *Social Forces* 78:779–91.

Hunt, Larry L., and Matthew O. Hunt. 2001. Race, region, and religious involvement: A comparative study of whites and African Americans. *Social Forces* 80 (2): 605–31.

Hunt, Matthew O. 1996. The individual, society, or both? A comparison of black, Latino, and white beliefs about the causes of poverty. *Social Forces* 75 (1): 293–322.

Hunt, Matthew O. 2002. Religion, race/ethnicity, and beliefs about poverty. *Social Science Quarterly* 83 (3): 810–31.

Hunt, Matthew O. 2007. African American, Hispanic, and white beliefs about black/white inequality, 1977–2004. *American Sociological Review* 72 (3): 390–415.

Kluegel, James R. 1985. "If there isn't a problem, you don't need a solution": The bases of contemporary affirmative action attitudes. *American Behavioral Scientist* 28 (6): 761–84.

Kluegel, James R. 1990. Trends in whites' explanations of the black-white gap in socioeconomic status, 1977–1989. *American Sociological Review* 55 (4): 512–25.

Kluegel, James R., and Eliot R. Smith. 1986. *Beliefs about inequality: Americans' views of what is and what ought to be.* Hawthorne, NY: Aldine de Gruyter.

Lincoln, C. Eric, and Lawrence H. Mamiya. 1990. *The black church in the African American experience.* Durham, NC: Duke University Press.

Morris, Aldon D. 1984. *The origins of the civil rights movement: Black communities organizing for change.* New York, NY: Free Press.

Paris, Peter J. 1985. *The social teachings of the black churches.* Philadelphia, PA: Fortress Press.

Pattillo-McCoy, Mary. 1998. Church culture as a strategy of action in the black community. *American Sociological Review* 63 (6): 767–84.

Robinson, Robert V., and Wendell Bell. 1978. Equality, success, and social justice in England and the United States. *American Sociological Review* 43:125–43.

Roof, Wade C., and William McKinney. 1987. *American mainline religion.* New Brunswick, NJ: Rutgers University Press.

Ryan, William. 1971. *Blaming the victim.* New York, NY: Random House.

Sewell, William H. 1992. A theory of structure: Duality, agency, and transformation. *American Journal of Sociology* 98 (1): 1–29.

Steensland, Brian, Jerry Z. Park, Mark D. Regnerus, Lynn D. Robinson, W. Bradford Wilcox, and Robert D. Woodberry. 2000. The measure of American religion: Toward improving the state of the art. *Social Forces* 79:291–318.

Swidler, Ann. 1986. Culture in action: Symbols and strategies. *American Sociological Review* 51:273–86.

Taylor, Marylee C., and Stephen M. Merino. 2010. *Assessing the racial views of white conservative Protestants: Who do we compare with whom?* University Park: Department of Sociology, Pennsylvania State University.

Taylor, Robert J., Linda M. Chatters, Rukmalie Jayakody, and Jeffrey S. Levin. 1996. Black and white differences in religious participation: A multisample comparison. *Journal for the Scientific Study of Religion* 35 (4): 403–10.

Wald, Kenneth D. 2003. *Religion and politics in the United States.* 4th ed. Lanham, MD: Rowman & Littlefield.

Weber, Max. 1958. *From Max Weber.* Translated and edited by H. H. Gerth and C. Wright Mills. New York, NY: Galaxy.

Including Oneself and Including Others: Who Belongs in My Country?

To be a full member of a country, must one have citizenship, the same ethnic or racial background, or the same religion as most citizens? What do people of different statuses believe about the criteria for inclusion? To answer these questions, the authors analyze the 2003 International Social Survey Programme survey on national identity, focusing on ten wealthy, democratic countries. They find a series of mismatches. A strong sense of being included is often coupled with a desire to exclude others. Countries with extreme public views are not always the countries with political controversy over inclusion. Views of citizens or members of the mainstream religion or race often differ from views of relative outsiders. Countries often cluster in ways that violate standard assumptions about geographic, cultural, or political affinities. Enjoying high status does not guarantee feeling included or seeking to include others. Given these mismatches, it is no surprise that politics and policies around inclusion are contentious, unstable, and fascinating.

Keywords: inclusion; exclusion; public opinion; OECD countries; immigrant incorporation; race; religion

By
JENNIFER L. HOCHSCHILD
and
CHARLES LANG

To be a full-fledged member of a country, does one have to have citizenship, the same ethnic or racial background, or the same religion as most citizens? Do well-off individuals feel

Jennifer L. Hochschild is Henry LaBarre Jayne Professor of Government at Harvard University, with a joint appointment in the Department of African and African American Studies. Recently, she coedited (with John Mollenkopf) Bringing Outsiders In: Transatlantic Perspectives on Immigrant Political Incorporation *(Cornell University Press 2009). Her current book projects are* Transforming the American Racial Order: Immigration, Multiracialism, DNA, and Cohort Change *(coauthored with Vesla Weaver and Traci Burch) and* Facts in Politics: What Do Citizens Know and What Difference Does It Make? *(University of Oklahoma Press forthcoming).*

Charles Lang is a doctoral student at Harvard Graduate School of Education, from which he holds a master's degree in mind, brain, and education. He has a bachelor's degree in biochemistry and political science from the University of Melbourne. He has worked as a research scientist and in database management and statistical analysis for Australia's Department of Health and Aging.

DOI: 10.1177/0002716210388990

secure enough to welcome in outsiders, or do they seek to protect their benefits and status from outsiders? Do poor members of a polity empathize with the excluded or raise barriers against potential competitors? Countries answer these questions differently, and residents of the same country disagree. To address this array of questions, this article examines how people in ten wealthy, Westernized states evaluate their own levels of inclusion and what criteria they set for including others.

Our goal is systematic comparison among and within countries that are, roughly speaking, socioeconomically and politically similar but that treat issues of inclusion differently. Such a comparison reveals starkly the trade-offs in many contemporary discussions of inclusion and exclusion. But it also reveals a broader set of attitudes than Americans usually consider, and it shows that governments resting on public opinion and seeking to deal with questions of inclusion have a wider set of policy choices than most Americans perceive.

We generate these comparisons from a public opinion survey, the International Social Survey Programme (ISSP). In 2003, analysts from forty-two countries asked a common set of seventy questions in a module on "national identity" (for illuminating uses of this survey, see Bail 2008; Kunovich 2009; Pehrson, Vignoles, and Brown 2009; and Davidov 2009. More generally, see Blank and Schmidt 2003). We use fourteen items to create indices that answer two seemingly simple questions: How included do I feel in my country? and What characteristics should a person have to be included in my country? We then analyze views about inclusion and exclusion of self and others across ten countries and by majority and minority groups within a country. We also show how views about inclusion relate to respondents' socioeconomic status.

Some results are not surprising: white Americans feel more included than nonwhites, Christians and Jews feel more included than people of other faiths or no faith, and citizens feel more included than noncitizens. Other findings were less predictable: nonwhite Americans resist bringing outsiders in as much as do whites, nonreligious Britons feel excluded but promote inclusion of others more than do those of any faith, and Canadians feel more included than do residents of most other countries but also express more exclusionary views than do most others.

The most powerful conclusion is one of mismatches, in five distinct ways. First, a strong sense of being included frequently accompanies a desire to exclude others from one's polity. Second, countries with extreme public opinion are not necessarily the countries with political controversy around questions of inclusion. Third, views of racial or religious insiders and of citizens typically differ from views of relative outsiders. Fourth, countries often cluster in groups that do not accord with our standard assumptions about geographic, cultural, or political affinities. Finally, enjoying high status does not guarantee feeling included or seeking to include others, and low status is not always associated with feeling excluded or preferring to exclude others. In short, attitudes about inclusion may not accord with one another or with one's social standing, the views of conationals, the level of political controversy about inclusion, or the views of people in purportedly

FIGURE 1
The Static Two-Dimensional Model of Group Standing

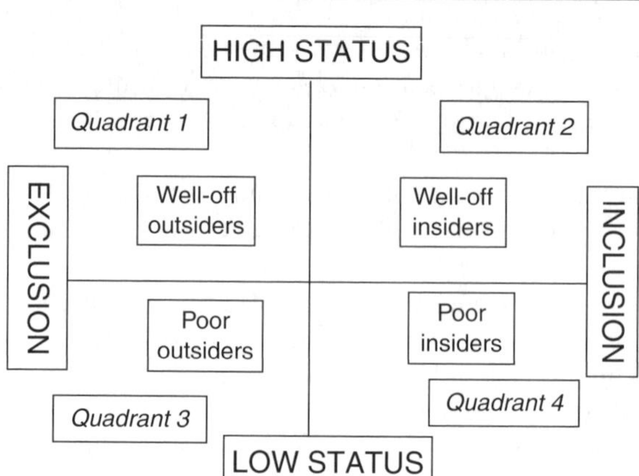

similar countries. No wonder the topic is endlessly fascinating, and policies to resolve issues of stratification and exclusion are extremely difficult to negotiate.

To explicate these mismatches, the article lays out a framework to show how, in theory, status and inclusion are related. Next, we specify our questions and explain the data and methods. We then provide results, and last, we discuss the numerous mismatches.

The Model of Status and Inclusion

We start from a model of a person's or group's position at a given time, conceptualized along two orthogonal dimensions. The vertical dimension is *status*, in which people are relatively dominant or subordinated based on some contextually specific combination of political power, socioeconomic standing, and cultural prestige. The horizontal dimension is one of *inclusion*, determined by some contextually specific combination of individual identity or preference, public policies, and the preferences and practices of others in the country (adapted from Kim 1999). In the static model, groups or individuals can be located in one of the four resulting quadrants, as in Figure 1.

The static model can be made dynamic, since the location of a group or person, or the elements determining the vertical or horizontal position, may change over time. Before the American Civil War, all whites had a higher status than all blacks, regardless of income; by the 2000s, some nonwhites arguably had a higher status than some whites, as nonwhites gained income or political power and as income or power sometimes has overridden race in determining high status. With regard to inclusion, from the Civil War through World War II, most Americans perceived

Asians to be outsiders, regardless of their wealth or nativity. By the end of the twentieth century, however, white Americans and Asians had intermarried, and whites' views had changed enough that Asians were arguably attaining insider status socially if not politically.

National context can affect a person's or group's location; dark-skinned Afro-Caribbeans might be high-status insiders at home but become low-status outsiders when they migrate to the United States or England. Even categories or individuals within a group may change their status with migration; different societal gender dynamics and laws may permit Muslim women to move from quadrant 3 to quadrant 1 or 4 when they move from Pakistan to England.[1]

Last, each person's or group's location is relative to others'. Insiders may, willingly or under pressure, open their symbolic gates to some outsiders, such as black Americans after the 1960s or Argentine-born ethnic Germans after World War II. Alternatively, a group may rise in status if another group enters the polity below it; Irish Americans became symbolically "more white" around the turn of the twentieth century as Southern and Eastern Europeans poured into the United States and as blacks migrated north. "To enter" here can be literal, as in migration, or metaphorical, as when homosexuals are identified as a distinct group with social and political import. Many political disputes can be interpreted as debates over whether and how a given group may move toward quadrant 2, and many intragroup conflicts revolve around whether a group or its members are willing to do what seems necessary to move toward quadrant 2.

Even boundaries between or understandings of the quadrants may evolve, as, for example, new groups enter quadrant 2 in sufficient numbers and with sufficient strength to change the meaning of "mainstream." Until at least the defeat of Alfred Smith's presidential candidacy in 1928, Catholicism was not part of the American mainstream; John Kennedy's election as president in 1960 signaled the acceptance of Catholics as insiders. Conversely, the attacks of September 11, 2001, contracted quadrants 2 and 4 (inclusion) and expanded quadrants 1 and 3 (exclusion) in the United States, at least with regard to Muslims and unauthorized immigrants. How expansive quadrant 2 can be—for example, can one be French and still retain citizenship in the country of origin?—is a vexed issue for most wealthy, Westernized countries.

This simple model is thus quite flexible historically, geographically, culturally, politically, and psychologically. It is especially useful if one treats the dimensions as continua rather than as sharply bounded quadrants and if the model is treated dynamically rather than statically. In this article, we use it to focus on *attitudes about* inclusion and exclusion rather than on groups' or individuals' *actual position or trajectory* across the four quadrants. That is, the model provides a systematic framework for analyzing components of political contestation or cooperation around immigrant incorporation, race relations, religious tolerance, and the meaning of citizenship in democratic countries. As we will show, these elements relate to one another in intelligible ways, but mostly through a poor fit with conventional wisdom.

Data and Methods

Independent institutions in individual countries around the world conduct the ISSP annually or biannually. The survey items are jointly negotiated and are as close to identical across countries as translation permits.[2] We created a four-item index to explore how included the respondent feels and a ten-item index to explore the conditions for including others within the respondent's national identity.[3] A third index of four items measures status.[4]

Methods. The analysis had two stages: we constructed the composite variables and then analyzed them with respect to respondents' country of residence, race, citizenship status, or religion. To do so, we needed to determine, first, if there was an underlying unidimensional construct that could be summed by the available variables, and second, if each included variable contributed equally to the final construct. If not, we needed to decide how to weight them to reflect their differing influence.

For the first determination, we correlated all variables from the dataset that were plausible candidates for measuring either status or inclusion. This provided a general idea of which variables might belong together. A classical composite analysis using Cronbach's alpha provided further evidence of how well the variables measured a single, latent construct.[5] Once these tests determined likely candidates for inclusion in the composites, we undertook Principal Component Analysis (PCA) to provide supporting evidence for the latent construct and to furnish appropriate weights to each included variable.[6] We identified which composites were relevant by plotting the estimated variance for each composite against their composite number in a scree plot.

Up to 10 percent of the values were missing for some variables, which required a way to deal with the implications of absent values. We used three strategies: listwise deletion (deleting the entire case if one value is missing), substituting the mean value for missing values, and multiple imputation of data.[7] None of these methods is ideal, and each has problems peculiar to it. Given this fact, and the fact that the analysis here is exploratory, we judged it most important that the same inferences could be made, regardless of the method used, to deal with missing data. Therefore, we repeated all statistical analyses—correlations, Cronbach's alpha, and PCA—using each method of dealing with missing data, and we present here only inferences that could be verified across all methods.

Countries. Where the data make it possible, we compare views of inclusion across ten countries. They are all relatively wealthy and democratic, and they all have a mix of races or ethnicities, religions, and residents with different legal statuses. All have engaged in political disputes with regard to questions of inclusion and stratification over recent decades, and none has fully resolved those issues. (Perhaps no country ever can.) Nevertheless, the countries vary in important ways. Three are Anglophone settler states: United States, Canada, and Australia. Four

TABLE 1
Feeling Included and Including Others, by Country, ISSP 2003

Country	Sample Size in Cells	Feeling Included		Including Others	
		1. Median View	2. Mean View	3. Median View	4. Mean View
United States	1,189 to 1,216	.83	.72	−1.20	−.77
Canada	1,174 to 1,211	.83	.46	−.50	−.33
Australia	2,041 to 2,183	.83	.55	.41	.42
Austria	972 to 1,006	.25	.78	−.47	−.17
Japan	1,065 to 1,072	.27	.19	.13	.18
Denmark	1,268 to 1,322	.21	.12	.03	.00
Great Britain	811 to 873	.03	−.19	.31	.27
France	1,513 to 1,669	.03	−.20	.27	.32
Sweden	1,110 to 1,168	−.33	−.30	1.00	.98
Germany	1,189 to 1,287	−.77	−.94	.78	.80

are large Western or Central European states: Great Britain, France, Germany, and Austria. Two are small Scandinavian states: Sweden and Denmark. One is non-Western: Japan. An initial hypothesis is that these clusters of states would correspond to clusters of attitudes—but that is not the case, as we show below.

Feeling Included and Including Others

Residents even of roughly similar countries vary a great deal in the degree to which they feel included in their own national identity (see Antonsich 2009) and in the terms that they set for welcoming outsiders in. Table 1 and Figure 2 show the evidence for this claim.

Looking at median or mean views of self-inclusion (columns 1 and 2 of Table 1) and at the distribution of views on self-inclusion (the dotted lines in Figure 2), we see three patterns. Especially in the United States and Australia, but also in Austria, Canada, and perhaps Japan and Denmark, most respondents see themselves as included in their polity (see Schildkraut 2007). British and French respondents are more evenly distributed around the midpoint, suggesting that they feel somewhat included but do not assert national identity as strongly as do residents of the first six countries. Swedes and especially Germans show a weak sense of inclusion or even exclusion compared with residents of the other states; respondents from those countries feel comparatively indifferent to or even alienated from their national identity, or they may prefer outsider to insider status (see Hjerm 1998; Jones and Smith 2001).[8] One would need to look much more closely at each country's political dynamics to understand just what this relative sense of self-exclusion entails. But German and Swedish political leaders may not be able

FIGURE 2
Feeling Included and Including Others, by Country, ISSP 2003

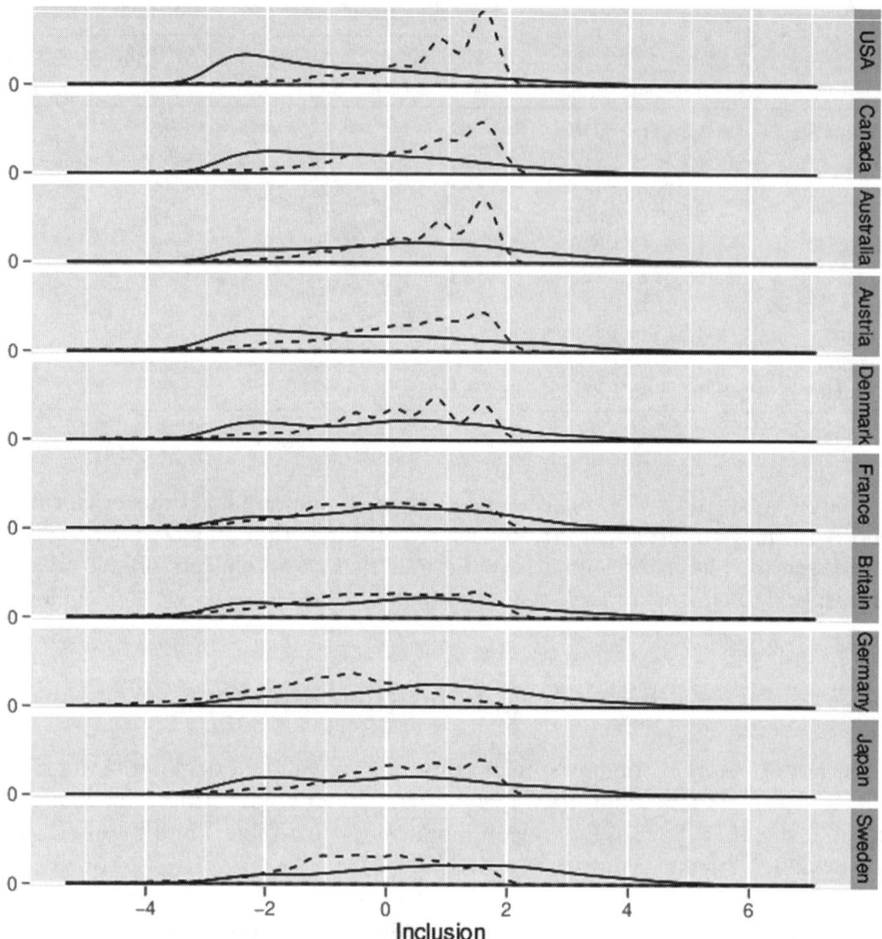

NOTE: Density distribution of self-inclusion (dotted line) and inclusion of others (solid line).

to draw on a powerful sense of patriotism as leaders in Australia and the United States can.

Now consider the median or mean views on inclusion of others (columns 3 and 4 of Table 1) and the distribution of views on including others (the solid lines in Figure 2). Here we see almost exactly the same three patterns. First, most strongly in the United States, Austria, and Canada, and to a lesser degree in Australia, Japan, and Denmark, respondents are exclusionary; they endorse using high hurdles for outsiders to overcome to attain national identity. These are the six countries with the highest levels of self-inclusion. Second, just as Britons and the French hold relatively moderate views about their own national identity, so too do they hold relatively moderate views with regard to permitting outsiders to attain national membership. Last, Swedish and German respondents welcome outsiders the most. Here too self-inclusion and inclusion of others move toward opposite ends of their distributions; Swedes and Germans are the least patriotic and the most hospitable to outsiders. Perhaps most important, all ten countries show a strong inverse relationship at the level of individual respondents between self- and other-inclusion.[9]

This simple statistical analysis invites a wealth of political analysis. Judging by only these data, one would expect the politics around the incorporation of outsiders to be less contentious in Great Britain and France—the states in which people feel neither deeply patriotic nor deeply protective against bringing outsiders in—and in Sweden and Germany—the states in which people claim to welcome outsiders. In contrast, one would expect the politics around incorporation to be highly problematic in the United States, Canada, and Austria and perhaps in Japan, Denmark, and Australia. Those are the countries in which residents are deeply patriotic and deeply concerned about bringing outsiders in. But that has not been the pattern of the politics of incorporation during the past several decades. Denmark, Great Britain, and France have seen violence and deaths, and Australia, Austria, and Germany have engaged in intense electoral and protest-based politics over immigration and immigrant inclusion. Conversely, Canada, Sweden, Japan, and the United States have been calm by comparison. Assuming that the survey accurately represents public opinion, we are left with intriguing questions for analysts and politicians. How and why have passionate advocates of one side in the immigration debate been able to override an underlying rough consensus in public opinion in Great Britain, France, and perhaps in Denmark and Germany? Why has political contention around incorporation been mild in Canada and relatively mild in the United States, in comparison with the riots, deaths, and successful nativist political parties in some European states?

The answers vary and cannot be pursued in this article. Sometimes (as in Denmark, Great Britain, and France), a particular incident has set off a chain of responses, with violence either at the beginning or the end of the chain. In countries that have been spared such an incident, perhaps the underlying moderation of public opinion has kept debates about immigration and immigrants less fraught. At other times (as in Germany, Australia, and Austria), strongly nationalist, even nativist, candidates or parties have emerged, but there has been little violence and passions have cooled somewhat after elections. (France has witnessed both strong nativism and violence.) Although a political scientist is loath to turn to contingency for explanations, it may be just luck that a galvanizing incident has not occurred in all countries where residents feel a strong sense of inclusion as well as a strong desire to exclude outsiders.

TABLE 2
Feeling Included and Including Others, by Race or
Ethnicity within Countries, ISSP 2003

			Feeling Included		Including Others	
Country	Ethnicity(ies)	Sample Size in Cells	1. Median View	2. Mean View	3. Median View	4. Mean View
United States	Majority	955 to 966	1.01	.82	−1.22	−.76
	Minority	228 to 244	.78	.33	−1.27	−.85
Austria	Majority	792 to 795	.78	.38	−.93	−.07
	Minority	130 to 150	−.36	−.29	1.07	.32
Canada	Majority	587 to 599	.44	.23	−.36	−.25
	Minority	456 to 470	.27	.13	−.29	−.20
Denmark	Majority	1,268 to 1,322	.21	.12	.03	.004
	Minority	32 to 33	−.36	−.33	1.46	1.25
France	Majority	1,322 to 1,449	.03	−.17	.21	.28
	Minority	34 to 43	−.36	−.35	1.32	1.17
Germany	Majority	1,021 to 1,052	−.59	−.90	.65	.65
	Minority	15	−1.30	−.81	2.46	2.44

Inclusion and Race or Ethnicity

We can gain more leverage on public views of inclusion and exclusion by disaggregating respondents into those more and less likely to be especially sensitive to such concerns. We first compare minority races or ethnicities (which we treat as synonyms) with majorities—the division that has been most fraught in the United States for centuries. Data constraints permit this analysis for only six countries; as above, we present the median and mean scores for self-inclusion and including others, as well as the subsample sizes (Table 2) and the distribution of views (Figure 3). The countries are arrayed from the most-included majority group to the least.

We see two different patterns with regard to self-inclusion, depending on what evidence we are considering. Focusing on median views permits the conclusion that minorities feel almost as included as do majorities in the United States and Canada (on the impact of that shared view, see Transue 2007) but less so in the other four states. Looking at means and the distribution of views, however, we see similarities across majority and minority ethnicities in a mostly different set of states—Canada, France, and Germany. Compared with medians, means also show weaker inclusion among both majorities and minorities in the United States and Canada but among only majority groups in the other four countries. That pattern suggests that most of the people with the strongest views feel comparatively less included, especially and surprisingly among members of majority races or ethnicities.

FIGURE 3
Feeling Included and Including Others, by Race
or Ethnicity within Countries, ISSP 2003

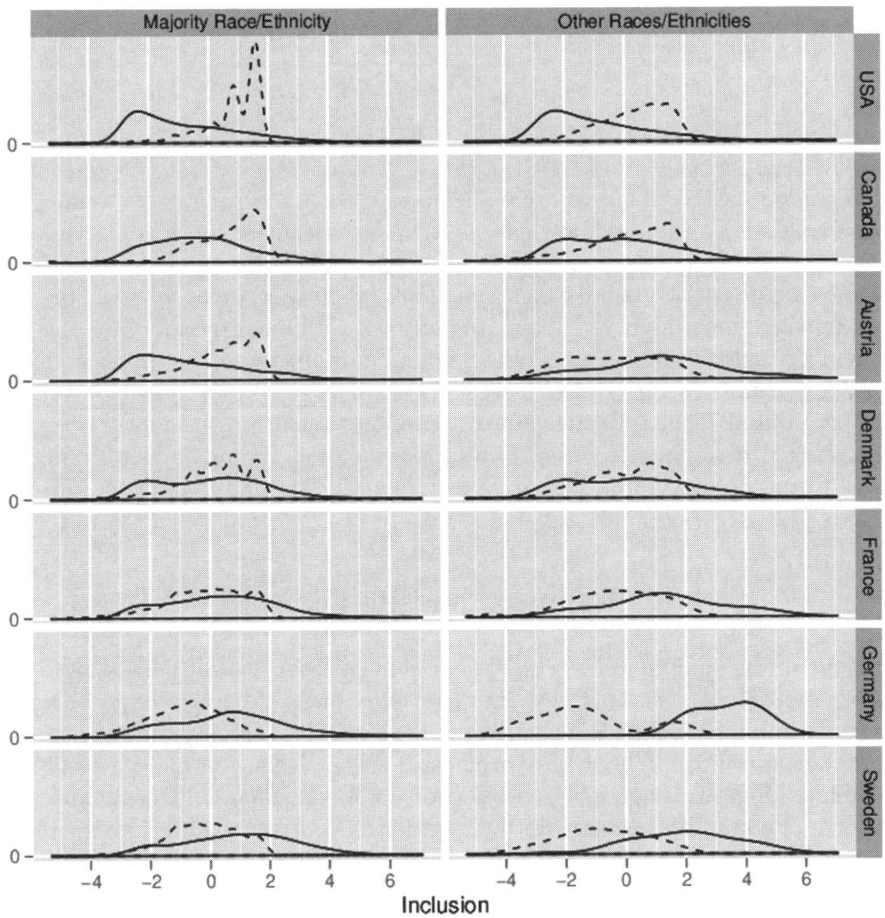

NOTE: Density distribution of self-inclusion (dotted line) and inclusion of others (solid line).

Turning to views about including others, the patterns are intriguingly different. In medians, means, and distribution of views, Canada and especially the United States are distinct; minority and majority ethnicities hold equally exclusionary views. In the other four countries, minority ethnicities favor bringing outsiders in more than do their majority counterparts. The Canadian case is partly explained by the fact that French Canadians compose a large part of the minority group in that country; they may view incorporation of non-French-speaking outsiders as a further threat to their highly contested position in the national power structure. A parallel situation may hold in the United States, where African Americans have a complex relationship with Latino immigrants, viewing them sometimes as rivals for jobs and political or social positions and sometimes as allies against the greater threat that whites pose (McClain et al. 2008; Marrow 2008). In the other four countries, minority groups may perceive outsiders to be much more like them and, therefore, likely allies in contests with majorities.

Inclusion and Citizenship

The 2003 ISSP contains few noncitizens in the countries we are examining, so this analysis is constrained. We can nevertheless compare the median views of citizens and noncitizens on including others in eight of the ten countries. Since citizens are the vast majority of respondents, their views closely resemble the countrywide views discussed above. In contrast, with one exception, the median noncitizen endorses inclusion of others much more than does the median citizen. Although countries vary in the location of their citizens and noncitizens along the continuum from full exclusion to complete inclusion, in almost all cases noncitizens are about a point or more supportive of inclusion. Only in France do citizens' and noncitizens' views about including others almost coincide.

Inclusion and Religion

Noncitizens (and, therefore, nonvoters in most cases) have little leverage over incorporative policies. That disadvantage does not hold for another form of minority status—religion. We divided the ISSP country samples into the majority or dominant religion (Christianity in all cases except Japan), all minority religions combined, and no religion.[10] Table 3 provides the median and mean views of majority and minority religions with regard to self-inclusion and including others; Figure 4 provides the distribution of views for majority and minority religions.

Since the bulk of respondents from a given country are members of the dominant religion, the views that they hold are similar to the views of that country's whole sample. The new information thus comes from the views of religious minorities. Table 3 shows that the median views of Christians and religious minorities with regard to self-inclusion (column 1) are similar in the United States, Canada, Denmark, Great Britain, and France; religious minorities in these states feel as much a part of their country, on average, as do religious majorities. In contrast, the median member of a religious minority feels less included in Australia, Austria, and Japan and feels excluded in Germany.[11] However, the mean view of religious minorities (column 2) is considerably lower than the median in seven of the ten countries—the United States, Canada, Austria, Denmark, Great Britain, France, and Sweden.[12] Given the patterns in median views of religious majorities and minorities and in the mean and median views of religious minorities, we conclude that some, if not most, religious minorities feel excluded in each of the ten states.

TABLE 3
Feeling Included and Including Others, by Religion within Countries, ISSP 2003

Country	Religion	Sample Size in Cells	Feeling Included		Including Others	
			1. Median View	2. Mean View	3. Median View	4. Mean View
United States	Christian	935 to 954	.83	.84	−1.48	−1.04
	Other	87 to 92	.78	.44	.45	.42
Canada	Christian	753 to 771	.83	.48	−.72	−.53
	Other	280 to 293	.83	.46	−.47	−.24
Denmark	Christian	1,109 to 1,153	.27	.23	−.07	−.12
	Other	36 to 40	.15	−.12	−.48	−.41
Great Britain	Christian	424 to 454	.21	.09	−.15	−.23
	Other	29 to 34	.21	−.01	1.38	1.10
France	Christian	869 to 947	.21	.10	−.15	−.12
	Other	112 to 142	.21	−.16	.29	.36
Australia	Christian	1,342 to 1,439	.83	.69	.09	.10
	Other	178 to 195	.27	.12	.96	.90
Japan	Buddhist	366 to 367	.78	.49	−.87	−.48
	Other	72 to 75	.36	.25	.20	.25
Austria	Christian	757 to 778	.78	.40	−.82	−.44
	Other	69 to 79	.03	−.32	.84	.82
Germany	Christian	756 to 802	−.53	−.84	.56	.56
	Other	21 to 43	−1.10	−.86	1.82	1.57
Sweden	Christian	778 to 808	−.30	−.21	.91	.86
	Other	31 to 33	.03	−.23	1.16	.84

The distribution of views in Figure 4 reinforces that conclusion. In the United States, Australia, and Austria and somewhat in Japan and Denmark, religious minorities feel less included than do religious majorities. Feelings of inclusion are similar for the two groups in Great Britain, Canada, France, and Sweden, and religious minorities feel slightly more included in Germany, if the small sample size can be trusted.

In Austria, and possibly in Denmark and Japan, all three measures—means, medians, and the distribution of views—show that religious minorities feel less included than do religious majorities. If public opinion underlies political contestation, we would expect religious tensions to be publicly manifested in these three states. That has occurred in Denmark and Austria but also in France, Germany, and Great Britain (and not in Japan). So we are again left with an open research question regarding the links between feeling more or less included and political contestation.

With regard to including others, religious minorities generally favor bringing outsiders in more than do religious majorities. The median view of minorities is higher than the median view of majority believers, except in Denmark (see Table 3,

FIGURE 4
Feeling Included and Including Others, by Religion within Countries, ISSP 2003

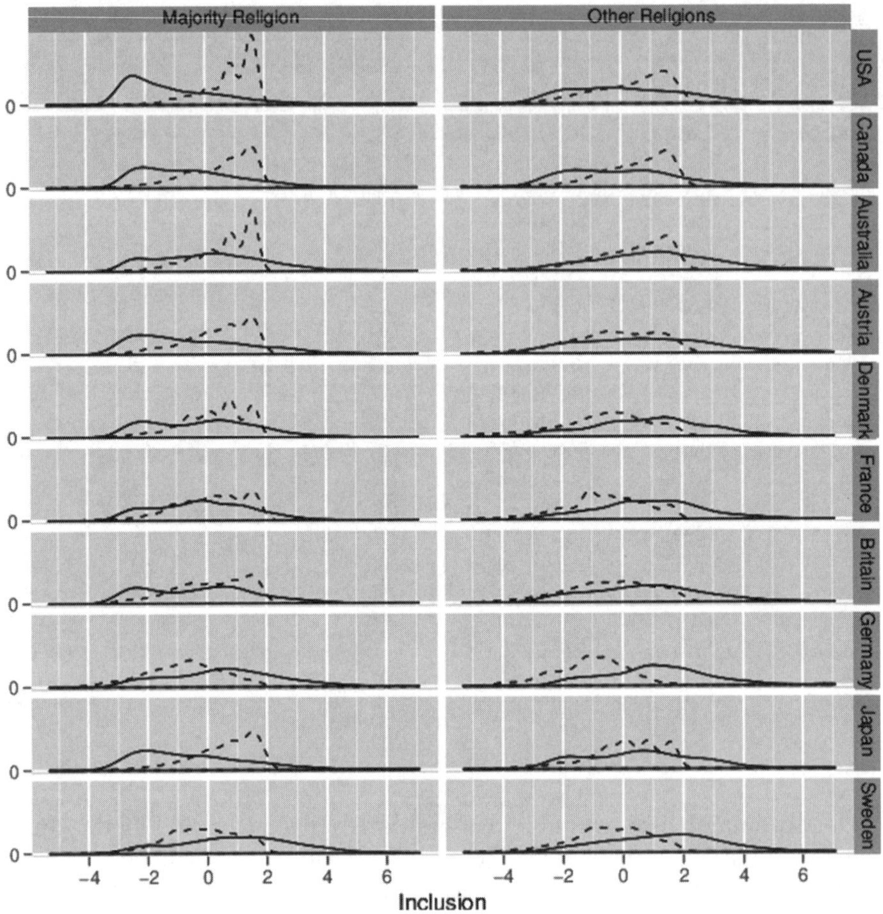

NOTE: Density distribution of self-inclusion (dotted line) and inclusion of others (solid line).

column 3), and in most cases the mean view among religious minorities is the same or higher than their median view (column 4); Great Britain, Sweden, and Germany are exceptions. The distribution of views of outsiders that religious minorities hold is much less skewed to the left than is the distribution of views of religious majorities in five of the ten countries (the United States, Austria, Australia, Denmark, and Japan).

Austria and Japan show great discrepancy between religious majorities and minorities on both self-inclusion and inclusion of others, which would lead us to expect political contests around religion or deep alienation among religious minorities (or both). That expectation is met in Austria and perhaps in Japan. We would expect the least contention in Sweden, an expectation that also has been met. Elsewhere, religious minorities diverge from religious majorities but not strongly or across all measures. In these places, particular incidents, leaders, or policy disputes could, but may not, lead to conflict over treatment of people divided by religion but united by residence. (For helpful comparative analyses of the relationship between religion and political incorporation, see Wright and Citrin 2009; Foner and Alba 2008; Norris and Inglehart 2009.)

Comparing Disparities by Citizenship, Religion, and Race

Which differences in a state—citizenship, religion, or race—seem likely to generate the most volatile politics around questions of inclusion? By one simple measure, citizenship disparities seem the most explosive. We determined the absolute difference between the median ratings of majority and minority groups with regard to including others, for each country and each difference. Differences between citizens and noncitizens averaged 1.30, compared with only 0.27 between religious majorities and minorities and 0.77 between racial or ethnic majorities and minorities. By this measure, we expect the most conflict among democratic publics around citizenship and the least around religion.[13] (This conclusion warrants caution, however, since sample size affects volatility. Noncitizen subsamples are small and perhaps not representative, so the survey results may not accurately reflect noncitizens' views in some or all of these countries.)

Countries vary in the number of differences that could prove volatile. In Australia and Austria, religious groups as well as citizens and noncitizens disagree strongly with each other; in Germany, there is disagreement between ethnic majorities and minorities as well. France, Canada, and the United States each show only one deep disagreement. Thus, if public opinion translated directly into political contestation, we would expect the most severe conflicts over inclusion in the two Germanic countries and Australia, and more conflict overall around immigrant incorporation than around religious tolerance or racial and ethnic stratification.

The Full Model: Dimensions of Status and Inclusion

We turn finally to the full model from Figure 1, by bringing in the status dimension. The model is probably best used in analyzing particular countries, so that one can consider change over time and across groups, as well as changing political dynamics and meanings of inclusion. Nevertheless, using the Figure 1 model to look across various countries at one point in time enables us to reveal one more— arguably the most important—mismatch. Figure 5 uses the indices of status and self-inclusion to locate four countries' respondents in the model's quadrants. We chose these four because they best typify distinctive patterns; each dot represents one respondent.[14]

FIGURE 5
Relating Status to Self-Inclusion in the Model of Group Standing, ISSP 2003

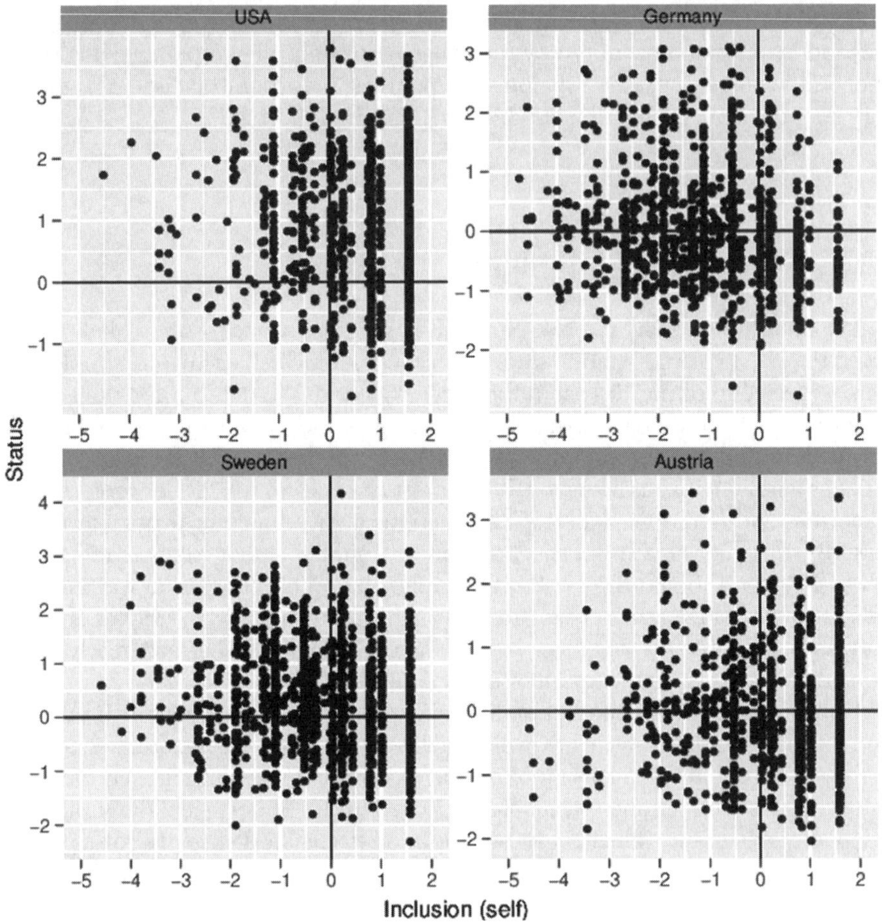

Presumably a country would prefer all residents to be in quadrant 2, in which people enjoy relatively high status and feel included. The United States comes closest to that ideal among these four countries, as one can see from the density of the dots in quadrant 2. The least desirable quadrant is 3, where people have relatively low status and feel excluded. Among these four countries, Germany is the unfortunate exemplar of that pattern.

Despite having extremely different political and personal valences, both quadrants 2 and 3 are analytically coherent. It is not surprising that high-status people feel included in their country or that low-status people feel excluded. Quadrants 1 and 4 are more analytically puzzling because they create two, quite distinct mismatches. Quadrant 1 is the most politically troubling, since it includes high-status people who nonetheless feel excluded or alienated from their country. In these

FIGURE 6
Relating Status to Inclusion of Others in the Model of Group Standing, ISSP 2003

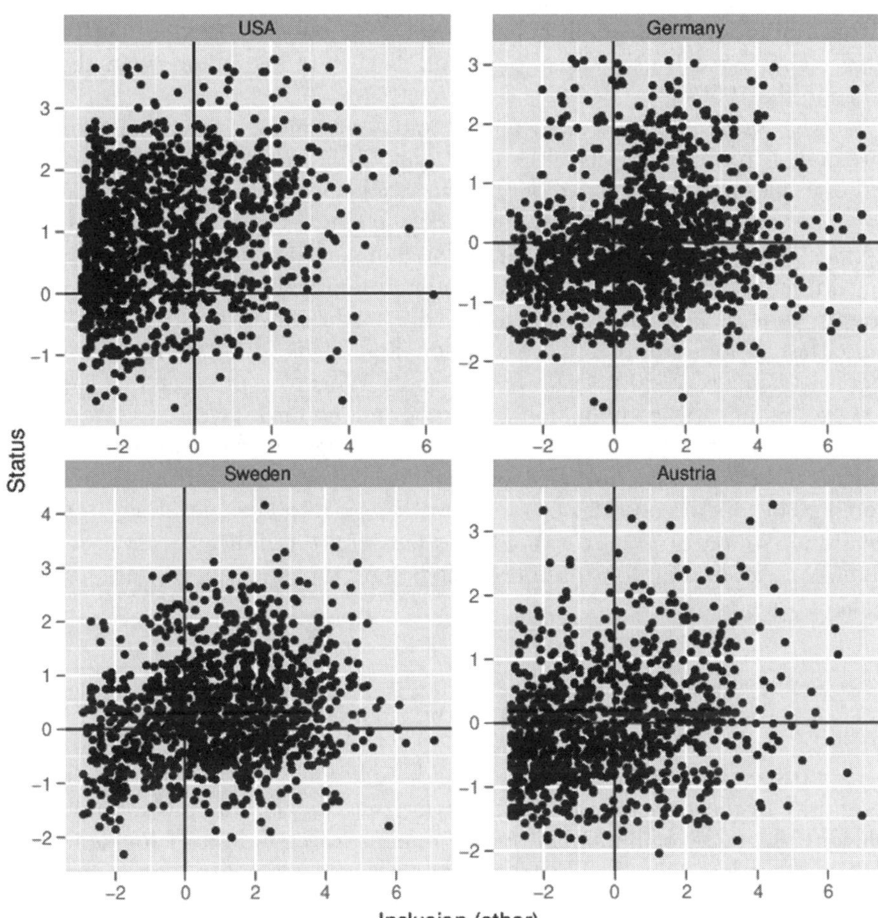

graphs, that is most clearly Sweden's situation. Finally, quadrant 4 is politically useful, since it serves as a buffer for a country's leaders and policies. It consists of low-status people who nonetheless feel included in or proud of their country. Among these four countries, Austria has the largest relative share of people who feel more included than one would predict from their situation in life.

The four countries in Figure 6 are divided into the same four quadrants except that the horizontal dimension focuses on inclusion of others rather than on self-inclusion. Again we have chosen countries that best typify the various patterns.

In the liberal cosmopolitan ideal, all of a country's residents would be in quadrant 2, with high status and strong support for bringing outsiders in. Sweden comes closest among our ten countries to this ideal, even though it also has a high proportion of disaffected high status residents (as we saw in Figure 5). The antithesis of the liberal cosmopolitan ideal lies in quadrant 3, with low-status people who are hostile to outsiders. Among our ten countries, Austria shows the strongest evidence of that confluence; this graph helps to explicate how the Freedom Party (FPÖ) of Jorg Häider, with its political platform of "zero immigration," gained prominence in the 1990s.

As with self-inclusion, quadrants 1 and 4 are more analytically complex. Quadrant 1 troubles liberals, although it gratifies a conservative nationalist. This is the arena of high-status residents who would prefer to exclude outsiders or make incorporation difficult. Among our ten countries, the United States shows the most high-status nationalism, manifested in periodic movements to eliminate illegal immigration, repatriate undocumented migrants, withhold governmental benefits to legal noncitizens, or even revoke birthright citizenship. Quadrant 4, in contrast, would gratify a liberal cosmopolitan. This is the arena of low-status people with inclusive attitudes toward outsiders. What is surprising is that Germany best exemplifies this combination among our ten countries.

As noted above, one could look further at changes in the distribution among quadrants through time, links between political disputes over inclusion and public opinion, clusters of countries or groups with regard to concentrations in a given quadrant, comparisons across quadrants between the indices of inclusion, and so on. We cannot develop those extensions here, but they suggest an intriguing research agenda.

Conclusion: Five Mismatches

Patterns of belief about inclusion and exclusion are complex. Even these descriptive results from one survey show why issues of racial or ethnic stratification, religious tolerance, or immigrant incorporation prove so difficult for democratic polities to resolve. They also show how cross-national comparisons open new vistas for analysis and politics.

We have identified five mismatches. Most important, patriotism is not associated with a warm welcome in any of our ten countries, although the consistently strong inverse relationship between feeling included and willingness to include varies slightly across countries. At a minimum, this dynamic makes it difficult for employers to bring in new workers or for elected officials to promote immigrant incorporation; at a maximum, it can generate virulent nativism.

A second mismatch grows out of the expectations that the first mismatch generates. From these data, one would expect political passions around inclusion to erupt in Austria, Canada, and the United States—the three countries with the greatest disparity in the distribution of views regarding personal inclusion and the desire to include others. But none of these three has experienced as much public turmoil around immigrant incorporation as have Denmark, Great Britain, and France. This mismatch points to the need for fine-grained analyses of the politics of stratification and incorporation, attention to conditions under which broad public opinion shapes policy disputes, and analyses of whether surveys reflect genuine public sentiment.

A third mismatch occurs among groups within a state. With some exceptions, noncitizens, members of religious minorities, and racial or ethnic minorities feel less included and are more willing to incorporate outsiders than their majority counterparts. That point is hardly news. But the details regarding disparities of opinion, gaps between median and mean views, and clusters of beliefs across these three distinctions reveal a great deal about feasible political coalitions in particular states.

However, the third mismatch does not always hold, which leads to the fourth. Countries do not always cluster in the same way across the indices of self- and other-inclusion, and when they do cluster, it is hard to tell why. For example, respondents in Australia, Canada, and the United States might be expected to feel equally included since those countries are Anglophone settler states. But why does Austria resemble those three, as it often does? Or why do racial and ethnic minorities in the United States and Canada mostly agree with majorities in seeking to exclude outsiders, given that Canadian noncitizens or American non-Christians feel differently? What appears to be a coherent cluster of countries along one dimension of inclusion often disintegrates when we consider a different dimension or another form of stratification.

The broadest angle of vision yields the final mismatch. The two-dimensional theory of status and inclusion would lead one to expect people of high status to feel included and people of low status to feel excluded. There may even be causal links there: high status leads to a sense of pride and inclusion, or a commitment to the country generates success that leads to high status. Nevertheless, a high proportion of people—more in some countries than in others—are in the "wrong" quadrants. They are well-off but feel alienated or rejected by their country, or they are poor but nonetheless proud of and attached to their country. The same two-dimensional theory points to complex views on including outsiders. To a cosmopolitan liberal, high-status nationalists or nativists generate the most troubling mismatch; to a nationalist conservative, people with low status who welcome outsiders are the misguided ones.

The United Nations predicts that 4 percent of the world's population will soon live outside their country of birth. People wept for joy in Grant Park the night that Barack Obama was elected president of the United States, but many of the same people still speak bitterly of continued racism and subordination. Mismatches between willingness to include others and feeling included in one's own polity will continue to shape political and policy disputes for decades to come.

Notes

1. Local context may also affect location on the quadrants. Homosexuals can become insiders more readily in San Francisco than in, say, Biloxi, Mississippi; Jews may feel excluded in Phoenix, Arizona, while fundamentalist Protestants hold a similar position in Manhattan. More generally, demographic composition, partisan competition, the nature of jobs, spatial segregation, local leadership, and other features of a city or region shape possibilities for upward mobility or, perhaps, exclusion.

2. ZACAT (the Central Archive for Empirical Social Research at the University of Cologne) documents and makes available the data. See www.issp.org/ and http://zacat.gesis.org/webview/index.jsp. Cautions about cross-national research using survey data are included in Medina, Smith, and Long (2009) and Heath, Martin, and Spreckelsen (2009).

3. Exact formatting of the questions included in the self-inclusion index can be found at www.gesis.org/en/services/data/survey-data/issp/modules-study-overview/national-identity/2003/. The self-inclusion index included the following: (1) Which in the following list is most important to you in describing who you are? Your current or previous occupation; Your race/ethnic background; Your gender; Your age group; Your religion; Your preferred political party, group, or movement; Your nationality; Your family or marital status; Your social class; The part of the country that you live in. [If nationality was chosen this question was coded as "nationality most important," if any other answer was chosen, nationality was not considered most important]. (2) How close do you feel to your country? (3) I would rather be a citizen of [country] (for example Austria) than any other country in the world. (4) How proud are you of being from [country] (for example Austria)? The index for inclusion of others included: To be truly [nationality] (for example, Austrian), how important is it to (1) have been born in [country]; (2) have [nationality] citizenship; (3) have lived in [country] for most of one's life; (4) be able to speak [country's recognized language(s)]; (5) to be a [member of the dominant religion or denomination in that country]; (6) to respect [country's] political institutions and laws.

4. The status measures were years of schooling, monthly income in euros, family income in euros, and employment class in Standard International Occupational Prestige Scale (SIOPS) status units. The latter is an international standardized prestige measure for occupations. It is highly reliable, with intercountry correlations of .97; thus, it can be used to measure the relative prestige of occupations within and across countries. We converted the International Standard for Classification of Occupations from 1988 (ISCO88) units used in the ISSP to SIOPS using SPSS macros developed by Harry B. G. Ganzeboom, downloaded from http://home.fsw.vu.nl/hbg.ganzeboom/harry/index.htm. See also Ganzeboom and Treiman (1996).

5. Cronbach's alpha measures the agreement among, or reliability of, respondents' answers on each variable. If the reliability were reduced by adding a particular variable, we deemed that added variable unnecessary to the composite.

6. PCA is a mathematical analysis of the variables that determines optimal weighted linear composites; in other words, it weights the variables to produce a set of possible composites that are most plausible. Plausibility is judged by maximum variance given the intercorrelations between variables, the first principal component being the composite with maximum variance.

7. Multiple imputation involves imputing several values for each missing value to represent the uncertainty about which values to impute. We used the Proc MI procedure from SAS for this task.

8. Social desirability could also account for the survey responses. It may be more difficult in some countries than in others to admit that one is not proud of one's country or does not feel fully included or to express hostility to outsiders or prejudice against minorities. We cannot, however, systematically test the possibility of variations in social desirability response sets across countries.

9. For all respondents by country, the correlations between self-inclusion and inclusion of others are as follows: Australia, –.805; Austria, –.984; Canada, –.658; Denmark, –.822; France, –.649; Germany, –.812; Great Britain, –.805; Japan, –.821; Sweden, –.635; United States, –.731. All are statistically significant at the .0001 level. R^2 ranges from .18 for Sweden to .40 for Austria.

10. Ideally one would disaggregate within Christianity and among minority religions, but sample sizes were too small or unrepresentative to permit that refinement. Our analysis does not address those with no religion, since the latter are not clearly within or outside the societal mainstream.

11. Sweden is the outlier; religious minorities feel more included than do Christians. However, the cell size for religious minorities is small, so these results may not be trustworthy.

12. In this case, Germany is the outlier, since the mean member of a minority religion feels slightly *less* excluded than does the median member. Here too, the cell size for religious minorities is small, so these results may not be trustworthy.

13. The small number of noncitizen responses on self-inclusion prevents a full comparison of that index. However, religious majorities and minorities differed by an average of .28 in their sense of inclusion, and racial or ethnic majorities and minorities differed by an average of .42.

14. We focus on only four because of space constraints. For graphs of the other countries, contact Jennifer Hochschild at Hochschild@gov.harvard.edu.

References

Antonsich, Marco. 2009. National identities in the age of globalization: The case of Western Europe. *National Identities* 11 (3): 281–99.

Bail, Christopher 2008. The configuration of symbolic boundaries against immigrants in Europe. *American Sociological Review* 73 (1): 37–59.

Blank, Thomas, and Peter Schmidt, eds. 2003. Special issue: National identity in Europe. *Political Psychology* 24 (2): 233–401.

Davidov, Eldad. 2009. Measurement equivalence of nationalism and constructive patriotism in the ISSP: 34 countries in a comparative perspective. *Political Analysis* 17 (1): 64–82.

Foner, Nancy, and Richard Alba. 2008. Immigrant religion in the U.S. and Western Europe: Bridge or barrier to inclusion? *International Migration Review* 42 (2): 360–92.

Ganzeboom, Harry, and Donald Treiman.1996. Internationally comparable measures of occupational status for the 1988 International Standard Classification of Occupations. *Social Science Research*, 25:201–39.

Heath, Anthony, Jean Martin II, and Thees Spreckelsen. 2009. Cross-national comparability of survey attitude measures. *International Journal of Public Opinion Research* 21 (3): 293–315.

Hjerm, Mikael. 1998. National identities, national pride, and xenophobia: A comparison of four European countries. *Acta Sociologica* 41:335–47.

Jones, Frank L., and Philip Smith. 2001. Diversity and commonality in national identities: An exploratory analysis of cross-national patterns. *Journal of Sociology* 37 (1): 45–63.

Kim, Claire. 1999. The racial triangulation of Asian Americans. *Politics and Society* 27 (1): 103–36.

Kunovich, Robert. 2009. The sources and consequences of national identification. *American Sociological Review* 74 (4): 573–93.

Marrow, Helen. 2008. Hispanic immigration, black population size, and intergroup relations in the rural and small-town South. In *New faces in new places: The changing geography of American immigration*, ed. Douglas S. Massey, 211–48. New York, NY: Russell Sage Foundation.

McClain, Paula D., Victoria M. DeFrancesco Soto, Monique L. Lyle, Niambi M. Carter, Gerald F. Lackey, Jeffrey D. Grynavisiki, Kendra Davenport Cotton, Shayla C. Nunnally, Thomas J. Scotto, and J. Alan Kendrick. 2008. Black elites and Latino immigrant relations in a southern city. In *New race politics in America: Understanding minority and immigrant politics*, eds. Jane Junn and Kerry Haynie, 145–65. New York, NY: Cambridge University Press.

Medina, Tait, Shawna Smith, and J. Scott Long. 2009. Measurement models matter: Implicit assumptions and cross-national research. *International Journal of Public Opinion Research* 21 (3): 333–61.

Norris, Pippa, and Ronald Inglehart. 2009. Muslim integration into Western cultures: Between origins and destinations. Working Paper RWP09-007, Harvard Kennedy School Faculty, Cambridge, MA.

Pehrson, Samuel, Vivian Vignoles, and Rupert Brown. 2009. National identification and anti-immigrant prejudice: Individual and contextual effects of national definitions. *Social Psychology Quarterly* 72 (1): 24–38.

Schildkraut, Deborah. 2007. Defining American identity in the twenty-first century: How much "there" is there? *Journal of Politics* 69:597–615.

Transue, John. 2007. Identity salience, identity acceptance, and racial policy attitudes: American national identity as a uniting force. *American Journal of Political Science* 51 (1): 78–91.

Wright, Matthew, and Jack Citrin. 2009. God and country: Religion, religiosity, and national identity in American public opinion. Paper presented at the annual meeting of the American Political Science Association, 3–6 September, Toronto, Canada.

On the Meaning, Measurement, and Implications of Racial Resentment

By
EDWARD G. CARMINES,
PAUL M. SNIDERMAN,
and
BETH C. EASTER

A new racism, it is claimed, has become a dominant feature of contemporary American politics. According to the theory's originators, the new racism has largely replaced the old racism, which was based on the alleged biological inferiority of blacks. The new racism, referred to as "symbolic racism" or, more recently, "racial resentment," by contrast, is defined as a conjunction of anti-black feelings and American moral traditionalism. According to its proponents, this new racism now structures and dominates the racial thinking of whites generally. Howard Schuman has suggested, however, that the index used to measure racial resentment may be fundamentally flawed because it may be conflated with the measurement of attitudes toward racial policies. The authors' analysis supports Schuman's suggestion. They conclude that racial resentment is not a valid measure of racism, which raises questions about the extent to which a new racism now dominates the thinking of white Americans.

Keywords: new racism; racial resentment; racial stereotypes; racial prejudice; racial policy preferences

Aprominent body of recent research contends that racism is the driving force behind whites' opposition to policies designed to assist blacks. This racism, to be sure, is not the blatant bigotry of the Jim Crow era, resting on assumptions about the biological inferiority of blacks. Rather, a new racism has taken hold, one that is more subtle than its predecessor but equally invidious, deriving its strength from a combination of anti-black sentiment and traditional American values, one of which, above all, is individualism (Kinder and Sears 1981).

According to this research, the new racism is not just one factor among many that influence people's racial policy preferences. Rather, this new racism is "the primary ingredient in white opinion on racial affairs," dominating and defining the views of white Americans, not on occasion or regarding an exceptionally controversial issue such as affirmative action, but across the whole spectrum of racial policies, including such

DOI: 10.1177/0002716210387499

mainstream issues as fair treatment in housing and employment (Kinder and Sanders 1996, 301). Emphasizing the predictive power of their measure of this new racism, these researchers conclude that racism has become "by a fair margin . . . the most important" force shaping the political thinking of white Americans about issues of race (Kinder and Sanders 1996, 124). Indeed, "to predict white opinion on issues of race, nothing works as well" (Kinder and Mendelberg 2000, 62).

This claim, if true, has important implications for both the understanding of American politics and the making of American public policy. It implies, at a minimum, that the nation's unfinished journey toward true racial equality has been derailed—perhaps permanently—by the power of a new force in American politics.

Though it may have declined in recent decades, no one disputes that racial prejudice continues to be a pervasive problem in American society. In this article,

---

Edward G. Carmines is Warner O. Chapman Professor of Political Science and Rudy Professor at Indiana University. He is also director of the Center on American Politics and research director at the Center on Congress at Indiana University. His research focuses on American politics, especially elections, public opinion, and political behavior. He has published widely in the major journals in the discipline, including American Political Science Review, American Journal of Political Science, *and* Journal of Politics. *He is the author/coauthor of seven books, two of which,* Issue Evolution: Race and Transformation of American Politics, *with James A. Stimson (Princeton University Press 1992), and* Reaching beyond Race, *with Paul M. Sniderman (Harvard University Press 1997), have won the American Political Science Association's Gladys M. Kammerer Award for best book in the field of U.S. national policy. Four of his papers presented at academic conferences have won outstanding paper awards, including the Franklin L. Burdette Pi Sigma Alpha Award, the Pi Sigma Alpha Award, and the Chastain Award.*

Paul M. Sniderman is the Fairleigh S. Dickinson Jr. Professor in Public Policy at Stanford University and a senior fellow at the Hoover Institution. His research focuses on public opinion and political psychology in the United States and Western Europe. His most recent coauthored book is When Ways of Life Collide: Multiculturalism and Its Discontents in the Netherlands *(Princeton University Press 2007). He has published many other books, including* Reasoning and Choice *(Cambridge University Press 1991),* The Scar of Race *(Belknap Press 1993),* Reaching beyond Race *(Harvard University Press 1997),* The Outsider: Prejudice and Politics in Italy *(Princeton University Press 2000), and* Black Pride and Black Prejudice *(Princeton University Press 2002), in addition to a plethora of articles. He initiated the use of computer-assisted interviewing, which integrates randomized experiments, into general population surveys. He is a fellow of the American Academy of Arts and Sciences and of the American Association for the Advancement of Science, and his books and articles have won a number of awards, including the Woodrow Wilson Prize, the Franklin L. Burdette Pi Sigma Alpha Award, the Gladys M. Kammerer Award, the Pi Sigma Alpha Award, and the Ralph J. Bunche Award.*

Beth C. Easter is a PhD candidate in the Department of Political Science at Indiana University. She holds a Juris Doctorate from Emory Law School and is a licensed member of the Michigan Bar. Her research interests include public opinion, elections, and judicial politics. Her dissertation examines the participation of political parties and organized interests in state Supreme Court elections. A grant from the National Science Foundation Law and Social Sciences Program has funded this project, which helped her to conduct a national survey of political parties and interest groups.

however, we show that racial resentment is not a valid measure of racial prejudice and, therefore, does not provide relevant, much less convincing, evidence about the extent to which racial animosity continues to dominate the thinking of white Americans.

This article first outlines the theoretical rationale underlying this line of research and then carries out a two-pronged assessment of the validity of the current measure of the new racism—or "racial resentment," as it now has been labeled. The first line of analysis assesses the most direct evidence offered in support of the claim that the measure of the new racism is, in fact, a measure of racism: notably, that it is interchangeable with a self-evidently valid measure of racism. The second line of analysis evaluates a conjecture of Schuman's (2000): namely, that this measure of the new racism is primarily a measure of the very thing that it is supposed to explain—racial policy attitudes.

The Concept of the New Racism

In our outlining of the theoretical rationale underlying the concept of the new racism, we pay particular attention to the only book-length treatment of the topic—Donald Kinder and Lynn Sanders's *Divided by Color* (1996). Their work is notable because it provides the most detailed explication of the concept and because it presents the most extensive evidence in support of the validity of the contemporary measure of the new racism.

As its name implies, the new racism shares many characteristics with the old. It is, as it were, racism in a new bottle. The older version was based on the presumption that African Americans were biologically inferior to whites—literally a race apart. This biological racism was racism in its rawest and most primitive form and gave rise to an ideology that at various times justified slavery, economic exploitation, political disenfranchisement, and legally enforced segregation.

The new racism differs from the old because of its disavowal of biological determinism. Most whites no longer regard African Americans as inherently inferior to them and, therefore, as intrinsically incapable of balancing the rights and responsibilities of full citizenship. But for the new racism researchers, the decline of biological racism does not mean that racism itself has disappeared from America or that racist impulses do not continue to dominate the political thinking of most white Americans. Quite the contrary: "The decline of biological racism must not be equated with the decline of racism generally for as biological racism has declined, a new form of racial prejudice has appeared" (Kinder and Sanders 1996, 97–98).

The new racism also differs from the old because the former represents an alliance between racial animosity on one hand and traditional American values, especially individualism, on the other. As Kinder and Sanders (1996, 293) put it, "Racial resentment is thought to be the conjunction of whites' feelings toward blacks and their support for American values, especially secularized versions of the Protestant ethic." It is this union of racial antagonism with American moral traditionalism that is the defining feature of the new racism and the main reason for its alleged potency in contemporary American politics.

On this account, the new racism is thus more refined and less offensive than the old. It claims not that blacks are genetically inferior to whites but that they lack the moral values of individualism, hard work, discipline, and self-sacrifice that whites believe are central to their race and American society as a whole. Blacks are faulted because they do not "try hard enough to overcome the difficulties they face and they take what they have not earned" (Kinder and Sanders 1996, 106). Since racial anger and indignation have now become disconnected from biological racism and joined with cherished American values, this new form of racism has not only become widespread in contemporary America but is expressed openly and without hesitation by many whites. Thus, the scar of racism continues to deform white America; the only difference is that "today prejudice is expressed in the language of American individualism" (Kinder and Sanders 1996, 106).

The Convergent Validity of Racial Resentment: The Test of Interchangeability

In *Divided by Color*, Kinder and Sanders employ a multiple-item scale to measure the new racism, which they refer to as "racial resentment."[1] They provide evidence pertaining to the scale's reliability, validity, and importance, concluding that "racial resentment is coherent and stable. . . . It powerfully predicts derogatory racial stereotypes . . . and it is associated with, but distinct from, biological forms of racism, which it has largely replaced" (Kinder and Sanders 1996, 109).

Kinder and Sanders (1996) maintain that their scale of racial resentment possesses two extremely important properties. First, they claim that the impact of racial resentment on white Americans' racial policy attitudes is unequaled. No other factor—including material threats to self-interest, support for limited government, ideology, the race of the interviewer, or a wide array of social background factors (age, region, gender, Hispanic ethnicity, family income, education, and occupational status)—has a comparable influence on the positions that white Americans take on a wide range of racial policies, including school desegregation, the fair treatment of blacks in employment, the role of the federal government in providing assistance to blacks, and affirmative action programs in employment and higher education. Second, Kinder and Sanders claim that their measure of racial resentment is characterized by a truly impressive degree of validity, presenting new evidence that it indeed measures what it is intended to measure.

The issue of validity has been a central concern since the introduction of measures of the new racism, with a succession of critical studies claiming that these measures are not really measures of racism (e.g., Hurwitz and Peffley 1998; Sniderman and Piazza 1993; Sniderman et al. 1991; Sniderman and Tetlock 1986a, 1986b; Sniderman, Crosby, and Howell 2000; Bobo 1988; Schuman et al. 1997; Stoker 1998; Tetlock 1994; Wood 1994). Huddy and Feldman (2009, 426) summarize the widely expressed criticism directed toward measures of the new racism as follows: "From a measurement perspective, new-racism questions remain ambiguous indicators of racial prejudice because they ask white Americans to agree with complex statements that could garner support for reasons other than racial prejudice."

Kinder and Sanders (1996) respond directly to this challenge in a variety of ways.[2] They argue, for example, that the questions they use to measure racial resentment are face valid—that is, that inspection of their manifest content shows them to be measures of the new racism. But arguments on the basis of face validity tend to be weak as a general matter. Their more original and impressive evidence focuses on the convergent validity of their measure of the new racism.

Convergent validity refers to the extent to which alternative measures of a given theoretical concept have similar relationships with other theoretically relevant variables (Carmines and Zeller 1979; Zeller and Carmines 1980). Kinder and Sanders (1996, 299) accordingly ask, "To what extent do our results depend on the particular ways we have measured racial resentment?" To answer this question, they introduce into their analysis an index of racial stereotypes, originally developed for the General Social Survey and later adopted by the American National Election Studies (ANES); the latter has long been considered a valid measure of racial prejudice (Levine, Carmines, and Sniderman 1999). (The racial stereotype items are listed in this article's appendix.) Kinder and Sanders substitute this alternative measure of racial prejudice for their measure of racial resentment and then reestimate the impacts each has on racial policy preferences. They find that the two measures of racism produce virtually identical results. Their conclusion is unequivocal:

> Our estimate of the role played by racial animosity in white opinion on racial policy is essentially unaffected by which measure we use—and in each case commands center stage. Whether by expressions of racial resentment or by endorsement of racial stereotypes, racial hostility is the primary ingredient in white opinion on racial affairs. (Kinder and Sanders 1996, 301)

The interchangeability of racial resentment and racial stereotyping as predictors of whites' racial policy positions would appear to provide compelling evidence of the convergent validity of Kinder and Sanders's measure of racial resentment. Since agreement with negative racial stereotypes is widely considered a valid measure of racial prejudice, if their measure truly can be substituted for a measure of racial stereotyping, then their measure, too, must be a valid measure of racism.

The proof of interchangeability is the equivalence of the regression coefficients of racial resentment and racial stereotypes in predicting whites' racial policy preferences. For example, taking attitudes toward fair employment as the dependent variable, the value of the unstandardized coefficient (scored from 0 to 1) of racial resentment, from the 1992 ANES survey, is .63; the value of the similarly calculated derogatory stereotype measure is .61. Kinder and Sanders (1996, 300) find a similar degree of equivalence with respect to all of the racial policies they analyze.

These results, however, may be an artifact of their scaling of the derogatory stereotype items. Even though they score the derogatory stereotype items between 0 and 1, Kinder and Sanders (1996) place white respondents who believe that blacks are every bit as meritorious as whites at the neutral midpoint of .5 rather than the logical endpoint of 0. Locating whites who believe that blacks are as good as whites at the midpoint is wrong. Such placement requires that, to be classified as racially tolerant, whites believe that blacks are superior to whites. More consequentially, since only a minuscule number of whites believe that blacks are superior to whites, this coding means that the distribution of scores for the derogatory stereotype measure, rather than running from the nominal minimum of 0 to the maximum of 1, is largely constrained between the midpoint, .5, and 1. Specifically, almost 97 percent of the white respondents are arbitrarily forced between the midpoint of the stereotype measure and its upper bound. This crowding, as we show, inflates substantially the regression coefficient.

The regression coefficient generated from least squares can be expressed as follows:

$$\hat{B} \equiv \frac{S_{xy}}{S_{xx}} = \frac{\sum (x_i - \overline{x})(y_i - \overline{y})}{\sum (x_i - \overline{x})^2} \ ,$$

where y is the dependent variable (support for a given racial policy) and x is the independent variable (level of prejudice measured by the endorsement of racial stereotypes). There are two main consequences of artificially constraining the range of scores on x from .5 to 1. First, $\overline{x}$ increases dramatically. In the 1992 ANES survey, $\overline{x}$ jumps from .19, when scores on prejudice are allowed to vary across the entire interval from 0 to 1, to .59, when virtually all of the scores are restricted to only the .5 to 1 range. Second, the distribution of x around its mean $(\overline{x})$ arbitrarily decreases. The variance decreases because only 3.4 percent of the white respondents score between 0 and .5. Accordingly, the standard deviation of x decreases from .20, when x can assume the full range of possible values, to .10, when it is artificially constrained to only one half of that range. The effect of increasing the mean and decreasing the standard deviation when scores are artificially constrained is straightforward: the ratio of S_{xy} to S_{xx} increases, substantially inflating the estimate of the regression coefficient.

The results presented in section A of Table 1 report a replication of the Kinder and Sanders (1996) analysis for the 1992 ANES, correcting for the truncation of scores in the racial stereotype measure. The first two columns compare the explanatory power of racial resentment and the derogatory racial stereotype measure, each entered separately as a predictor of whites' racial policy preferences. Instead of the effects of the two measures being (approximately) equal in size, the impact of racial resentment on racial policy preferences is markedly larger—for the three racial policies, more than twice the size of the racial stereotype measure. For example, on the issue of the government making an effort to improve the economic and social position of blacks, the coefficient for racial resentment is .48;

TABLE 1
The Impact of Racial Resentment and Derogatory Racial Stereotypes
on Whites' Racial Policy Preferences, Calculated Independently and Jointly

	Independently Estimated		Jointly Estimated	
	Racial Resentment	Derogatory Stereotypes	Racial Resentment	Derogatory Stereotypes
Section A: 1992 ANES				
Government effort	.48°	.21°	.46°	.09°
Preferential hiring	.33°	.03	.35°	−.05
Government spending	.41°	.17°	.39°	.07°
Section B: 2000 ANES				
Preferential hiring	.31°	.06	.32°	−.02
Government spending	.37°	.15°	.36°	.06
Section C: 2004 ANES				
Government effort	.51°	.20°	.49°	.09°
Preferential hiring	.46°	.10°	.46°	−.01

NOTE: Standardized regression coefficients reported.
°Significant at .01.

for the measure of derogatory stereotypes, .21. Similarly, the coefficient for government spending is .41 for racial resentment and .17 for the stereotype measure.

The third and fourth columns of section A in Table 1 report the impact of both racial resentment and derogatory stereotypes when the contributions of the two are calculated simultaneously. The contrast could not be more striking. For every issue, the impact of racial resentment is large, that for racial stereotypes trivial (when distinguishable from 0, barely so). Thus, for the issue of government effort, the coefficient for racial resentment is .46; for the racial stereotypes, .09; for the issue of preferential hiring, .35; and for racial stereotypes, −.05.

Sections B and C in Table 1 provide comparable results for the 2000 and 2004 ANES, the two other surveys that contain measures of racial resentment, racial stereotypes, and racial policies. These results parallel those from 1992. In each case, the coefficients for racial resentment are strikingly higher than those for racial stereotypes. For example, in 2000, the simple correlation between preferences for government spending on programs to assist blacks and racial resentment is .37, but for derogatory stereotypes the coefficient is .15.

In sum, Kinder and Sanders's (1996) measure of racial resentment is not substitutable for a measure of racial stereotypes when it comes to predicting whites' racial policy preferences. It appeared so only because of Kinder and Sanders's arbitrary scoring of the measure of racial stereotypes, which has the effect of artificially inflating the magnitude of the regression coefficient. Since the two measures are not interchangeable, it follows that they cannot be measures of the same thing. Since derogatory racial stereotypes are widely seen as a valid measure of racial prejudice, it follows that, whatever the Kinder and Sanders measure of racial resentment is measuring, it cannot be a measure of racial prejudice.

The Risk of Tautology: Racial Resentment and Racial Policy Preferences

The strongest piece of evidence in support of the new racism is its predictive power. No one disputes the fact that there is a very strong relationship between racial resentment and racial policy preferences. But while highlighting the apparent strength of the new racism, researchers have done little to investigate its actual meaning.

Howard Schuman (2000, 304–7) questions the meaning of the relationship between racial resentment and racial policy preferences. For Kinder and his collaborators, this relationship of course demonstrates the powerful role that the new racism plays in shaping whites' attitudes toward contemporary racial issues. That is, they see the relationship as being one of cause and effect. But as Schuman points out, this is not the only reason that racial resentment and opposition to racial policies may be strongly related. He notes that the wording of some of the items in the racial resentment scale and the wording of the racial policy questions overlap to a substantial extent. Given this similarity, he speculates that the "strong association between them might be thought of as indicating somewhat different aspects of the same general construct, negative attitudes toward the need to help blacks, rather than as distinguishing cause from effect" (Schuman 2000, 307).

In other words, according to Schuman, racial resentment—at least as measured by Kinder and Sanders's (1996) scale—might not be a valid measure of racial prejudice—new or old—at all, but rather an alternative way of asking respondents whether blacks need, require, or are entitled to help and assistance. If so, racial resentment and racial policy would simply be, as Schuman (2000, 305) puts it, "different aspects of the same general construct." And the astonishing power of the racial resentment measure to predict whites' racial policy positions, rather than being proof of the continuing power of racial hostility to dominate the political thinking of white Americans, instead would constitute evidence that it is essentially another way of measuring what it purports to explain. As Schuman (2000, 304) elaborates,

> Attitudes are mental entities or constructs based on verbalizations, and they all swim around in the same heads with no temporal or other labels to conveniently indicate causal order. Any correlation between the two attitudes, therefore, starts with the burden of proof on the investigator to show that the two are not just somewhat different ways of asking about the same construct, or at least about constructs that overlap greatly in meaning.

The basis for Schuman's (2000) concern is evident on examination of the wording of the items that make up the racial resentment index. For example, consider the following racial resentment item: "It's really a matter of some people not trying hard enough; if blacks only try harder they could be just as well off as whites." Is this item really very different from the following question concerning racial policy?

> Some people feel that the government in Washington should make every effort to improve the social and economic position of blacks. Others feel that the government should not make any special effort to help blacks because they should help themselves.

Both of these items seem to capture a similar underlying concept—namely, whether blacks make sufficient effort to help themselves. The main difference between the statements is that the latter explicitly mentions government while the former does not.

As another example, take this item from the racial resentment scale: "Over the past few years, blacks have gotten less than they deserve." Compare this item to the following question about race policy: "Should federal spending on programs that assist blacks be increased, decreased, or kept about the same?" Again, these two items seem to tap into essentially the same basic attitude—whether more should be done to assist blacks—the primary difference between them being that the latter invokes government as the sponsor of the assistance. The substantial overlap in the content of the two sets of items does not prove, of course, that the two scales basically measure the same underlying concept, but it does suggest that this is a distinct possibility.

Does Kinder and Sanders's (1996) measure of racial resentment and racial policy preferences reflect the same or highly overlapping phenomenon, as Schuman (2000) suggests? Or is racial resentment the primary determinant of whites' racial positions, as Kinder and Sanders and others contend? Factor analysis can help to answer this question by indicating whether it requires one or two principal factors to account for the pattern of observed correlations between the racial resentment and racial policy items. If both sets of items measure the same underlying phenomenon, then an exploratory factor analysis should reveal a single dominant factor. Conversely, if these items represent two separate, though related, concepts, then there should be compelling evidence of a two-factor solution with the two factors corresponding to racial resentment and racial policy.

Fortunately, the ANES has included a version of Kinder and Sanders's (1996) measure of racial resentment in seven surveys; each of these surveys includes a battery of racial policy questions as well. Thus, we are able to conduct seven separate tests of the dimensionality of these measures. Table 2 presents the eigenvalues of the first two extracted factors derived from the correlations between the racial resentment and racial policy items for each of the seven surveys. The higher the eigenvalue, the greater the capability of the given factor to account for the correlation among the items. The general rule, as Bollen (1989, 229) observes, is to "rank the eigenvalues and use a cutoff value of one or a sharp drop in the size of the eigenvalues to determine the number of factors." Based on this criterion, the evidence is unequivocal: the correlations between these items are accurately represented by a single major factor. In all seven surveys, the first extracted factor has an eigenvalue well above 1.0, in the 2.0 to 3.0 range. But none of the second factors has an eigenvalue approaching 1.0. This evidence is consistent with Schuman's (2000) conjecture that both the racial resentment and racial policy measures reflect a single underlying phenomenon, not two different concepts.

TABLE 2
Factor Analysis of Racial Resentment and Race Policy
Items: Eigenvalues of First Two Extracted Factors

	1986	1988	1990	1992	1994	2000	2004
Eigenvalue factor 1	2.79	2.70	2.96	2.57	2.29	2.08	2.75
Eigenvalue factor 2	0.46	0.57	0.54	0.47	0.48	0.34	0.37

SOURCE: American National Election Studies Cumulative Data File.

It should be said that the strength of association between the measure of racial resentment and racial policy is, ironically, a reason for concern. Correcting for measurement error, the correlation between the two scales for the seven ANES studies varies between .72 and .94, with the average being .85. The magnitude of these coefficients suggests again that, for all practical purposes, these measures of racial resentment and racial policy represent the same, rather than a different, phenomenon.

Yet it can be argued that these results, instead of demonstrating that the racial resentment and the racial policy items measure the same underlying phenomenon, show the sheer power of racial resentment in determining white Americans' positions on issues of race. That the two sets of items load on the same factor indicates just how close the causal connection between the two is. A factor analysis of these two sets of items cannot differentiate between these two competing interpretations.

The question of causal proximity does suggest a further test. If racial resentment fundamentally reflects racial prejudice, then it should be more closely tied to measures of racial prejudice than to measures of racial policy. Conversely, just as the racial resentment measure is another way of measuring racial policy preferences, it should be more closely tied to indicators of racial policy positions than to indicators of racial prejudice.

We therefore have conducted an exploratory factor analysis of the indicators of all three constructs—racial resentment, racial stereotypes, and racial policy—for the three ANES surveys in which there are measures of all three concepts: 1992, 2000, and 2004. If Kinder and Sanders (1996) are correct in maintaining that racial resentment and racial stereotypes are basically alternative measures of the same underlying construct—racism—then both sets of indicators should define one factor, while racial policy positions should define a separate second factor. Conversely, if, as Schuman (2000) suggests, racial resentment and racial policy are really measuring the same underlying phenomenon, then measures of these constructs should define the one factor, while racial stereotypes—being the only measure of racial prejudice—should define a second factor. It is not the number of substantive factors, but rather their structure, that distinguishes these two alternative interpretations.

An exploratory factor analysis indicates that in all three surveys, the three sets of items reflect two main factors. Only the first two extracted factors have eigenvalues

TABLE 3
Factor Analysis of Racial Resentment, Racial Policy,
and Racial Stereotype Items: Factor Loadings

Item	1992		2000		2004	
	Factor 1	Factor 2	Factor 1	Factor 2	Factor 1	Factor 2
Government effort	.62	.14	—[a]	—[a]	.59	.15
Preferential hiring	.43	−.04	.41	.01	.55	.04
Government spending	.55	.11	.46	.10	—[a]	—[a]
Past discrimination	.56	.14	.62	.11	.63	.08
Special favors	.67	.08	.65	.07	.74	.09
Try harder	.61	.16	.63	.19	.67	.19
Blacks have gotten less	.65	.12	.61	.17	.70	.09
Blacks not intelligent	.06	.64	.04	.81	.01	.81
Blacks don't work hard	.17	.66	.18	.69	.19	.77
Blacks violent	.12	.53	—[a]	—[a]	—[a]	—[a]
Blacks not trustworthy	—[a]	—[a]	.09	.76	.09	.76

SOURCE: 1992, 2000, and 2004 American National Election Studies.
a. Question was not available for that particular year.

greater than 1.0, and there is a sharp drop in the size of the eigenvalues associated with the factors beginning with the third extracted factor. When the two factors are rotated according to the varimax criterion, a crystal-clear pattern emerges in each survey, as shown in Table 3. The racial stereotype items are distinct in loading almost entirely on the second factor, while both the racial resentment and racial policy items load strongly on the first factor but not at all on the second factor. The racial resentment and racial policy items, this evidence strongly suggests, represent the same underlying concept, while the three racial stereotypes constitute a separate concept.

Finally, we can assess the meaning of the racial resentment scale—whether it primarily measures a new form of racism or simply reflects preferences about racial policies—by formally comparing the structural equation models represented by the Kinder and Sanders (1996) and Schuman (2000) formulations. The causal model that Kinder and Sanders implied is depicted in Figure 1. In this model, racial prejudice is measured by the racial resentment and racial stereotype items, which, in turn, have a causal impact on whites' racial policy preferences. Conversely, in Figure 2, which is based on Schuman's alternative causal model, the racial resentment items actually represent attitudes toward racial policy, while racial stereotypes represent the only measure of racial prejudice.

A vast array of indexes now exist to assess the extent to which observed correlations fit alternative structural models, and sometimes they can lead to different conclusions about which structural model provides a better fit (Bentler and Bonett 1980; Bollen 1989). Fortunately, in this case, this complexity does not complicate our evaluation because all of the evidence supports the same conclusion. As can be seen in Table 4, all of the coefficients indicate that the Schuman

FIGURE 1
Kinder and Sanders's Structured Model: Racial Resentment
Items and Racial Stereotype Items as Components of Racial Prejudice

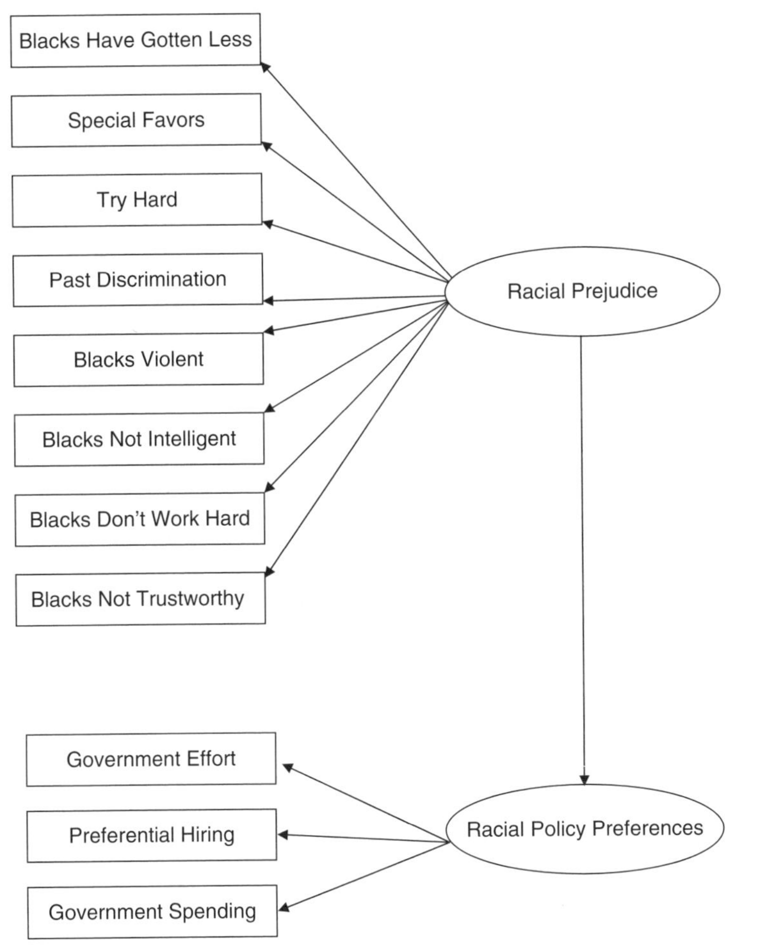

model provides a better fit to the data estimated in all three surveys than does the Kinder and Sanders model, and it provides an acceptable overall fit.

Summary and Conclusions

Does racial prejudice still dominate the political thinking of white Americans, not just with respect to controversial issues such as affirmative action but also with regard to mainstream racial issues such as whether the government should

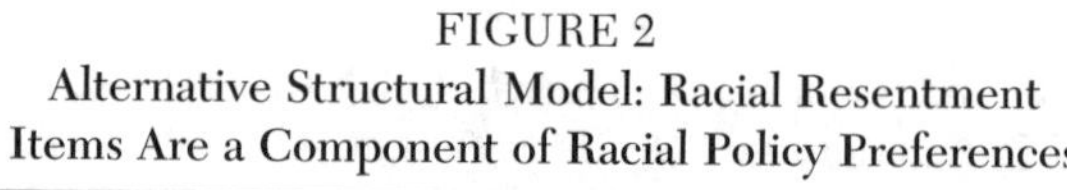

FIGURE 2
Alternative Structural Model: Racial Resentment
Items Are a Component of Racial Policy Preferences

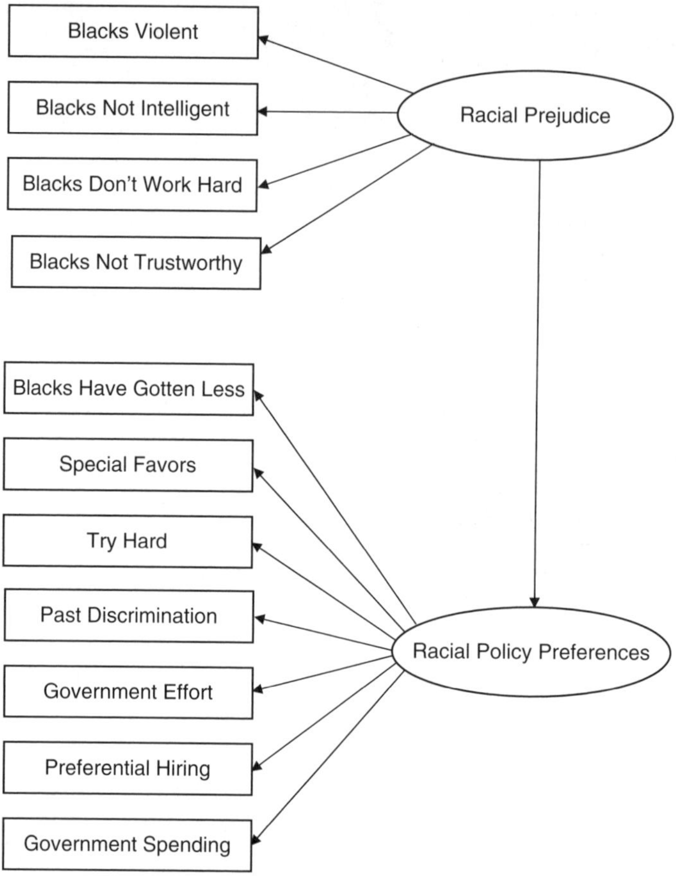

guarantee equal rights for blacks and whites and whether the government should make an effort to improve the social and economic position of African Americans? According to proponents of the new racism, the answer to this question is an unequivocal yes. While acknowledging that old-fashioned biologically based racism has declined among white Americans, they maintain that a new form of racism has taken its place. Moreover, this new racism may be more insidious than its predecessor because it combines racial animosity with traditional American moral values, especially individualism. Today, expressions of racism are openly uttered and socially accepted because they are entwined with the language of American values.

Empirical evidence supporting the new racism rests not only on its alleged powerful and unequaled impact on shaping the political thinking of white Americans

TABLE 4
Fit Indices for the Two Structural Equation Models

	1992		2000		2004		
	Kinder/ Sanders Model	Alternative Model	Kinder/ Sanders Model	Alternative Model	Kinder/ Sanders Model	Alternative Model	Suggested Criteria Acceptable Fit
Goodness-of-fit index	0.90	0.94	0.77	0.96	0.78	0.95	> .90
Adjusted goodness-of-fit index	0.84	0.91	0.60	0.94	0.61	0.92	> .90
Normed fit index	0.86	0.92	0.70	0.95	0.73	0.95	> .90
Incremental fit index	0.87	0.93	0.71	0.95	0.73	0.95	> .90
Relative fit index	0.81	0.89	0.59	0.93	0.63	0.93	> .90
Parsimonious goodness-of-fit index	0.56	0.58	0.44	0.56	0.45	0.55	higher value
Parsimonious normed goodness-of-fit index	0.65	0.69	0.51	0.68	0.53	0.68	higher value
Root mean squared error of approximation	0.12	0.09	0.23	0.08	0.22	0.09	< .10

SOURCE: American National Election Studies.

but also on the truly impressive degree of construct validity apparently exhibited by the scale used to measure new racism, most recently, Kinder and Sanders's (1996) racial resentment scale. Their strategy for assessing the validity of their measure of racial resentment is straightforward and, on its face, convincing. Having shown that racial resentment is a powerful predictor of whites' racial policy preferences—no other predictor approaches its potency—they substitute a different measure of racial prejudice for their measure of racial resentment and reestimate its effects on these same racial policy preferences. The two sets of estimates are virtually the same, seemingly putting to rest any concern one might have about the validity of their measure of racial resentment. One's confidence is only heightened by the fact that racial stereotypes have long been considered a valid measure of racism. If these two measures of racial attitudes are interchangeable, then there is little doubt that the Kinder and Sanders measure of racial resentment is valid. Ipso facto, a new racism is currently dominating the racial and political views of white Americans.

The burden of this article has been to argue that this conclusion, concerning the stranglehold that racial prejudice has on white Americans, is doubtful to the extent that it is based on the presumed validity of the racial resentment scale. Our evidence strongly indicates that racial resentment is not a valid measure of racial prejudice.

Our results show, contrary to the claim of Kinder and Sanders (1996), that the measure of racial resentment or symbolic racism is not substitutable for a measure of racial stereotypes—a direct, clear-cut, and widely accepted measure of racial prejudice. But if racial resentment does not reflect primarily racial prejudice, what does it represent? Several studies indicate that it is confounded with measures of political ideology, a criticism that its defenders strongly deny (Feldman and Huddy 2005; Sniderman and Tetlock 1986a, 1986b; Sears and Henry 2005; Tarman and Sears 2005). Howard Schuman (2000) suggests instead that the racial resentment measure primarily reflects racial policy attitudes, hence the extraordinary strength of the relationship between the two. In his view they are, if not quite the same thing, so closely related that one cannot be treated as an explanation of the other.

Our results support Schuman's (2000) conjecture. A variety of statistical analyses show that, rather than being a measure of racism, racial resentment measures primarily racial policy attitudes. This casts the results of the new racism research in a quite different light. The strongest part of such research has been the sheer strength of the correlation between the measure of racial resentment and racial policy attitudes. In retrospect, the very strength of this relationship points to the weakness of the measure. Racial resentment's relationship with racial policy attitudes is so exceptionally strong precisely because the measure of "racial resentment" is primarily a measure of racial policy attitudes.

We believe this result is of substantial importance. According to the new racism researchers, racism in the United States declined after World War II. But it rebounded in response to race riots in cities and the rise of the Black Power Movement in the middle of the 1960s. Indeed, racism regained so much of its strength that it became in the 1960s and has remained "by a fair margin . . . the most important" force shaping the political thinking of white Americans about issues of race (Kinder and Sanders 1996, 124).

Consider what it would mean if this were true. Between the 1940s and 1960s, America went through a profound social and political transformation. Economic opportunities expanded at an unprecedented rate. Educational opportunities exploded. The new mass medium of television helped to nationalize the American experience. The civil rights movement caught the conscience of the country. Americans' commitment to the principle of racial equality and to tolerance—racial, political, and social—was transformed. The change in American beliefs about race during this time may be the largest recorded in the study of public opinion. But if all of these changes sufficed to cause only a *temporary* decline in white Americans' racism, then racism in one form or another will almost certainly be the driving force behind white Americans' responses to issues of race for the foreseeable future.

Such a pessimistic conclusion is unwarranted in our judgment. Racial prejudice is far from having vanished from contemporary American politics. But the only evidence that it dominates the thinking of white Americans is based on a single measure—a measure, we have shown, that should not be considered a valid measure of racial prejudice.

Appendix
Racial Resentment, Racial Policy, and Racial Stereotype Items

Racial Resentment

Blacks Have Gotten Less: Over the past few years, blacks have gotten less than they deserve.

Special Favors: Irish, Italians, Jews, and many other minorities overcame prejudice and worked their way up. Blacks should do the same without any special favors.

Try Hard: It's really a matter of some people not trying hard enough; if blacks would only try harder they could be just as well off as whites.

Past Discrimination: Generations of slavery and discrimination have created conditions that make it difficult for blacks to work their way out of the lower class.

Racial Policy

Guaranteed Equal Opportunity: Please tell me how much you agree or disagree with the following statement. Equal opportunity for blacks and whites is very important but it's not really the government's job to guarantee it. Do you agree strongly, agree somewhat, neither agree nor disagree, disagree somewhat, or disagree strongly with that statement?

(continued)

Appendix (continued)

Fair Employment: Some people feel that if black people are not getting fair treatment in jobs, the government in Washington should see to it that they do. Others feel that this is not the government's business. Should the government in Washington see to it that black people get fair treatment in jobs or is this not the government's business?

Government Spending: If you had a say in making up the federal budget this year, on which of these programs would you like to see spending increased and which decreased? Should federal spending on programs that assist blacks be increased, decreased, or kept about the same?

Government Effort: Some people feel that the government in Washington should make every effort to improve the social and economic position of blacks. Suppose these people are at one end of the scale at point number 1. Others feel that the government should not make any special effort to help blacks because they should help themselves. Suppose these people are at the other end, at point 7. And of course, some other people have opinions somewhere in between at points 2, 3, 4, 5, or 6. Where would you place yourself on this scale, or haven't you thought much about it?

Preferential Hiring: Some people say that because of past discrimination against blacks, preference in hiring and promotion should be given to blacks. Others say preferential hiring and promotion of blacks is wrong because it gives blacks advantages they have not earned. What about your opinion—are you for or against preferential hiring and promotions of blacks?

Racial Stereotypes

Blacks' (whites') intelligent: Where would you rate blacks (whites) on a scale of 1 to 7? (Where 1 indicates unintelligent, 7 means intelligent, and 4 indicates most blacks [whites] are not closer to one end or the other.)

Blacks' (whites') violent: Where would you rate blacks (whites) on a scale of 1 to 7? (Where 1 indicates violent, 7 means peaceful, and 4 indicates most blacks [whites] are not closer to one end or the other.)

Blacks' (whites') hardworking: Where would you rate blacks (whites) on a scale of 1 to 7? (Where 1 indicates lazy, 7 means hardworking, and 4 indicates most blacks [whites] are not closer to one end or the other.)

Blacks' (whites') trustworthy: Where would you rate blacks (whites) on a scale of 1 to 7? (Where 1 indicates untrustworthy, 7 means trustworthy, and 4 indicates most blacks [whites] are not closer to one end or the other.)

SOURCE: American National Election Study, Cumulative Data File.

Notes

1. In his more recent work, Kinder refers to racial resentment as simply racial prejudice (Kinder and Kam 2009, 209–10); there is no longer any claim that it is "subtle" (by implication, just the opposite), nor that it also measures values. But if this were true, it is even more important that the racial resentment items load on the standard prejudice measure rather than policy.

2. For other defenses of the measurement of racial resentment, see Henry and Sears (2002), Sears and Henry (2005), and Tarman and Sears (2005).

References

American National Election Studies. 1992, 2000, 2004, and Cumulative File. Time series study. Ann Arbor, MI: University of Michigan, Center for Political Studies.

Bentler, P. M., and D. G. Bonett. 1980. Significance tests and goodness-of-fit in the analysis of covariance structures. *Psychological Bulletin* 88:588–600.

Bobo, Lawrence. 1988. Group conflict, prejudice, and the paradox of contemporary racial attitudes. In *Eliminating racism: Profiles in controversy*, eds. Phyllis A. Katz and Dalmas A. Taylor. New York, NY: Plenum.

Bollen, Kenneth A. 1989. *Structural equations with latent variables*. New York, NY: John Wiley.

Carmines, Edward G., and Richard A. Zeller. 1979. *Reliability and validity assessment*. Sage University Papers Series on Quantitative Applications in the Social Sciences, 7–17. Thousand Oaks, CA: Sage Publications.

Feldman, Stanley, and Leonie Huddy. 2005. Racial resentment and white opposition to race-conscious programs: Principle or prejudice? *American Journal of Political Science* 49:168–83.

Henry, P. J., and David O. Sears. 2002. The symbolic racism 2000 scale. *Political Psychology* 23 (3): 253–83.

Huddy, Leonie, and Stanley Feldman. 2009. On assessing the political effects of racial prejudice. *Annual Review of Political Science* 12:423–47.

Hurwitz, Jon, and Mark Peffley. 1998. Introduction. In *Perception and prejudice: Race and politics in the United States*, eds. Jon Hurwitz and Mark Peffley. New Haven, CT: Yale University Press.

Kinder, Donald R., and Cindy D. Kam. 2009. *Us against them: Ethnocentric foundations of American opinion*. Chicago, IL: University of Chicago Press.

Kinder, Donald R., and Tali Mendelberg. 2000. Individualism reconsidered: Principles and prejudice in contemporary American opinion. In *Racialized politics: The debate about racism in America*, eds. David O. Sears, James Sidanius, and Lawrence Bobo. Chicago, IL: University of Chicago Press.

Kinder, Donald R., and Lynn M. Sanders. 1996. *Divided by color: Racial politics and democratic ideals*. Chicago, IL: University of Chicago Press.

Kinder, Donald R., and David O. Sears. 1981. Prejudice and politics: Symbolic racism versus racial threats to the good life. *Journal of Personality and Social Psychology* 40:414–31.

Levine, Jeffrey, Edward G. Carmines, and Paul M. Sniderman. 1999. The empirical dimensionality of racial stereotypes. *Public Opinion Quarterly* 63:371–84.

Schuman, Howard. 2000. The perils of correlation, the lure of labels, and the beauty of negative results. In *Racialized politics: The debate about racism in America*, eds. David O. Sears, James Sidanius, and Lawrence Bobo. Chicago, IL: University of Chicago Press.

Schuman, Howard, Charlotte Steeh, Lawrence Bobo, and Maria Krysan. 1997. *Racial attitudes in America: Trends and interpretations*. Cambridge, MA: Harvard University Press.

Sears, David O., and P. J. Henry. 2005. Over thirty years later: A contemporary look at symbolic racism and its critics. In *Advances in experimental social psychology*, ed. Mark P. Zanna. New York, NY: Academic Press.

Sniderman, Paul M., Gretchen C. Crosby, and William G. Howell. 2000. The politics of race. In *Racialized politics: The debate about racism in America*, eds. David O. Sears, James Sidanius, and Lawrence Bobo. Chicago, IL: University of Chicago Press.

Sniderman, Paul M., and Thomas Piazza. 1993. *The scar of race*. Cambridge, MA: Harvard University Press.

Sniderman, Paul M., Thomas Piazza, Philip E. Tetlock, and Ann Kendrick. 1991. The new racism. *American Journal of Political Science* 35:423–47.

Sniderman, Paul M., and Philip E. Tetlock. 1986a. Reflections on American racism. *Journal of Social Issues* 42:173–87.

Sniderman, Paul M., and Philip E. Tetlock. 1986b. Symbolic racism: Problems of motive attribution in political debate. *Journal of Social Issues* 42:129–50.

Stoker, Laura. 1998. Understanding whites' resistance to affirmative action: The role of principled commitments and racial prejudice. In *Perception and prejudice: Race and politics in the United States*, eds. Jon Hurwitz and Mark Peffley. New Haven, CT: Yale University Press.

Tarman, Christopher, and David O. Sears. 2005. The conceptualization and measurement of symbolic racism. *Journal of Politics* 67:731–61.

Tetlock, Philip E. 1994. Political psychology or politicized psychology: Is the road to scientific hell paved with good moral intentions? *Political Psychology* 15:509–29.

Wood, Jeremy. 1994. Is "symbolic racism" racism? A review informed by intergroup behavior. *Political Psychology* 15:673–86.

Zeller, Richard A., and Edward G. Carmines. 1980. *Measurement in the social sciences: The link between theory and data*. New York, NY: Cambridge University Press.

Reexamining Racial Resentment: Conceptualization and Content

By
DAVID C. WILSON
and
DARREN W. DAVIS

There is an ongoing debate in the racial attitudes literature about the degree to which new racism measures
actually tap negative racial beliefs. Racial resentment is
one construct that has been criticized on such grounds.
To date, Kinder and Sanders (1996) have proposed the
most commonly utilized measure of racial resentment,
which is largely based on a similar construct—symbolic
racism. The authors enter this discussion by proposing
and testing an alternative racial resentment measure,
one that is more explicit. They analyze data from two
convenience samples of college students and from two
national adult samples. They find the Explicit Racial
Resentment (EXR) measure to have strong measurement properties and associations with known correlates
of racial attitudes, suggesting promise as a survey-based
indicator of underlying racial resentment.

Keywords: racial attitudes; measurement; resentment;
prejudice; racism

Few areas of research have been more
intensely debated than the conceptualization and measurement of contemporary racial
attitudes. As a result of this attention, we now

*David C. Wilson is an assistant professor in the
Department of Political Science and International
Relations and holds joint appointments in the
Department of Psychology and the Black American
Studies program, all at the University of Delaware. His
research focuses on political psychology, public opinion, discrimination and prejudice, and survey research
methodology. His research has been published in* Public
Opinion Quarterly, *the* Journal of Applied Psychology,
and the Du Bois Review. *Prior to his appointment
at the University of Delaware, he was a senior statistical researcher at the Gallup polling organization in
Washington, D.C.*

*Darren W. Davis is a professor of political science
at Notre Dame University. He specializes in political
psychology, political behavior, public opinion, research
methods, and racial politics. He is the author of*
Negative Liberty: Public Opinion and the Terrorist
Attacks on America *(Russell Sage Foundation 2007).
His work has appeared in journals such as the* American
Political Science Review, American Journal of Polit-
ical Science, Journal of Politics, *and* Public Opinion
Quarterly.

DOI: 10.1177/0002716210388477

know a great deal about racial perceptions and their complexity. The major controversy centers on the conceptualization and content of contemporary racial animosity. While it is clear that the behavioral nature of racism has changed—based on peoples' expressed willingness to reject racial stereotypes and biological explanations for racial differences in survey interviews—exactly what racism has morphed into is open to debate. Thus, a core problem with contemporary racial attitudes research has been measuring and defining perceptions of African Americans and other minorities in ways that are uncontaminated by other simultaneously evolving attitudes of individualism, conservatism, perceptions of government, and social desirability (Feldman and Huddy 2005). Since racial attitudes are theorized to have significant effects on both racial and non-race-targeted policy opinions (Alvarez and Brehm 2002; Kinder and Sanders 1996; Kinder and Sears 1981; Sears et al. 1997; Sniderman and Piazza 1993), as well as evaluations of political candidates (Mendelberg 2001; Reeves 1997), it is important to dissect and assess the nature and levels of current racial beliefs and the ways in which they are measured.

Attempts to capture the range of racist attitudes seemed to have accepted the conceptual and operational framework of racial resentment (Feldman and Huddy 2005; Kinder and Sanders 1996). Unfortunately, racial resentment has been met with criticism that calls into question its validity as a measure of racism. It is argued that racial resentment conflates ostensibly racist views with individualism and conservatism as well as with predispositions about government policy (Feldman and Huddy 2005; Sniderman et al. 1991; Sniderman, Crosby, and Howell 2000; Sniderman and Tetlock 1986). While some research has substantiated the claim that racial attitudes matter more than ideology (Kinder and Mendelberg 2000; Sears et al. 1997), the continued use of the same controversial measures has led to further division than agreement and has, according to some scholars, "hindered the advancement of research on white racial policy attitudes" (Feldman and Huddy 2005, 168). Adding to the controversy is the view that racial resentment may be a rehashed version of "symbolic racism" (see, for example, Feldman and Huddy 2005), given the similarity of the items contained in the scales (Henry and Sears 2002; Kinder and Sears 1981; Kinder and Sanders 1996; Schuman 2000).

The goal of this article is to hold racial resentment to greater scrutiny. We build off of an existing literature on the general construct of resentment (Feather 2006), propose a new racial resentment scale, and validate the proposed measure. Results suggest that we have a valid and powerful new measure that we term Explicit Racial Resentment (EXR).

The Existing Measurement of Racial Resentment

The stated rationale of racial resentment is to "distinguish between those whites who are generally sympathetic toward blacks and those who are unsympathetic" (Kinder and Sanders 1996, 106). The creation of a measure to reflect such resentment was intended to tap into the broader beliefs that promote the expression of subtle racial hostility without violating democratic norms of racial egalitarianism. The racial resentment items that Kinder and Sanders (1996) proposed are stated as assertions (i.e., the extent of agreement or disagreement with a statement), refer to blacks as a whole, contain strong evaluative components designed to reveal racial antipathy without referencing white supremacy, and focus on character (e.g., effort, determination, and enterprise) rather than racial superiority.

Kinder and Sanders propose that levels of racial resentment hang on the contention that "blacks do not try hard enough to overcome the difficulties they face and they take what they have not earned" (1996, 105–6). Thus, according to Kinder and Sanders, racial resentment differs from old-fashioned racism in that it raises questions about effort and determination on the part of African Americans, as opposed to references regarding genetic or biological differences. Racial resentment features annoyance and fury as its central emotional themes, and these emotions are provoked by the sense that "blacks Americans are getting and taking more than their fair share" (1996, 293). That is, black Americans are undeserving of special considerations on the basis of racial group membership alone. Herein lies the problem with racial resentment and its measurement: while it is not clear from a conceptual standpoint if resentment underlies these racial motivations, the items have to reflect a great deal more than simple resentment or sympathy. The items must also go further than implicating resentment through beliefs about racial stereotypes related to the personal efforts of blacks; believing a racial stereotype is true does not necessarily equate to racial resentment. It raises the question of whether resentment is a simple retrofitting of symbolic racism.

The original Racial Resentment Scale (RRS) relied on a set of items conceptualized around the sense that blacks have been handed advantages; that government has provided these advantages and special favors; and that hard work, personal responsibility, sacrifice, and self-discipline no longer matter. Yet none of the RRS items explicitly connects this basis of resentment with both blacks and the underlying notion of unfairness or special consideration. What is more, the items do not *explicitly* measure the sentiment of racial resentment; rather, they *allege* that the underlying source of the response is resentment.

For example, Kinder and Sanders (1996) pose the following assertion: "Over the past few years blacks have gotten less than they deserve." Disagreement with this question is presumed to indicate racial resentment. However, the item only indicates resentment if one believes that blacks have gotten more than they deserve. One could have disagreed with the question—a prejudiced response— and still feel as though blacks have gotten exactly what they deserve, which is not necessarily resentful or racist. Moreover, it is not clear what blacks have gotten less of or less of relative to what. In another question, respondents evaluate whether "generations of slavery and discrimination have created conditions that make it difficult for blacks to work their way out of the lower class." Disagreement with this statement presumably indicates resentment; however, one could disagree with this statement but still believe that some other structural conditions, other than slavery and discrimination, have made it difficult for blacks to work their way out of the lower class. Also, similar to the first item mentioned, the resentment is implicit, not explicit. A third statement asserts, "Government officials usually pay less attention to a request or complaint from a black person than from a white person." Disagreement with this item also presumably indicates resentment. However, once again, the resentment seems implicit. One must believe that government officials pay more attention to a request or complaint from a black person than a white person, and one must be angry or resentful about it. One could disagree with this statement, yet be angry at government officials, or believe that whites and blacks receive the same treatment; neither belief is racially resentful. Thus, there is some ambiguity about the nature of the underlying source and meaning of resentment within these items.

In our view, the most troubling, but most commonly employed, RRS item makes the following assertion: "Irish, Italians, Jews and many other minorities overcame prejudice and worked their way up. Blacks should do the same without any special favors."[1] Agreement with the statement signifies resentment; however, there are a number of confounding issues. First, the item implies that blacks do not already work their way up, or that they do not work their way up at the same level as the other groups listed in the statement. It also implies that Irish, Italian, and Jewish groups have not received "any special favors" in their efforts to overcome prejudice. There is also ambiguity about to whom the "other minorities" part of the statement is referring; could they be other "blacks"—Haitians, Brazilians, or Africans—who live in America but would not consider themselves American blacks? Second, the item is double-barreled in that there is more than one assertion being made in the statement; individuals must judge whether other minority groups have worked their way up, whether blacks should do the same (as the other groups), and, potentially, whether blacks should do the same (as the other groups) without "any special favors." One could agree that the other groups have worked their way up but disagree that blacks should do the same without special considerations or vice versa. This second concern is less that it is double-barreled and more that the statements are almost independent, with a respondent making assertions about one set of groups (i.e., Irish, Italians, Jews, and other minorities) and a second assertion about blacks. Thus, in our view, the items composing the RRS need revision.

Measurement of Explicit Racial Resentment (EXR)

Before we get into the measurement details, it is important to explain our conceptualization of racial resentment. At the most basic level, *resentment* is an explicit feeling of animosity or antipathy toward a person or group of people who are perceived to be unfair or unjust recipients of some outcome. While resentment can emanate from a variety of sources, it departs from simple envy or jealousy by including a sense of injustice originating from judgments about the deservingness of some other individual or group (Feather 2006; Feather and Sherman 2002).

Applying this to racial perceptions, *racial resentment* may also encompass anger, bitterness, or concern related to one racial group's beliefs about the deservingness of special considerations on the basis of race for another group. "Special considerations" violate norms of fairness and values related to deservingness. Thus, the racially resentful person is offended by claims of racism and racial discrimination and other racial justifications for special consideration because he or she believes racism and discrimination are events of the past and, thus, attempts to present race as a rationale for social problems, inequality, or celebration are invalid and unfair.

The EXR items mainly differ from past resentment measures in their explicit connection between the source of the resentful feelings and the targeted racial group. As mentioned in previous conceptualizations, racial resentment is not overt racial prejudice (Kinder and Sanders 1996); rather, it is a general annoyance and antipathy related to race. Observe the EXR statements presented to respondents.

> *Question 1:* I resent all of the special attention/favors that African Americans receive; other Americans like me have problems too.
>
> *Question 2:* African Americans should not need any special privileges when slavery and racism are things of the past.
>
> *Question 3:* How concerned are you that the special privileges for African Americans place you at an unfair disadvantage when you have done nothing to harm them?
>
> *Question 4:* For African Americans to succeed they need to stop using racism as an excuse.

The first item explicitly considers resentment in terms of what African Americans get relative to oneself (a non–African American). Agreement with the item acknowledges that African Americans receive special advantages and that this is an unfair situation. However, the item does subtly imply that African Americans do have problems (i.e., "too"); it is just that these problems are no different from those of non–African Americans. This subtle suggestion taps into the belief that while all races may have problems, African Americans are getting more attention and support for their problems than other races and such attention is undeserved and unfair. Thus, stronger agreement on this item indicates that the respondent believes he or she is placed at a disadvantage because of African Americans.

The second statement assesses the basis of special privileges for African Americans. It requires the respondent to consider two ideas: (1) that African Americans should not need special privileges and (2) that slavery and racism are not currently relevant to the situation of African Americans. Stronger agreement with this item indicates that currently, African Americans have virtually no excuse by which to claim special considerations.

The third item measures the extent to which individuals view special privileges for African Americans as unfair because they place the individual in a disadvantaged position for something for which he or she is not responsible. The statement also asserts that African Americans already receive undeserved special privileges. This is an important feature of resentment because it reverses the blame from the past behavior of whites to the current behavior of African Americans. Thus, it is because African Americans are making such a big deal of race that contemporary whites are blamed for the past sins of their race. Notice the response options for this item are "very concerned," "concerned," "not concerned," or "not at all concerned." More concern implies that the respondent is aware of his or her racial group's current position and that his or her position is affected by what African Americans potentially get (in terms of special considerations). This item can also be presented on an agreement scale using the following wording: "The special privileges for African Americans place me at an unfair disadvantage when I have done nothing to harm them."

The fourth statement taps into the beliefs about the prevalence of racism and its affect on African Americans' success. Agreement assumes (1) the individual believes that African Americans use racism as a reason for their social position in society, and (2) the individual does not believe that racism is a valid reason for the position of African Americans. An underlying premise of this question is the belief that blacks often use racism as a convenient defense rather than accept responsibility for their lot in life.

Together, these four items compose our EXR scale. We hypothesize that this scale is aptly suited for the measure of racial resentment because the items are descriptive of the content of the racial resentment concepts and because the items explicitly state the nature of the resentment toward blacks. Thus, the EXR, on its surface, has strong face validity and contains suitable content as a parsimonious measure of racial resentment. What is more, the items do not contain any references to government programs or politics, nor is there ambiguity in the meaning of agreement with the items.

We expect our EXR scale to be characterized by strong validity and reliability and to have strong associations with other known correlates of racial attitudes.

Data

We assessed the EXR items and their scale properties in four separate studies, two—studies 1 and 2—using student convenience samples and two—studies 3 and 4—using national samples of registered voters. Brief descriptions of the data are presented below.

Study 1. Participants in this study were respondents from surveys administered to an interdisciplinary course at a midwestern university in fall 2006.[2] We removed self-identified nonwhites and those who did not provide a racial-ethnic classification, since there is no way of knowing whether they are racial minorities.[3] The sample contains 98 (65 percent) females and 51 (34 percent) males; 2 (1.3 percent) respondents provided no gender. Our final sample size for study 1 was 129.

Study 2. Respondents in this study were a convenience sample of students who volunteered to participate in a research project at a mid-Atlantic university. Participants were solicited campuswide and had the option of choosing one of three consecutive days in October 2007 to take part in the survey. Similar to study 1, we removed all nonwhites and those who did not provide a race, bringing the final working sample to 520.[4] Of this group, 352 (68 percent) were females and 163 (31 percent) males; 5 (1 percent) respondents provided no gender.

Studies 3 and 4. These studies contain survey data from the 2008 Cooperative Campaign Analysis Project (CCAP). The CCAP data contain a national sample of registered voters, stratified by political geography, with oversampling of populations in "battleground" states.[5] The YouGov Polimetrix research firm collected the data online using a six-wave preelection and postelection panel design. Our data were collected from a random subsample of respondents in two of the waves—September (study 3) and October (study 4)—preceding the 2008 presidential election. For consistency with previous studies, we include only self-reported white respondents (Study 3 $N = 556$ and Study 4 $N = 564$).

Our goal in each study was to examine the construct validity and the internal consistency of the four items composing the EXR scale. Construct validity is the degree to which collected measures in a study correspond to the theoretical constructs on which they were based, and internal consistency is the extent to which items show similar patterns of response as for items designed to measure the same characteristic. On the surface, the EXR items appear to be measuring resentment as we define it; that is, they have face validity. However, we conducted the four studies in search of empirical confirmation. We ran Principal Components Analysis (PCA) and Confirmatory Factor Analysis (CFA) to assess validity and calculated reliability (Cronbach's alpha [α]) statistics to assess internal consistency.[6] Statistically speaking, good constructs will form a single factor and explain a large amount of variance in the items (e.g., 50 percent or more), have sufficient reliability (i.e., internal consistency), and have a good "fit" with the data to which they are applied. We set our reliability (α) standards at .600 or higher and assessed fit through multiple indicators: a nonsignificant ($p > .05$) chi-square (χ^2) statistic; confirmatory (CFI), normed (NFI), relative (RFI) fit indices of $> .95$, $> .90$, and $> .90$, respectively; and a root mean square error of approximation (RMSEA) $< .08$ (Tabachnick and Fidell 2006). The scale and measurement statistics for the EXR in all four studies are provided in Table 1.

Findings

Study 1. The EXR items formed a single factor and produced an adequate reliability statistic of .644. Also, CFA showed the proposed EXR measures are well modeled by the data (i.e., have good fit). Thus, our initial examination reveals the EXR items to have strong psychometric properties in our first student sample.

TABLE 1
Descriptive Statistics and Scale Metrics for Racial Resentment

| | Explicit Racial Resentment (EXR) Statistics | | | |
Statistics	Study 1 ($n = 116$)[a]	Study 2 ($n = 502$)[b]	Study 3 ($n = 556$)[c]	Study 4 ($n = 564$)[d]
Descriptive statistics				
Mean (SD)[e]	10.1 (2.1)	10.4 (2.4)	11.9 (3.0)	12.1 (3.0)
Reliability				
Cronbach's alpha (α)	.644	.752	.894	.908
PCA results				
Eigenvalues (% variance explained)	1.95 (48.7)	2.32 (58.7)	3.0 (76)	3.1 (78)
CFA Results				
χ^2 ($df = 2$), sig.	1.47, $p = .48$	10.1, $p = .01$	16.9, $p = .01$	2.7, $p = .26$
NFI	.98	.98	.99	.99
CFI	1.00	.98	.99	1.00
RFI	.95	.94	.94	.99
RMSEA	.00	.09	.07	.02

NOTE: White respondents only.
a. Student sample, midwestern university.
b. Student sample, mid-Atlantic university.
c. Cooperative Campaign Analysis Project (CCAP), September.
d. CCAP, October.
e. The scales range from 4 to 16 (higher scores indicate more resentment), and the mean is the average of the sum of the four items.

Study 2. Here, the EXR items once again form a single factor with good reliability ($\alpha = .752$), and the CFA shows a good to moderate fit. The larger size of this college student sample may help to explain the stronger alpha value and larger amount of explained variance in the items by the factor.

Studies 3 and 4. For both these studies, the PCA revealed single factors with excellent reliability metrics of .894 and .908, respectively. Most impressive with the EXR scale is that across both studies all but one indicator—a significant χ^2 fit statistic in study 3—meet the statistical standard. This is solid evidence that the EXR items are likely capturing the theoretical construct that they are designed to measure in the data.

While sufficient, our student samples in studies 1 and 2 were not optimal in terms of their factor analysis and reliability results, so we took an extra step to assess the scales' ability to converge with other relevant variables. This approach allows us to say whether the effects of a proposed measure are consistent with theory and should therefore correlate ("converge") with known predictors of concept of interest, already accepted measures of the concept, or expected outcomes.

In studies 1 and 2, we collected data on several well-established correlates of racial attitudes. For complete information on the measures and their questions, see the appendix. We measured Social Dominance Orientation (SDO) using a set of eleven items reported in Sidanius and Pratto (2003). Examples of these survey items include statements such as, "Some groups of people are simply not the equal of others" and "Inferior groups should stay in their place." Authoritarianism is measured using six items from Altemeyer's (1981) Right-Wing Authoritarianism (RWA) scale. For example, "People can be divided into two distinct classes: the weak and the strong." Dogmatism is measured using a subset of eight items from Rokeach's D-scale (Dogmatism scale) (Christie 1991; Rokeach 1960), which includes, for example, "There are two kinds of people in this world: those who are for the truth and those who are against it." We also take account of explanations for black-white socioeconomic differences—which we will call "stratification beliefs"—using five items, such as, "On average Blacks have worse jobs, income, and housing than white people. Do you think these differences are mainly 1) due to discrimination or 2) because most Blacks are irresponsible in their daily lives?"[7] Items on the stratification beliefs index were coded such that higher values supported more individualistic explanations for racial inequality (see the appendix). All of the above mentioned variables were rescaled to range from zero to one, with higher values indicating more influence by the underlying construct.[8] We also consider a measure of racial affect: a ten-point feeling thermometer question asked students to indicate the extent to which they like (dislike) blacks. We call this "black affect." In addition, we tapped social distance with other races by asking students to indicate what percentage of their close friends and associates belong to a different racial/ethnic group. We call this variable "interracial friendships."

Since racial resentment is theorized to stem from early preadult attitudes and beliefs about race, along with a blend of traditional values and conservatism, we expect that individuals who are more closed-minded or dogmatic, more authoritarian, more conservative, hold more individualistic racial stratification beliefs, have lower affect toward blacks, have fewer interracial friends, and have a stronger social dominance orientation will have higher EXR scores (see Sears and Henry 2003). We tested these hypotheses with bivariate correlations (Pearson's r), which are shown in Table 2.

In study 1, a social dominance orientation and authoritarianism strongly characterized the EXR measure, but it was also significantly related to lower black affect, fewer interracial friendships, and stronger self-reported conservatism. Study 1 confirms that the EXR measure is related to known correlates of negative racial attitudes. Note, the EXR measure, which contains no references to politics or government, is significantly related to self-reported political ideology (higher values equate to stronger conservatism). This is consistent with the conceptualizations of new racism that are hypothesized to contain conservative value orientations. But the significant relationship also indicates that resentment is not simply political but an orientation that is likely to occur among conservatives. This is counter to the findings of Feldman and Huddy (2005).

TABLE 2
Correlates of Racial Resentment for Studies 1 and 2

	Study 1[a]
	Explicit Racial Resentment
Affect toward blacks	−.204*
Interracial friendships	−.214*
Conservatism (ideology)	.200*
Stratification beliefs	.136
Social dominance orientation	.417**
Authoritarianism	.359**
Dogmatism	.201
	Study 2[b]
	Explicit Racial Resentment
Affect toward blacks	−.271**
Interracial friendships	−.089*
Conservatism (ideology)	.347**
Stratification beliefs	.638**
Social dominance orientation	.343**
Authoritarianism	.308**
Dogmatism	.312**

NOTE: White respondents only.
a. Student sample, midwestern university.
b. Student sample, mid-Atlantic university.
*$p < .05$. **$p < .01$.

In study 2, the EXR measure is most strongly associated with stratification beliefs, stronger self-reported conservatism, and a higher social dominance orientation. That the EXR was not related to stratification beliefs in the first study, but was the strongest predictor of EXR in the second study, suggests that context (e.g., region, university, classroom setting, or the race of the study's presenter) may have played a role in some way. Nevertheless, study 2 also confirms that EXR stands as a consistent indicator of negative racial attitudes and also replicates the finding that conservatism is correlated with politically neutral racial attitudes (Federico and Sidanius 2002).

Discussion

The study of racial attitudes over the past five decades has led to the conclusion that racial antagonisms have "changed" to be more subtle and covert

(Sears, Sidanius, and Bobo 2000). Current measures of racial resentment are criticized for their content and validity (Feldman and Huddy 2005; Sniderman, Crosby, and Howell 2000), yet the theoretical arguments regarding the need for a more accurate measurement and understanding of the contemporary forms of racism are not questioned. Thus, in our view, progress in the study of racial attitudes depends largely on clarifying the operationalization and meaning of these concepts and improving their measurement.

Our goal was to design and test a new, more explicit measure of resentment, and we believe that we have done so with great promise. First, we believe our questions are more explicit in their connection to resentment. Our measures contain updated wording using the label of "African American" instead of "black"; the questions are free of wording related to government or policy; and most important, they explicitly connect the sources of the resentment (e.g., special attention/favors or racial excuses) to the target (African Americans). Second, our EXR scale measure has strong validity and reliability properties. Both PCA and CFA results show a single factor, and the data have a good fit with the theoretical model of resentment. As with all measures, the items should continue to undergo revision, testing, and scrutiny, and we encourage more, rather than less, dialogue regarding our items.

By making the measurement more explicit, we believe the construct of resentment becomes more pronounced and has the ability to detect nongovernment-based racial attitudes (e.g., attitudes toward African Americans' progress in economic and social arenas) while avoiding many of the criticisms levied against traditional measures of resentment. While some will claim that the proposed EXR is nothing more than the "same thing using different words," the fact that we have explicitly and empirically connected our concept of racial resentment to its operationalization and measurement is a marked improvement over what currently exists, which is essentially a different name—"resentment"—for an existing symbolic racism measure. For example, four of the six RRS items are found on the Symbolic Racism 2000 (SR2K) scale (see Henry and Sears 2002). Overall, our results signal to us that measures of contemporary racial attitudes should continue to undergo scrutiny with the goal of improving our understanding of the content, origins, and effects of racial considerations.

While we are hopeful about the ability to offer an alternative measure of racial resentment, there are caveats and limitations to our findings. First, that our items form a single factor does not mean that they are an independent construct from existing "new racism" measures. It is possible that the EXR items could be used in conjunction with the existing symbolic and modern racism items, as well as with the Kinder and Sanders's (1996) racial resentment items, to form a multidimensional measure of government/policy based on racial resentment. Second, and related to the previous point, none of the items in the EXR scale is expressly political. This is intentional, so as to identify the general source of racial resentment toward African Americans; however, the exclusion of political references may take away from the theory related to the new racism theses: it is both caused by and affects policy and political judgments.

Conclusion

A refocus on the concept of resentment helps to bring about new questions related to racial attitudes. The racial resentment term was applied to what is symbolic racism, yet resentment is something much more explicit. We have defined resentment as a general feeling related to notions of deservingness for racial groups. Such a conceptualization allows researchers to answer and address many new questions connecting political science and psychology.

One example lies in the motivations for resentment. Because of social identity concerns, resentment may result from seeking pleasure in another's misfortune (*Schadenfreude*) (Feather 2006; Feather and Sherman 2002).[9] The perceived competitive nature of racial differences in society (e.g., equality can only be gained if whites give up some of their prerogatives to blacks) may heighten group identities, with in-groups becoming more protective of their prerogatives by "cutting down" out-groups. Whites who feel that they have been unfairly disadvantaged may gain pleasure (i.e., experience positive emotion) in seeing black Americans lose out on various political and policy issues, so as to not gain an advantage over their white in-group. Their internal rationale is that blacks are undeserving of anything they get that they have not presumably worked hard to get; being members of a racial group that has faced past discrimination is not enough. Thus, racial resentment may serve a positive psychological purpose (i.e., it is self-serving), which manifests itself when whites are asked to evaluate certain policies, institutions, programs, and candidates.

Another thought is that resentment may act to reduce dissonance in the minds of subtle racists. Many whites may believe that blacks are undeserving of special considerations or favors based on race, while simultaneously believing that equality is important in American society. Instead of accepting arguments that blacks should receive positive special considerations because of past racism and discrimination, they instead alter their thinking to believe that no one should receive anything special. This allows their racial and egalitarian beliefs to become balanced. By being resentful of any special favors, especially those based on race, the subtle racist can hold anti-black beliefs without being "anti-black."

In general, we believe that the importance of contemporary racial attitudes has been renewed with the election of President Barack Obama. Obama's popularity has altered stereotypes about black candidates, but it has also increased racial resentment through the subtle framing of Obama as a person who receives "special treatment" from the media. Perhaps unwittingly, as the media played up Obama's race and his status as the first African American nominated by a major party, they also likely primed feelings about deservingness that were then assimilated to statements about his experience. Moreover, Obama was consistently characterized as an eloquent speaker who was high on presentation but low on substance, and political figures such as former Democratic vice presidential nominee Geraldine Ferraro suggested that Obama's race was the main reason for his early Democratic primary success. In an interview with a local

California paper, Ferraro said, "If Obama was a white man, he would not be in this position. And if he was a woman of any color, he would not be in this position. He happens to be very lucky to be who he is. And the country is caught up in the concept" (quoted in Seelye and Bosman 2008).[10] Such comments implied that Obama's race was his sole political skill and that he was benefiting by using it. Together these characterizations, or "frames," of Obama may have racialized him and heightened concerns that he was gaining an unfair advantage because of his race.

While some of the events of the 2008 presidential campaign are a sad commentary on racial thinking in America (e.g., constant references and imagery of Obama as a monkey), they highlight why the measurement of racial attitudes and beliefs is so important. Without accurate measures, we may miss the opportunity to thoroughly understand why some people opposed Obama and his policies based more on their political principles and partisanship than on Obama's race and qualifications.

The added value of our new measure is that it explicitly takes into consideration the conceptual notion of resentment and ties it to the chief source of antipathy toward African Americans: special considerations on the basis of race. Thus, researchers now have a competing indicator of racial feelings through which policy attitudes and political behaviors can be evaluated.

Appendix

Social Dominance Orientation Scale

Please indicate whether you strongly disagree, disagree, agree, or strongly agree.

1. Some groups of people are simply not the equal of others.
2. Some people are just more worthy than others.
3. This country would be better off if we cared less about how equal all people were.
4. Some people are just more deserving than others.
5. It is not a problem if some people have more of a chance in life than others.
6. Some people are just inferior to others.
7. To get ahead in life, it is sometimes necessary to step on others.
8. If people were treated more equally we would have fewer problems in this country.
9. We should treat one another as equals as much as possible.
10. It is probably a good thing that certain groups are at the top and other groups are at the bottom.
11. Inferior groups should stay in their place.

(continued)

Appendix (continued)

Dogmatism Scale

Please indicate whether you strongly disagree, disagree, agree, or strongly agree.

1. There are two kinds of people in this world: those who are for the truth and those who are against it.
2. A group which tolerates too many differences of opinions among its members cannot exist for long.
3. To compromise with our political opponents is dangerous because it usually leads to the betrayal of our own side.
4. Of all the different philosophies that exist in the world there is probably only one that is correct.
5. In the long run the best way to live is to pick friends and associates whose tastes and beliefs are the same as one's own.
6. Most of the ideas that get printed nowadays aren't worth the paper they are printed on.
7. In this complicated world of ours the only way we can know what's going on is to rely on leaders or experts who can be trusted.
8. There are a number of people I have come to hate because of the things they stand for.

Authoritarianism Scale

Please indicate whether you strongly disagree, disagree, agree, or strongly agree.

1. America is getting so far from the true American way of life that force may be necessary to restore it.
2. No matter how they act on the surface, men are interested in women for only one reason.
3. Human nature being what it is, there will always be war and conflict.
4. What this country needs is fewer laws and agencies, and more courageous, tireless, devoted leaders whom the people can put their faith in.
5. What the youth needs most is strict discipline, rugged determination, and the will to work and fight for your family and country.
6. People can be divided into two distinct classes: the weak and the strong.

(continued)

Appendix (continued)

Stratification beliefs

Please indicate whether you strongly disagree, disagree, agree, or strongly agree.

1. On the average Blacks have worse jobs, income, and housing than white people. These differences are mainly due to discrimination? (disagree)
2. Because most blacks don't have the chance for education that it takes to rise out of poverty. (disagree)
3. Because most blacks just don't have the motivation or will power to pull themselves up out of poverty. (agree)
4. Because most blacks enjoy or have no problems with being where they are in life. (agree)
5. Because most blacks are irresponsible in their daily lives. (agree)

Anti-black affect

On a scale from 0 to 10, with 0 being cold (I really dislike this group) and 10 being warm (I really like this group), how would you rate your feelings towards black people?

Interracial friendships

What percentage of your close friends and associates (people with whom you normally hang-out—including friends back home) are from a different racial or ethnic group?

Notes

1. This question has been asked in the General Social Survey (GSS) since 1994, and over the past three administrations—2004, 2006, and 2008—it has been presented as a stand-alone resentment measure. The American National Election Study (ANES) has asked this item since 1986 along with other variations of the RRS items; however, the 2008 ANES removed the wording "Irish, Italians, Jews, and many" from the assertion.

2. As a required course intended to expose entering college students to multidisciplinary treatment of social inequality, the class contained a cross-section of students.

3. Of 208 students interviewed, at least sixty majors were represented. Seventy-four percent were freshmen, 18 percent sophomores, 4 percent juniors, and 1 percent seniors. The original sample contained 129 (62 percent) whites, 11 (5.3 percent) blacks, 11 (5.3 percent) Asians, and 3 (1.4 percent) Latinos. Pacific Islanders and American Indians each had one respondent from their respective group, and six respondents (2.9 percent) said they belonged to some "other" race not listed. Finally, forty-six (22.1 percent) respondents did not provide their racial background when asked. The human subjects consent form explicitly stated subjects may opt out of any question they felt uncomfortable answering, and given the anonymity of response, we could not gather much information on those who did not provide their race or ethnic classification. However, those who did not provide a racial-ethnic classification were more likely to be male than female and were more conservative than liberal, but these differences were not statistically significant.

4. The original sample consisted of 622 respondents, including 520 (85 percent) white, 28 (5 percent) black, 23 (4 percent) Asian, and 25 (4 percent) Latino students. Pacific Islanders and American Indians each had three (0.5 percent) respondents from their respective group, and twelve respondents (2 percent) said they belonged to some "other" race not listed. Finally, eight (1 percent) respondents did not provide their racial background when asked.

5. "Registered voter" identification is based on a self-report. The political geographic strata are early primary battleground (FL, WI, PA, IA, NH, MN, NM, NV, and OH) and nonbattleground (all others) states. The sampling frame was designed by YouGov Polimetrix, using target estimates based on the 2007 American Community Study (ACS) that the U.S. Census Bureau conducted. Sample targets were created within each strata according to age, race, gender, education, and voter registration battleground/nonbattleground state location. While the data contain sample design weights, our analyses are unweighted because of our experimental design and our focus on measurement. The baseline study (wave 1) took place between December 17, 2007 and January 3, 2008; wave 2 took place between January 24 and February 4, 2008; wave 3 took place from March 21 to April 14, 2008; wave 4 took place from September 17 to September 29, 2008; wave 5 took place between October 22 and November 3, 2008; and the postelection study (wave 6) took place from November 5 to December 1, 2008.

6. The PCAs were estimated using oblique rotated (Promax) factor structures, and our interpretations were based on the estimated "structure" matrices (Tabachnick and Fidell 2006). In cases where all items loaded on a single factor, no rotation was needed. With the PCA analyses, we are looking for a single-factor solution with factor loadings greater than .500 (Comrey and Lee 1992). The CFAs were conducted in AMOS 16 using maximum likelihood estimation.

7. Three of these items have been asked in the GSS and are understood to tap support for structural (e.g., discrimination, education) and individualistic (e.g., motivation) explanations for black-white socioeconomic differences (see Hunt 2007). Although structuralist and individualistic explanations are generally analyzed as separate constructs, in both studies the items have sufficient internal consistency to fit together as a single scale (study 1: $n = 102$, $M = .73$, $SD = .10$, $\alpha = .614$; study 2: $n = 521$, $M = .58$, $SD = .12$, $\alpha = .706$), with higher values indicating stronger individualistic beliefs.

8. All items on the SDO, RWA, and Dogmatism scales were coded such that more agreement on a four-point Likert scale equates to higher levels of the construct.

9. *Schadenfreude* is a sense of pleasure gained by witnessing another's misfortune.

10. The Torrance, California paper was the *Daily Breeze*.

References

Altemeyer, Robert. 1981. *Right wing authoritarianism*. Winnipeg, Canada: University of Manitoba Press.

Alvarez, R. Michael, and John Brehm. 2002. *Hard choices, easy answers: Values, information, and American public opinion*. Princeton, NJ: Princeton University Press.

Christie, Richard. 1991. Authoritarianism and related constructs. In *Measures of personality and social psychological attitudes*, vol. 1, eds. John P. Robinson, Phillip R. Shaver, and Lawrence S. Wrightsman, 501–72. San Diego, CA: Academic Press.

Comrey, Andrew L., and Howard B. Lee. 1992. *A first course in factor analysis*. 2nd ed. Hillsdale, NJ: Lawrence Erlbaum.

Feather, N. T. 2006. Deservingness and emotions: Applying the structural model of deservingness to the analysis of affective reactions to outcomes. *European Review of Social Psychology* 17:38–70.

Feather, N. T., and Rebecca Sherman. 2002. Envy, resentment, Schadenfreude, and sympathy: Reactions to deserved and undeserved achievement and subsequent failure. *Personality and Social Psychology Bulletin* 28:953–61.

Federico, Christopher, and Jim Sidanius. 2002. Racism, ideology and affirmative action revisited: The antecedents and consequences of principled objections to affirmative action. *Journal of Personality and Social Psychology* 82:488–502.

Feldman, Stanley, and Leonie Huddy. 2005. Racial resentment and white opposition to race-conscious programs: Principles or prejudice? *American Journal of Political Science* 49:168–83.

Henry, Patrick J., and David O. Sears. 2002. The symbolic racism scale. *Political Psychology* 23:253–83.

Hunt, Matthew O. 2007. African-American, Hispanic, and white beliefs about black/white inequality, 1977–2004. *American Sociological Review* 72:390–415.

Kinder, Donald R., and Tali Mendelberg. 2000. Individualism reconsidered. In *Racialized politics: Values, ideology, and prejudice in American public opinion*, eds. David O. Sears, James Sidanius, and Lawrence Bobo. Chicago, IL: University of Chicago Press.

Kinder, Donald R., and Lynn M. Sanders. 1996. *Divided by color*. Chicago, IL: University of Chicago Press.

Kinder, Donald R., and David O. Sears. 1981. Prejudice and politics: Symbolic racism versus racial threats to the good life. *Journal of Personality and Social Psychology* 40:414–31.

Mendelberg, Tali. 2001. *The race card: Campaign strategy, implicit messages, and the norm of equality*. Princeton, NJ: Princeton University Press.

Reeves, Keith. 1997. *Voting hopes or fears? White voters, black candidates and racial politics in America*. New York, NY: Oxford University Press.

Rokeach, Milton. 1960. *The open and closed mind*. New York, NY: Basic Books.

Schuman, Howard. 2000. The perils of correlations, the lure of labels, and the beauty of negative results. In *Racialized politics: Values, ideology, and prejudice in American public opinion*, eds. David O. Sears, James Sidanius, and Lawrence Bobo. Chicago, IL: University of Chicago Press.

Sears, David O., and Patrick J. Henry. 2003. The origins of symbolic racism. *Journal of Personality and Social Psychology* 85:259–75.

Sears, David O., Colette van Laar, Mary Carrillo, and Rick Kosterman. 1997. Is it really racism? The origins of white Americans' opposition to race-targeted policies. *Public Opinion Quarterly* 61:16–53.

Sears, David O., James Sidanius, and Lawrence Bobo, eds. 2000. *Racialized politics: The debate about racism in America*. Chicago, IL: University of Chicago Press.

Seelye, Katherine Q., and Julie Bosman. 12 March 2008. Ferraro's Obama remarks become talk of campaign. *New York Times*. Available from www.nytimes.com.

Sidanius, James, and Felicia F. Pratto. 2003. Social dominance theory and the dynamics of inequality: A reply to Schmitt, Branscombe, & Kappen and Wilson & Liu. *British Journal of Social Psychology* 42:207–13.

Sniderman, Paul M., Gretchen C. Crosby, and William G. Howell. 2000. The politics of race. In *Racialized politics: Values, ideology, and prejudice in American public opinion*, eds. David O. Sears, James Sidanius, and Lawrence Bobo. Chicago, IL: University of Chicago Press.

Sniderman, Paul M., and Thomas Piazza. 1993. *The scar of race*. Cambridge, MA: Harvard University Press.

Sniderman, Paul M., Thomas Piazza, Philip E. Tetlock, and Ann Kendrick. 1991. The new racism. *American Journal of Political Science* 35:423–47.

Sniderman, Paul M., and Phillip Tetlock. 1986. Symbolic racism: Problems with motive attribution in political analysis. *Journal of Social Issues* 42:129–50.

Tabachnick, Barabara G., and Linda S. Fidell. 2006. *Using multivariate statistics*. 5th ed. Boston, MA: Pearson.

Whites' Racial Policy Attitudes in the Twenty-First Century: The Continuing Significance of Racial Resentment

By
STEVEN A. TUCH
and
MICHAEL HUGHES

A topic of long-standing interest in racial attitudes research is whites' support for principles of racial equality on one hand coupled with their intransigence on policies designed to redress that inequality on the other. Much has been written on possible explanations of this "principle-policy gap" and what the gap reveals about the state of contemporary American race relations. In this article, the authors provide an update and partial replication of their 1996 study of whites' views of racial policies in what has been referred to as our post-racial society. Using both General Social Survey and American National Election Survey data, the authors assess the current state of whites' racial policy attitudes and the factors that shape those attitudes and consider whether any meaningful change has occurred in recent decades. Among the explanations of the principle-policy gap that the authors examine, one stands out as especially powerful: racial resentment, a variant of stratification ideology that focuses on the role of racial individualism in shaping white resistance to meaningful policy change. Moreover, the authors find no evidence that whites' racial policy views have changed since the 1980s.

Keywords: racial policy attitudes; principle-policy gap; stratification ideology; racial resentment

Steven A. Tuch is a professor of sociology at George Washington University. His primary research interests are in race and ethnicity, social stratification and inequality, and public opinion. He is especially interested in whites' and blacks' racial attitudes and changes in these attitudes over time. He is coeditor (with Yoku Shaw-Taylor) of The Other African Americans: Contemporary African and Caribbean Immigrants in the United States *(Rowman & Littlefield 2007) and coauthor (with Ronald Weitzer) of* Race and Policing in America: Conflict and Reform *(Cambridge University Press 2006).*

Michael Hughes is a professor of sociology at Virginia Polytechnic Institute and State University (Virginia Tech). He is currently studying mental health and use of services following the shootings at Virginia Tech in April 2007. Most of his research focuses on mental health and the social psychology of race, particularly on racial identity, racial differences in mental health, and whites' racial attitudes. He is coauthor (with Carolyn J. Kroehler) of Sociology: The Core *(McGraw-Hill forthcoming 2011).*

DOI: 10.1177/0002716210390288

Few issues are as controversial as race-targeted social policies. Viewed by proponents as appropriate remedies for the lingering effects of past racial injustices and by opponents as unfair "reverse discrimination," racial policy was one of the most divisive issues in late-twentieth-century American social and political life. In this article, we examine whites' racial policy views in what has been referred to recently in some mainstream press accounts as our "post-racial" society (Schneider 2008; Noonan 2009; Tierney 2008; for opposing viewpoints, see Hutchings 2009; Pettigrew 2009; and Smith and King 2009). Focusing on a range of racial policies, from preferences in hiring and promotion of blacks to spending on programs to improve African Americans' social and economic conditions to ensuring racial fairness in jobs, we assess the current state of whites' racial policy attitudes, the factors that shape those attitudes, and whether any meaningful change in these views has occurred over the past several decades.

Background

A topic of long-standing interest in racial attitudes scholarship is the discrepancy between whites' strong support for principles of racial equality on one hand and their intransigence on policies designed to redress that inequality on the other (Schuman et al. 1997; Krysan 2000). Much has been written on possible explanations of this "principle-policy gap," the factors that shape it, and what the gap reveals about the quality of whites' racial thinking (Bobo 2000; Bobo, Kluegel, and Smith 1997; Hughes 1997; Hunt 1996; Sears, Sidanius, and Bobo 2000; Sniderman and Piazza 1993; Tuch and Hughes 1996a, 1996b). Our purpose here is to update and partially replicate our 1996 study (Tuch and Hughes 1996b) on this topic by examining recent patterns in, and sources of, whites' racial policy attitudes. There are two primary reasons why an update is warranted. First, our original study used data that are now more than two decades old—the 1986 American National Election Survey (ANES) and 1990 General Social Survey (GSS); and second, as noted above, Barack Obama's election as our nation's first African American president has been heralded in some circles as evidence that race no longer plays the dominant role it once did in American society and politics. If this argument is valid, we would expect to find an upswing since the 1980s in support for remedies designed to ameliorate structured racial disadvantage and a decrease in the role of racial affect in shaping this support. Thus, this is an opportune moment to reexamine trends in, and explanations of, racial policy attitudes.

Several explanations of the sources of the principle-policy gap have been discussed in the research literature. Some analysts equate whites' intransigence on policies with thinly veiled racism, but other accounts are more nuanced, pointing to the widespread denial of continuing racial discrimination and thus the necessity for policies designed to redress its consequences, group self-interest (Bobo and Kluegel 1993; Bobo 1988), a "principled conservatism" that rejects government intrusion into private affairs (Sniderman and Piazza 1993), "laissez-faire" racism

(Bobo, Kluegel, and Smith 1997), minority threat and the defense of white privilege (Quillian 1995, 1996), and what is currently referred to as "racial resentment." Racial resentment is a variant of stratification ideology that focuses on the role of racial individualism in shaping white resistance to meaningful policy change. Work on this topic by Hughes (1997) and Kinder and Sanders (1996), and earlier work by Sears (1988), Sears and Kinder (1971), and Kinder and Sears (1981) on the conceptually similar notion of "symbolic racism," posits that traditional or "Jim Crow" racism has been replaced by a "modern" version of anti-black affect that is rooted in early racial socialization experiences and in the beliefs of many whites that African Americans violate such traditional values as self-reliance and hard work. According to this theoretical account, racial resentment is the principal ideological dimension influencing whites' racial policy views (Hughes 1997).

Some research on the principle-policy gap has used a causal attribution theoretical framework that differentiates between "individualist" and "structuralist" accounts of the factors that shape economic outcomes (Feagin 1975; Kluegel and Smith 1986). Those who invoke individualist attributions of wealth and poverty point to supposed characteristics of the wealthy or poor—such as superior motivation or ability in the case of the wealthy and lack of effort or weak attachment to a work ethic in the case of the poor—in accounting for economic differentials; those who attribute inequality to structuralist forces, on the other hand, point to the role of such systemic factors as poor educational opportunity or discrimination or lack of jobs in structuring economic outcomes. Causal attributions of inequality are of key theoretical importance in stratification research generally because citizen accounts of the prerequisites for success or failure reflect the very legitimacy with which stratification systems are viewed: if the wealthy are not considered as deserving of their advantages, and the poor of their disadvantages, the stratification system is likely to be challenged as unfair and illegitimate. In the case of racial inequality specifically, whether one explains the black-white socioeconomic gap in individualist or structuralist terms has been shown to be an important predictor of racial policy views (Hughes and Tuch 2000).

Our objective is to examine both recent and longer-term trends in racial resentment and assess its explanatory power, compared to other theoretical accounts, in shaping racial policy views (Kluegel 1990; Hunt 2007).

Data and Methods

Data

We use both 1991–2008 GSS and 2008 ANES data in our analyses. As described below, these datasets incorporate several common items, but each includes measures of key variables that the other does not.[1] Utilizing both datasets provides for a more nuanced analysis of the factors that shape policy views and allows us to examine the replicability of our findings across surveys.[2] The National Opinion Research Center at the University of Chicago administers the GSS. The University of Michigan's Institute for Social Research conducts the ANES. Both of these national surveys are based on full probability sampling designs and are representative of the noninstitutionalized adult population of the continental United States. For a complete discussion of GSS sampling methodology, see Davis, Smith, and Marsden (2008); for the ANES, see Hutchings, Jackman, and Segura (2008). We limit our analyses to white respondents only.

Measures

Racial policy attitudes. We combine three GSS questions into an index of whites' racial policy attitudes: (1) "Some people say that because of past discrimination, blacks should be given preference in hiring and promotion. Others say that such preference in hiring and promotion of blacks is wrong because it discriminates against whites. What about your opinion—are you for or against preferential hiring and promotion of blacks?" Responses are coded 1 (*strongly support*), 2 (*support*), 3 (*oppose*), and 4 (*strongly oppose*). (2) "Some people think that African Americans have been discriminated against for so long that the government has a special obligation to help improve their living standards. Others believe that the government should not be giving special treatment to African Americans. Where would you place yourself on this scale, or haven't you made up your mind on this?" Responses range from 1 (*government should help*) to 5 (*no special treatment*). (3) "We are faced with many problems in this country, none of which can be solved easily or inexpensively. I am going to name some of these problems, and for each one I would like you to tell me whether you think we are spending too much money on it, too little money, or about the right amount. Are we spending too much, too little, or about the right amount on improving the conditions of blacks?" Responses are coded 1 (*too little*), 2 (*about the right amount*), and 3 (*too much*). The alpha for the index is .61. The index is factor weighted with a mean of 100 and a standard deviation of 10.

In the ANES, we measure racial policy views with an index of three items: (1) "Some people say that because of past discrimination, blacks should be given preference in hiring and promotion. Others say that such preference in hiring and promotion of blacks is wrong because it gives blacks advantages they have not earned. What about your opinion—are you for or against preferential hiring and promotion of blacks?" Respondents who reported being either for or against the policy were then asked how much they favored or opposed the policy. We coded responses to this variable as follows: *agree (and strongly favor)* = 1; *agree (and favor not strongly)* = 2; *neither agree nor disagree* = 3; *disagree (and oppose not strongly)* = 4; *disagree (and oppose strongly)* = 5. (2) "Should the government in Washington see to it that black people get fair treatment in jobs or is this not the federal government's business?" Responses to this question are coded from 1 to 5, as follows: *strongly favor fair treatment* = 1; *favor fair treatment not strongly* = 2; *not enough interest in the issue to favor one alternative over the other* = 3; *believe (not strongly) this is not the government's business* = 4; *strongly believe this is not the government's business* = 5. (3) Respondents were asked to respond to the following item by indicating their support or opposition on a scale from 1 to 7: "Some people feel that the government in Washington should make every effort to improve the social and economic position of blacks. Suppose these people are at one end of a scale, at point 1. Others feel that the government should not make any special effort to help blacks because they should help themselves. Suppose these people are at the other end, at point 7. And, of course, some other people have opinions somewhere in between, at points 2, 3, 4, 5, or 6." The response that the government in Washington should make every effort to improve the social and economic position of blacks was coded 1; the response indicating that blacks should help themselves was coded 7; other responses were coded from 2 to 6 as indicated in the question. The alpha for the index is .62. The index is factor weighted with a mean of 100 and a standard deviation of 10.[3]

Racial resentment. The GSS measure of racial resentment is a three-item index: "On average blacks have worse jobs, income, and housing than white people. Do you think these differences are: (1) Mainly due to discrimination?" (1 = yes, 2 = no), (2) "Because most blacks just do not have the motivation or willpower to pull themselves up out of poverty?" (1 = no, 2 = yes), (3) "Do you strongly agree, agree somewhat, neither agree nor disagree, disagree somewhat, or disagree strongly with the following statement? Irish, Italians, Jews, and many other minorities overcame prejudice and worked their way up. Blacks should do the same without special favors" (1 = *disagree strongly*, 2 = *disagree somewhat*, 3 = *neither agree nor disagree*, 4 = *agree somewhat*, 5 = *strongly agree*). Each of these questions taps the kind of race-conscious individualism in causal attributions about disadvantage that is central to racial resentment theory (Sears 1988). The alpha for the index is .57. The index is factor weighted with a mean of 100 and a standard deviation of 10.

Racial resentment in the ANES data is an index of four items: (1) "Irish, Italians, Jews, and many other minorities overcame prejudice and worked their way up. Blacks should do the same without any special favors." (2) "Generations of slavery and discrimination have created conditions that make it difficult for blacks to work their way out of the lower class." (3) "Over the past few years, blacks have gotten less than they deserve." (4) "It's really a matter of some people not trying hard enough; if blacks would only try harder they could be just as well off as whites." Responses for all four items were *agree strongly, agree somewhat, neither agree nor disagree, disagree somewhat,* or *disagree strongly*. The items were coded from 1 to 5, with 5 indicating the greatest degree of resentment. The alpha for the index is .77. The index is factor weighted with a mean of 100 and a standard deviation of 10.

Traditional prejudice. In the GSS, two questions are used to tap traditional prejudice: (1) "Now I have some questions about different groups in our society. I am going to show you a seven-point scale on which the characteristics of people in a group can be rated. In the first statement a score of 1 means that you think almost all of the people in that group tend to be hardworking. A score of 7 means that you think almost everyone in the group tends to be lazy. A score of 4 means that you think that the group is not toward one end or another, and of course you may choose any number in between that comes closest to where you think people in the group stand. Where would you rate [blacks/whites] in general on this scale?" (2) "Do people in these groups tend to be unintelligent or tend to be intelligent?" In the ANES, the traditional prejudice measure is the combination of two items that are nearly identical to those in the GSS. The questions were prefaced with the following statement: "Next are some questions about different groups in our society. Please look, in the booklet, at a seven-point scale on which the characteristics of the people in a group can be rated." Respondents were asked to rate whites and blacks on two continua, an intelligence continuum (*intelligent* [coded 1] to *unintelligent* [coded 7]) and a hardworking continuum (*hardworking* [coded 1] to *lazy* [coded 7]). In both the GSS and ANES, we subtracted the white rating from the black rating, so the resulting variable taps how much more unintelligent or lazy the respondent thought blacks are as compared with whites. The final variable is the mean of the two continua for each respondent.

Economic individualism in the GSS is measured with a three-item index: (1) "Some people think that the government in Washington is trying to do too many things that should be left to individuals and private businesses. Others disagree and think that the government should do even more to solve our country's problems. Still others have opinions somewhere in between. Where would you place yourself on this scale, or haven't you made up your mind on this?" Response options range from *government should do more* (coded 1) to *agree with both* (coded 3) to *government is doing too much* (coded 5). (2) "Some people think that the government in Washington should do everything possible to improve the standard of living of all poor Americans; they are at point 1 on this card. Other people think it is not the government's responsibility and that each person should take care of himself; they are at point 5. Where would you place yourself on this scale?" (3) "Some people think that the government in Washington ought to reduce the income differences between the rich and the poor, perhaps by raising the taxes of wealthy families or by giving income assistance to the poor. Others think that the government should not concern itself with reducing this income difference between the rich and the poor. Here is a card with a scale from 1 to 7. Think of a score of 1 as meaning that the government ought to reduce the income differences between rich and poor, and a score of 7 meaning that the government should not concern itself with reducing income differences. What score between 1 and 7 comes closest to the way you feel?" The alpha for the index is .68. The index is factor weighted with a mean of 100 and a standard deviation of 10.

In the ANES, economic individualism is an index of three items. Respondents were read three statements prefaced with the following introduction: "Next, I am going to ask you to choose which of two statements I read comes closer to your own opinion. You might agree to some extent with both, but we want to know which one is closer to your own views." The three pairs of statements were as follows: (1) "One, the main reason government has become bigger over the years is because it has gotten involved in things that people should do for themselves; or two, government has become bigger because the problems we face have become bigger"; (2) "One, we need a strong government to handle today's complex economic problems; or two, the free market can handle these problems without government being involved"; (3) "One, the less government the better; or two, there are more things that government should be doing." The response favoring the nongovernment preference was coded 1, and a government preference response was coded 0. The index has an alpha of .70. The index we use is factor weighted with a mean of 100 and a standard deviation of 10.

The ANES (though not the GSS) dataset also contains *feeling thermometers* for whites and blacks that are ratings of how "warm" or "cold" the respondent feels toward each racial group. Respondents were instructed to rate each group between 50 and 100 if they were favorable toward them, between 0 and 50 if they were unfavorable, and at 50 if they felt neither favorable nor unfavorable toward the group.

Political views are measured in the GSS with the following question: "We hear a lot of talk these days about liberals and conservatives. I am going to show you a seven-point scale on which the political views that people might hold are arranged from extremely liberal—point 1—to extremely conservative—point 7. Where would you place yourself on this scale?" Response categories are (1) *extremely liberal*, (2) *liberal*, (3) *slightly liberal*, (4) *moderate, middle of the road*, (5) *slightly conservative*, (6) *conservative*, (7) *extremely conservative*.

The ANES political views measure is nearly identical to the GSS question above: "We hear a lot of talk these days about liberals and conservatives. I am going to show you a seven-point scale on which the political views that people might hold are arranged from extremely liberal—point 1—to extremely conservative—point 7. Where would you place yourself on this scale, or haven't you thought much about this?" Response options were the same as in the GSS on the 1 to 7 scale, but if respondents indicated "moderate, middle of the road," they were asked if they had to choose, would they be liberal, conservative, or moderate. We coded responses to this second question along with those to the first as follows: *liberal* = 2, *conservative* = 6, and *moderate* = 4.

The *egalitarianism* measure in the ANES data is an index of five items: (1) "Our society should do whatever is necessary to make sure that everyone has an equal opportunity to succeed"; (2) "We have gone too far in pushing equal rights in this country"; (3) "One of the big problems in this country is that we do not give everyone an equal chance"; (4) "This country would be better off if we worried less about how equal people are"; and (5) "It is not really that big a problem if some people have more of a chance in life than others." Responses were 1 = *agree strongly*, 2 = *agree somewhat*, 3 = *neither agree nor disagree*, 4 = *disagree somewhat*, and 5 = *disagree strongly*. Items were coded so that a high score indicated support for equality. The index has an alpha of .66. The index we use is factor weighted with a mean of 100 and a standard deviation of 10.

We also include in our models a range of *sociodemographic* controls: gender (1 = female; 0 = male), age (age of the respondent in years), education (four dummy variables: 12 years, 13 through 15 years, 16 years, and 17 or more years; the comparison category is 0 through 11 years), income (a standardized variable with mean of 0 and standard deviation of 1, generated in the ANES using twenty-five categories ranging from less than $2,999 to $150,000 or more; in the GSS the range is from less than $1,000 to $75,000 or more in survey years 1991–1996, in survey years 1998–2002 the upper-income category is $110,000, and in survey years 2006 and 2008 the highest category is $150,000), region (three dummy variables: Northeast,[4] Midwest,[5] and South;[6] the comparison category is West[7]), and employment status (five dummy variables: unemployed, retired, disabled, full-time student, homemaker; the comparison category is working full time).

Findings

Racial policy attitudes

The top panel of Table 1 presents the percentage distributions on each of the racial policy questions in the GSS; the bottom panel of the table presents the distributions on the ANES items. In the GSS, on question 1, which asks respondents whether they favor or oppose preference in hiring and promotion of African Americans, only 11.5 percent strongly favor or favor such preferential policies while 88.5 percent of interviewees oppose or strongly oppose preferential hiring and promotion. Question 2 solicits views on whether the government should help to improve the living standards of blacks as a remedy for past discrimination. On this item, only 4.5 percent of respondents unequivocally endorse the idea of government giving special treatment to blacks; 33.2 percent unequivocally reject such help. On question 3, which asks respondents whether we are spending too much, too little, or about the right amount on assistance to blacks, only 28.2 percent think spending levels are too little.

Percentage distributions on each of the racial policy questions in the 2008 ANES are presented in the bottom panel of Table 1. On the first item, regarding support for preferences in hiring and promotion for African Americans, 82.8 percent are opposed or strongly opposed. Few respondents have no opinion (6.7 percent), and few support such a policy (10.6 percent, with only 5.3 percent voicing strong support). A plurality of respondents (49.4 percent) has no opinion on the second question regarding whether the U.S. government should see to it that blacks get fair treatment in jobs, with 23.1 percent supporting government action of this kind and 27.8 percent being opposed. On the third item asking respondents to rate their support for the government making efforts to improve the social and economic position of blacks on a 7-point scale, 34.5 percent are neutral, with 13.2 percent indicating some degree of support (scores from 1 through 3) and 52.4 percent responding that the government should not make such efforts (scores from 5 through 7). Though the items are not always identical,

TABLE 1
Whites' Racial Policy Attitudes

General Social Survey

Some people say that because of past discrimination, blacks should be given preference in hiring and promotion. Others say that such preference in hiring and promotion of blacks is wrong because it discriminates against whites. What about your opinion—are you for or against preferential hiring and promotion of blacks?

Strongly support	5.5%
Support	6.0
Oppose	27.0
Strongly oppose	61.5

Some people think that African Americans have been discriminated against for so long that the government has a special obligation to help improve their living standards. Others believe that the government should not be giving special treatment to African Americans. Where would you place yourself on this scale, or haven't you made up your mind on this?

1 Government should help	4.5%
2	7.8
3 Agree with both	30.5
4	23.9
5 No special treatment	33.2

We are faced with many problems in this country, none of which can be solved easily or inexpensively. I'm going to name some of these problems, and for each one I'd like you to tell me whether you think we're spending too much money on it, too little money, or about the right amount. Are we spending too much, too little, or about the right amount on improving the conditions of blacks?

Too little	28.2%
About the right amount	51.0
Too much	20.9

American National Election Study

Some people say that because of past discrimination, blacks should be given preference in hiring and promotion. Others say that such preference in hiring and promotion of blacks is wrong because it gives blacks advantages they haven't earned.

Agree (and strongly favor)	5.3%
Agree (and favor not strongly)	5.3
Neither agree nor disagree	6.7
Disagree (and oppose not strongly)	19.1
Disagree (and oppose strongly)	63.7

Should the government in Washington see to it that black people get fair treatment in jobs OR is this not the federal government's business?

Strongly favor fair treatment	18.0%
Favor fair treatment not strongly	4.7
Not enough interest in the issue to favor one alternative over the other	49.4
Believe (not strongly) this is not the government's business	5.8
Strongly believe this is not the government's business	22.0

(continued)

TABLE 1 (continued)

Some people feel that the government in Washington should make every effort to improve the social and economic position of blacks. Suppose these people are at one end of a scale, at point 1. Others feel that the government should not make any special effort to help blacks because they should help themselves. Suppose these people are at the other end, at point 7. And, of course, some other people have opinions somewhere in between, at points 2, 3, 4, 5, or 6.

1 Government should make every effort	3.0%
2	3.9
3	6.3
4	34.5
5	12.1
6	16.0
7 Blacks should help themselves	24.3

NOTE: Percentages do not always sum to 100 due to rounding.

overall these distributions are remarkably similar to those we reported in our 1996 study (Tuch and Hughes 1996b, 731). In other words, whites' racial policy attitudes have shown almost no change since the 1980s.

Racial resentment

Analyses of ANES data show that since 1986 there has been little overall change in the level of racial resentment among whites in the United States. Figures 1 and 2 show trends in the individual items and in the overall index, respectively, from 1986 to 2008. Items have been coded as indicated above so that a high score reflects a more "resentful" response. Figure 1 shows that there have been fluctuations in all four items, with a clear increase in the likelihood that respondents downplay the role of slavery and discrimination in making it difficult for blacks to move out of the lower class. As can be seen in Figure 2, there appears to have been an extremely small overall increase in racial resentment, due apparently to the change in the item regarding slavery and discrimination. What is particularly significant about these findings is that there has been no decline in racial resentment among whites over this 20-year period.

Figure 3 displays scores on the racial resentment items for the eight GSS survey years since 1994; Figure 4 displays the index scores. As in the ANES, what is remarkable about both of these figures is the near total absence of change in racial resentment since 1994, whether measured by the individual items or by the composite index. At least since 1994, white Americans' levels of racial resentment have remained virtually the same.

Multivariate results

Table 2 presents findings from regressing racial policy attitudes on the set of sociodemographic and attitudinal predictors separately in the GSS and ANES

FIGURE 1
ANES Racial Resentment Items, White Respondents Only

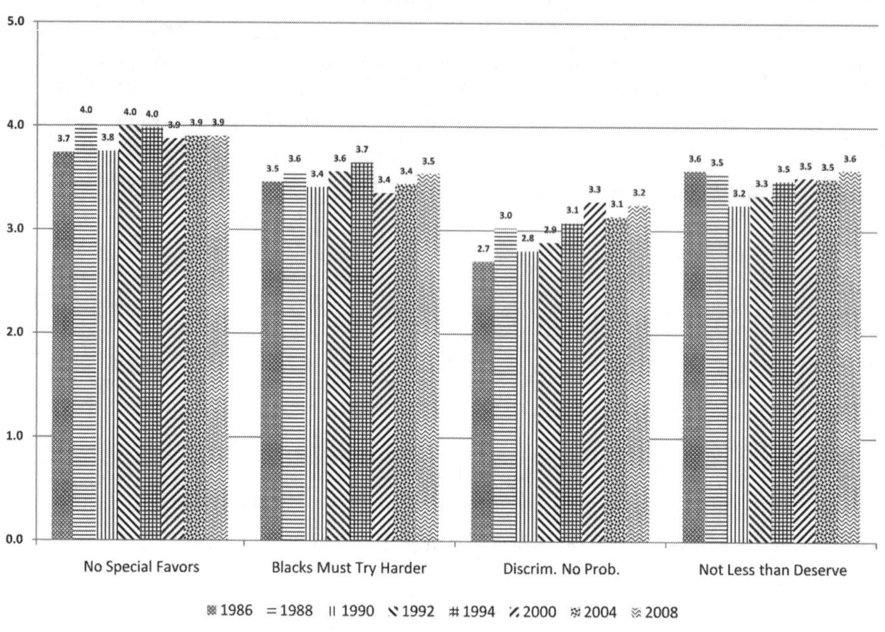

NOTE: Each item is scored 1 to 5, with 5 indicating the most "resentful" response.

datasets. We fit the models in blocks, entering the sociodemographic variables first, followed by the attitudinal variables.

Analysis of the GSS data. Focusing first on the sociodemographic predictors in the first block, gender, urban residence, education, and region significantly shape racial policy views. Women and those living in urban locales are less opposed to racial policies than their male and nonurban counterparts, and those with some college education and residents of the South are more opposed than those in other educational categories and non-southerners. The sociodemographic factors alone account for 4.8 percent of the variance in the racial policy index.

Next we increment the model in step 1 with the attitudinal predictors. In the full model, the effects of the sociodemographics are generally, though not always, attenuated. Age and employment status become significant, with older respondents less opposed, and the unemployed more opposed, to racial policies; gender and urban residence are no longer significant; and those with some college education and southerners remain significantly more opposed to policy interventions. Overall, consistent with the results of previous research, the sociodemographic variables tend not to be especially cogent predictors of racial policy attitudes (Schuman et al. 1997).

FIGURE 2
ANES Racial Resentment Index by Year, White Respondents Only

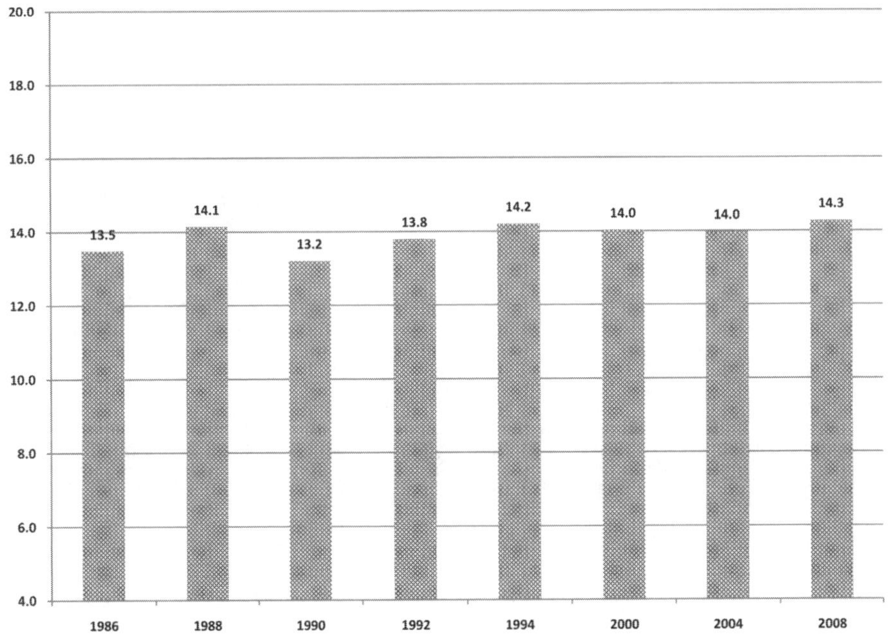

NOTE: Additive index of four items. Each item is scored 1 to 5, with 5 indicating the most "resentful" response. Maximum possible score is 20, lowest is 4; a neutral on Racial Resentment would be a 12.

The strongest effects in the model are those of the attitudinal predictors, all four of which significantly shape policy views: net of the effects of the sociodemographics, racial resentment, traditional prejudice, economic individualism, and political views all exert significant effects, in each case increasing opposition to racial policies. The effect of racial resentment (beta = .402) is the strongest in the model, followed by individualism (beta = .269); the effects of political views (beta = .121) and traditional prejudice (beta = .067) are second in strength only to the "some college" category in increasing opposition to racial policies. Clearly, the attitudinal variables, taken together, are the most important explanatory factors in the model. R-squared increases from .048 in the initial model to .398 in the full model, an indication that our explanatory variables provide meaningful insights into the process by which whites formulate their racial policy views. Year is not significant in any model, indicating that there is no significant linear change in racial policy views over time. We also fit interaction terms between year on one hand and racial resentment, traditional prejudice, and economic individualism on the other (results not shown) to determine whether the effects of these predictors differ over time. None of the interactions was significant.

FIGURE 3
GSS Racial Resentment Items, White Respondents Only

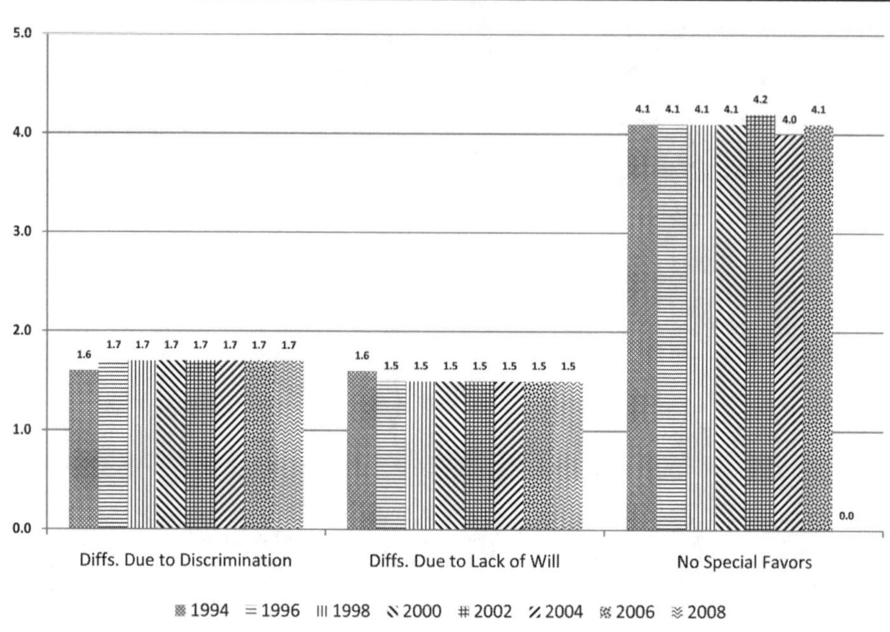

NOTE: The first two items are scored 1 or 2; the third item is scored 1 to 5; high scores indicate the most "resentful" response.

Analysis of the ANES data. With a few exceptions, the effects of the sociodemographic variables in the ANES analysis are similar to those in the GSS analysis. Age, gender, income, education, region, and being disabled are significant predictors of racial policy attitudes, with older people, those with higher incomes, those with a high school or some college education (compared with those with less than high school), and those from regions other than the West (particularly the South and the Midwest) more opposed to racial policies, and women and the disabled more in favor. When we add the attitudinal variables in step 2, all of these associations are changed. The impacts of age and gender disappear, and those of income, region, and being disabled are reduced. Those with a high school education or some college are less different from those with less than high school, and those with more education are now significantly more opposed to racial policies than are those with less than high school education.

The notable differences in findings at step 2 compared with the GSS findings are that age has no impact on racial policy attitudes in the ANES analysis, income is associated with greater opposition, and unemployment has no significant association. Similar to the GSS findings, those with a college education or some college are the most opposed to racial policies, and those with less than high school education are least opposed; gender has no association with racial policy attitudes; and

FIGURE 4
GSS Racial Resentment Index by Year, White Respondents Only

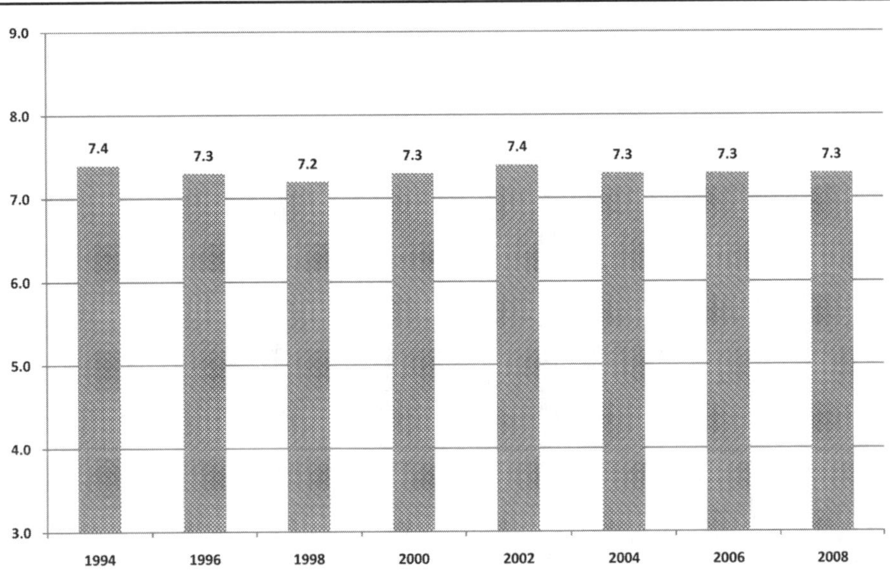

NOTE: Additive index of three items. Two items are scored 1 or 2, with 2 indicating the most "resentful" response. The third item is scored 1 to 5, with 5 indicating the most "resentful" response. Maximum possible score is 9, lowest is 3; a neutral on Racial Resentment would be a 6.

across regional categories, the greatest opposition is in the South, followed by the Midwest, with the lowest opposition occurring in the West. In contrast to the GSS data, the ANES has an employment status category for "disabled," and compared with other employment status categories, this category is the least opposed to racial policies and is significantly different from the employed.

The attitudinal variables are the most important predictors of opposition to racial policies. As in the GSS analysis, the strongest impact among the attitudinal variables, and indeed among all variables in the model, is racial resentment, with beta = .497. This is followed by significant effects of individualism (beta = .138); the black thermometer rating (–.111), indicating that whites with "warm" feelings toward blacks are more supportive of racial policies, and those with "cold" feelings are less supportive; the equality index (–.081); and political views (conservative vs. liberal, beta = .043). Traditional prejudice has no significant association with racial policy attitudes in this model specification.

Some of the differences between the ANES and the GSS analyses are due to the different model specifications. For example, the equality index and the feeling thermometers included in the ANES analysis (which are absent in the GSS analysis) reduce the effect of traditional prejudice to insignificance, suggesting that the weak effect of traditional prejudice without these variables in the equation

TABLE 2
OLS Estimates from Regression of Opposition to Racial Policies on
Sociodemographic and Attitudinal Predictors, 1991–2008 General Social
Survey (GSS) and 2008 American National Election Survey (ANES) Data

	GSS				ANES			
	b	beta	b	beta	b	beta	b	beta
Sociodemographic								
Age	−.005	−.008	−.045*	−.072	.060**	.109	−.002	−.003
Female	−1.406*	−.070	−.016	−.001	−1.085*	−.055	−.222	−.011
Urban	−1.619*	−.071	−.388	−.017	—	—	—	—
Income	.212	.021	−.312	−.031	1.478**	.149	.659**	.066
High school	1.588	.070	1.160	.051	4.080**	.191	2.179**	.102
Some college	3.149**	.147	2.712**	.127	3.733**	.168	2.885**	.129
College	.613	.022	1.672	.061	1.374	.053	3.335**	.130
Postgrad	−2.205	−.077	.657	.023	.042	.001	2.238**	.079
South	3.065**	.153	1.309*	−.065	4.808**	.242	1.356**	.068
Northeast	.519	.012	−.028	−.001	1.745*	.061	.934	.033
Midwest	1.274	.056	.436	.019	2.676**	.114	1.306*	.056
Unemployed	.512	.011	2.217*	.048	−.653	−.014	−1.035	−.022
Retired	−1.108	−.040	−1.085	−.039	−1.260	−.051	.292	.011
In-home	.025	.001	−.179	−.005	−.059	−.001	.780	.019
Student	−.513	−.008	−.958	−.015	.225	.003	.722	.011
Disabled	—	—	—	—	−4.594**	−.101	−2.000*	−.044
Attitudinal								
Racial resentment	—	—	.401**	.402	—	—	.478**	.497
Traditional prejudice	—	—	.306*	.067	—	—	.092	.024
Individualism	—	—	.274**	.269	—	—	.136**	.138
Political views	—	—	.854**	.121	—	—	.246*	.043
Black thermometer	—	—	—	—	—	—	−.056**	−.111
White thermometer	—	—	—	—	—	—	.014	.028
Equality	—	—	—	—	—	—	−.080**	−.081
Year	—	—	−.007	−.002	—	—	—	—
Adjusted R^2	.048		.398		.100		.461	
F	4.548**		35.878**		11.802**		57.430**	
Constant	99.491		28.514		93.464		45.477	

$*p < .05.$ $**p < .01.$

(beta = .058, similar to the effect in the GSS analysis) is explained by antipathy
toward blacks and lack of support for equality in general (both factors are required
to eliminate the significance of traditional prejudice).

In both datasets, the effects of racial resentment are notable for their strength.
Some researchers have criticized the measurement of racial resentment, however,

noting that items in some racial resentment (or symbolic racism) indices include measures of the belief that blacks should get ahead on their own and should not rely on help from the government (see Hughes 1997). Of course, a belief of that kind is similar to a belief that government policy should not be designed to help blacks, perhaps confounding our independent and dependent variables. In our indices, the item that is closest to tapping an aspect of racial policy is the following: "Irish, Italians, Jews, and many other minorities overcame prejudice and worked their way up. Blacks should do the same without any special favors." To deal with this possible confounding of the dependent variable with racial resentment, we respecified both our GSS and ANES models in several different ways using various combinations of the racial resentment items, including specifications of each item individually in separately fit models, and all items as single items in one model.

In both datasets, when we used different combinations of two- (in the GSS) and three- (in the ANES) variable indices, selecting items from among the full indices (see the discussion above on variables used in the construction of the composite indices), the respecified racial resentment variable was always the strongest variable in the model. In the separate regressions in which we reduced the measurement of racial resentment to only a single item, we observed the same outcome. Regardless of which single item, or which two- or three-variable combinations of items, we used as our measure of racial resentment, this variable always emerged as the strongest predictor. When we put all racial resentment items in the model as separate variables, the strongest of these in the ANES was the (reverse coded) item tapping the belief that blacks have gotten less than they deserve (beta = .271), followed by the item noted above about special favors (beta = .178). Each of these effects was stronger than any other variable in the model. Somewhat less strong was the item concerning blacks needing to "try harder" (beta = .085) and the (reverse coded) item about slavery and discrimination being barriers to advancement (beta = .098). In the GSS, similarly, the strongest effect among the racial resentment items, and the strongest overall in the model, was the special favors variable (beta = .331), followed by the willpower attribution item (beta = .152), one of the strongest effects in the model. The third item, discrimination, exerted a lesser effect (beta = .055). Overall, then, racial resentment is a powerful predictor of racial policy attitudes, and it emerges as the most important predictor regardless of how it is specified.

Below, we discuss some implications of our findings and suggest directions for future research.

Summary and Conclusion

We concluded our 1996 study of racial policy attitudes by stating, "In sum, whites who fail to support government-sponsored intervention policies do so because they do not believe that blacks face a significant degree of discrimination or are particularly burdened by the legacy of past discrimination; [and] because they attribute racial inequality to perceived lack of effort or ability on the part of blacks" (Tuch and Hughes 1996b, 741). Those conclusions were based on analyses of 1986 ANES and 1990 GSS data.

In the current study, using 2008 ANES and 1991–2008 GSS data, we reach similar conclusions regarding the salience of racial affect in shaping whites' views of policy initiatives. Among the several explanations of the principle-policy gap that we examine, one factor especially resonates: racial resentment, a variant of stratification ideology that focuses on the role of racial individualism in shaping white resistance to meaningful policy change. Net the effects of a range of demographic variables, as well as several alternative explanations of the principle-policy gap—including traditional prejudice, economic individualism, egalitarianism, and political ideology—racial resentment is by far the strongest predictor of policy attitudes in both the GSS and ANES data.

What does this finding of the continuing significance of racial resentment imply for the argument that America is on the threshold of becoming a post-racial society? At best, such an argument is grossly premature; at worst, it ignores the continuing consequences for African Americans of past and, in many instances, present discrimination and racism in virtually every institution in American society.

Consistent with other recent research, we also find that whites' racial policy attitudes have changed little over the past two decades (see especially Hutchings 2009) and that attitudinal factors play a much more important role in shaping policy views than do sociodemographic factors. The fact that racial resentment has remained virtually unchanged since the 1980s is a key part of the explanation of whites' continued reluctance to support meaningful racial policy change.

In his 1997 study, Hughes concluded that racial resentment was the principal ideological dimension influencing whites' racial policy views. Based on the analyses presented here, it is fair to say that this conclusion is just as applicable today. An important goal of future research should be to probe the reasons why whites' racial belief systems are so slow to change.

Notes

1. We combine several GSS years because not all survey years contain each of our variables of interest. To control for time effects, we include a term for year in all GSS multivariate analyses.

2. See Firebaugh (2007) for an excellent discussion of the utility of replicating findings across datasets in a single study.

3. See Hutchings (2009) for a similar analysis of the ANES policy items.

4. States included were CT, ME, MA, NH, NJ, NY, PA, RI, VT.

5. States included were IL, IN, IA, KS, MI, MN, MO, NE, ND, OH, SD, WI.

6. States included were AL, AR, DE, DC, FL, GA, KY, LA, MD, MS, NC, OK, SC, TN, TX, VA, WV.

7. States included were AK, AZ, CA, CO, HI, ID, MT, NM, NV, OR, UT, WA, WY.

References

Bobo, Lawrence. 1988. Group conflict, prejudice, and the paradox of contemporary racial attitudes. In *Eliminating racism: Profiles in controversy*, eds. Phyllis Katz and Dalmas A. Taylor, 85–114. New York, NY: Plenum.

Bobo, Lawrence. 2000. Race and beliefs about affirmative action: Assessing the effects of interests, group threat, ideology, and racism. In *Racialized politics: The debate about racism in America*, eds. David Sears, James Sidanius, and Lawrence Bobo, 137–64. Chicago, IL: University of Chicago Press.

Bobo, Lawrence, and James R. Kluegel. 1993. Opposition to race-targeting: Self-interest, stratification ideology, or racial attitudes? *American Sociological Review* 58:443–64.

Bobo, Lawrence, James R. Kluegel, and Ryan A. Smith. 1997. Laissez-faire racism: The crystallization of a kinder, gentler, antiblack ideology. In *Racial attitudes in the 1990s: Continuity and change*, eds. Steven Tuch and Jack K. Martin, 15–41. Westport, CT: Praeger.

Davis, James A., Tom W. Smith, and Peter V. Marsden. 2008. *General Social Surveys, 1972–2008: Cumulative codebook*. Chicago, IL: National Opinion Research Center.

Feagin, Joe. 1975. When it comes to poverty, it's still "God helps those who help themselves." *Psychology Today* 6:101–29.

Firebaugh, Glenn. 2007. *Seven rules for social research*. Princeton, NJ: Princeton University Press.

Hughes, Michael. 1997. Symbolic racism, old-fashioned racism, and whites' opposition to affirmative action. In *Racial attitudes in the 1990s: Continuity and change*, eds. Steven Tuch and Jack K. Martin, 45–75. Westport, CT: Praeger.

Hughes, Michael, and Steven A. Tuch. 2000. How beliefs about poverty influence racial policy attitudes: A study of whites, African Americans, Hispanics, and Asians in the United States. In *Racialized politics: The debate about racism in America*, eds. David Sears, James Sidanius, and Lawrence Bobo, 165–90. Chicago, IL: University of Chicago Press.

Hunt, Matthew O. 1996. The individual, society, or both? A comparison of black, Latino, and white beliefs about the causes of poverty. *Social Forces* 75:293–322.

Hunt, Matthew O. 2007. African American, Hispanic, and white beliefs about black-white inequality, 1977–2004. *American Sociological Review* 72:390–415.

Hutchings, Vincent. 2009. Change or more of the same? Evaluating racial attitudes in the Obama era. *Public Opinion Quarterly* 73:917–42.

Hutchings, Vincent, Simon Jackman, and Gary M. Segura. 2008. American National Election Studies. Available from www.electionstudies.org.

Kinder, Donald R., and Lynn M. Sanders. 1996. *Divided by color: Racial politics and democratic ideals*. Chicago, IL: University of Chicago Press.

Kinder, Donald R., and David O. Sears. 1981. Prejudice and politics: Symbolic racism versus racial threats to the good life. *Journal of Personality and Social Psychology* 40:414–31.

Kluegel, James R. 1990. Trends in whites' explanations of the black-white gap in socioeconomic status, 1977–1989. *American Sociological Review* 55:512–25.

Kluegel, James R., and Eliot R. Smith. 1986. *Beliefs about inequality: Americans' views of what is and what ought to be*. New York, NY: Aldine de Gruyter.

Krysan, Maria. 2000. Prejudice, politics, and public opinion: Understanding the sources of racial policy attitudes. *Annual Review of Sociology* 26:135–68.

Noonan, Peggy. 16 January 2009. Suspend your disbelief. *Wall Street Journal*, A11.

Pettigrew, Thomas F. 2009. Post-racism? Putting President Obama's victory in perspective. *Du Bois Review* 6:279–92.

Quillian, Lincoln. 1995. Prejudice as a response to perceived group threat: Population composition and anti-immigrant and racial prejudice in Europe. *American Sociological Review* 60:586–611.

Quillian, Lincoln. 1996. Group threat and regional change in attitudes toward African Americans. *American Journal of Sociology* 102:816–60.

Schneider, William. 8 November 2008. What racial divide? *National Journal Magazine*. Available from www.nationaljournal.com/njmagazine/pl_20081108_6997.php.

Schuman, Howard, Charlotte Steeh, Lawrence Bobo, and Maria Krysan. 1997. *Racial attitudes in America: Trends and interpretations*. Rev. ed. Cambridge, MA: Harvard University Press.

Sears, David O. 1988. Symbolic racism. In *Eliminating racism: Profiles in controversy*, eds. Phyllis Katz and Dalmas A. Taylor, 53–84. New York, NY: Plenum.

Sears, David O., and Donald R. Kinder. 1971. Racial tensions and voting in Los Angeles. In *Los Angeles: Viability and prospects for metropolitan leadership*, ed. Werner Z. Hirsch, 51–88. New York, NY: Praeger.

Sears, David O., James Sidanius, and Lawrence Bobo. 2000. *Racialized politics: The debate about racism in America*. Chicago, IL: University of Chicago Press.

Smith, Rogers M., and Desmond S. King. 2009. Barack Obama and the future of American racial politics. *Du Bois Review* 6:25–35.

Sniderman, Paul M., and Thomas Piazza. 1993. *The scar of race*. Cambridge, MA: Belknap Press.

Tierney, John. 2008. Where have all the bigots gone? *New York Times*. Available from http://tierneylab.blogs.nytimes.com/2008/11/07.

Tuch, Steven A., and Michael Hughes. 1996a. Whites' opposition to race-targeted policies: One cause or many? *Social Science Quarterly* 77:778–88.

Tuch, Steven A., and Michael Hughes. 1996b. Whites' racial policy attitudes. *Social Science Quarterly* 77:723–45.

Racial Attitudes in City, Neighborhood, and Situational Contexts

Multiple social contexts have been shown to affect racial attitudes both positively and negatively when considered at different levels. In this article, context is simultaneously considered at three different levels: the metropolitan area, the census block group, and the interview situation (as measured by race of interviewer/race of respondent matching). Significant effects can be classified into three categories: the effects of the racial composition of the city, the effects of the racial composition of the neighborhood, and the effects of a "different-race" interviewer. Neighborhood income and race of interviewer effects are direct; by contrast, racial composition effects are typically cross-level interaction effects. This indicates that the modeling of cross-level interactions is essential for future studies of the effects of racial composition on attitudes.

Keywords: racial attitudes; context; stereotypes; prejudice

By
MONICA McDERMOTT

In recent years, the importance of considering environmental effects on individual-level phenomena has been reflected in a burgeoning research literature. Especially with regard to racial attitudes, a number of researchers have used multilevel models to assess the impact of local population composition on intergroup beliefs (Fossett and Kiecolt 1989; Quillian 1996; Taylor 1998). The central finding to emerge from these studies is that the percentage of black respondents in a metropolitan area is positively related to negative racial stereotypes (see Oliver

Monica McDermott is an assistant professor of sociology at Stanford University. Her primary research interests involve race and ethnic relations in the United States, especially white identity, racial attitudes, and race/class interactions. She is the author of Working-Class White: The Making and Unmaking of Race Relations *(University of California Press 2006), which is based on her participant observation research on interracial interactions in Atlanta and Boston, where she worked as a convenience store clerk for a year.*

NOTE: The author wishes to thank Matthew Hunt, George Wilson, Rebecca Sandefur, Tomas Jimenez, and Paolo Parigi for helpful comments on earlier drafts of this article.

DOI: 10.1177/0002716210388388

and Wong 2003). The strength of this finding is such that large North/South differences are reduced to statistical insignificance after considering percentage black (Taylor 1998). Some form of the group threat model that Blumer (1958) formulated and that Bobo (1999) extended is often adopted to explain these findings.

While the primary focus of studies of contextual effects on racial attitudes is on racial context, class context has gained renewed attention in recent years (e.g., Oliver and Mendelberg 2000; Gay 2006; Branton and Jones 2005). Findings from studies that consider both class and racial contexts are mixed—Branton and Jones (2005) conclude that this is due to an interaction effect between diversity and class, such that highly diverse areas with high socioeconomic status (SES) support racial policy measures while highly diverse areas with low SES oppose racial policy measures. As Taylor (1998, 533) notes in her analysis of contextual effects on racial attitudes, "A better understanding is needed of the dynamics that account for the observed macro/micro links."

Part of the reason these linkages have been difficult to make, based on our current understanding of contextual effects, is the level of aggregation of the data. Many of the major analyses of the effects of local context on group attitudes are undertaken at the level of the metropolitan area, although there are notable exceptions (e.g., Gay 2006; Adelman 2005; Oliver and Wong 2003). While this is a useful level of aggregation for assessing group threat in some arenas, especially the political one, it is less useful for analyzing true "neighborhood" effects. Labor markets, social networks, residential patterns, and class composition can vary wildly within the same metropolitan area. Furthermore, the ethnographic research upon which the development of macro-micro linkages depends is almost always conducted at the level of the neighborhood rather than at the level of the metropolitan area (e.g., McDermott 2006). Baybeck (2006, 386) notes that "racial context needs to be considered as a complex system of overlapping spatial units," one that might overlap with the socioeconomic context in unexpected ways.

Taylor (1998) identifies another area for research on local context effects: the effect of perceived status and physical threat on whites' attitudes. While Blumer (1958) identifies status threat as an important factor in black-white relations, it is difficult to assess the extent to which the size of the minority population is activating status or physical threat (as distinct from economic or political threat). Since one's immediate surroundings, rather than the larger setting of the metropolitan area, tend to activate status and physical threat, a multilevel analysis of contextual effects based at the census block group level can shed more light on status and physical threat. For example, one would not expect a white person living in a gated community in an affluent suburb to be beset by the same fears and worries as a white person living in a lower-income, mixed-race neighborhood in the inner city. However, the studies of contextual effects, using only the metropolitan area as the level of analysis, do just that (Baybeck 2006).

At an even more micro level than the neighborhood context is the situational context, or the context in which the survey interview occurs. One of the major influences on responses to questions about race is a match between the race of the interviewer and the race of the interviewee. A concern with providing the socially desirable response often leads those who are interviewed by someone of another race to give more racially tolerant responses than someone interviewed by a "same-race" interviewer (Hatchett and Schuman 1975; Krysan and Couper 2003).

In this article, the metropolitan area, the census block group,[1] and the interview situation (as measured by race of interviewer/race of respondent matching) are considered. By doing so, I find that the neighborhood context amplifies the effects of individual variables, such as race and class, in terms of both the racial context and the class context. The situational context of an interview matters in many, but not all, cases.

Effects of local context on racial attitudes

Classic texts, such as Allport (1954) and Key (1949), have identified the size of a local black population as important for influencing white racial attitudes and voting behavior. Blumer's (1958) theory of "group threat" as the primary motivation for negative white racial attitudes has become the primary lens through which contextual effects on beliefs have been understood. Group threat assumes that whites are motivated to be hostile toward blacks via competition for scarce resources, including jobs and political power. Consequently, areas in which there is a high proportion of blacks are expected to be characterized by high degrees of racial animosity (Blalock 1967). This perspective can explain, in part, why the South has exhibited persistently higher levels of racial prejudice than other regions of the United States.

With the development of sophisticated multilevel linear models, the hypothesis about the impact of the size of the black population on white racial attitudes has been rigorously tested (Fossett and Kiecolt 1989; Glaser 1994; Quillian 1996; Taylor 1998; Oliver and Mendelberg 2000). Most studies find that the size of the black population in a metro area has a huge effect on white racial attitudes. Quillian (1996) estimates that this effect is sufficiently large to explain 50 percent of the difference in racial hostility between the South and the non-South. Many of the studies of contextual effects of the black population, with the notable exception of Oliver and Mendelberg (2000), have been conducted at the county or metro area level (Soss, Langbein, and Metelko 2008; Campbell, Wong, and Citrin 2006), and it is telling that only Oliver and Mendelberg find ambiguous support for the black population size effect. While they attribute their divergent findings to the effects of the socioeconomic context, Quillian finds that the effect of percentage black holds even after controlling for average per capita income of the area. Oliver and Wong (2003) argue that the effect of racial composition at the neighborhood level is conditioned by the racial composition of the metropolitan area, with neighborhood composition making a bigger difference in cities with large black populations.

The mechanism through which the size of the black population affects white attitudes is a matter of some debate. While a group threat model is often employed, the nature of this threat can be multivalent. For example, Cohen (1998) identifies the threat as racial inequality in the labor market; the proportion of a metropolitan area that is black increases black-white earnings inequality, with whites earning more relative to blacks as the black population increases. Thus, the threat to whites' economic interests actually lessens as the black population increases. Taylor (1998), who gives qualified support to the group threat hypothesis, echoes Kinder and Sanders's (1996) concern with distinguishing "personal threat" from "group threat." For example, status anxieties combined with preexisting resentment against an "out-group" may result in the observed effects of black population size. Rocha and Espino (2009) explain away previous ambiguous findings about the effect of racial context on attitudes by correlating racial composition with residential segregation; the more segregated a metropolitan area is, the more likely an increase in the size of the Latino population will result in an increase in anti-immigrant attitudes. And Stolle, Soroka, and Johnston (2008) find that those who interact more with their neighbors are less likely to be influenced by racial context; this could account for some of the variability across studies on the impact of context on attitudes.

Class effects on racial attitudes

While much of the research on the effects of local context on white racial attitudes has focused on the size of the black population, higher-level class effects also have been demonstrated. Quillian (1996, 853) finds that "regional income per capita is inversely related to traditional prejudice and opposition to race targeting, even when controlling at the individual level for income." The income effects are in addition to substantial observed effects of black population size on attitudes. Branton and Jones (2005) find an interaction between racial context and class context, with racially diverse, low-SES communities having the least tolerant racial attitudes as well as the most antiegalitarian attitudes.

Oliver and Mendelberg (2000) make an even stronger claim for the primacy of the contextual effects of class on racial attitudes; they insist that the effects of percentage black on perceptions of group threat are valid only insofar as they interact with socioeconomic characteristics. They go so far as to say that "living amongst more uneducated whites has a greater impact on whites' racial attitudes than does living amongst more blacks" (p. 574). Education is only one measure of socioeconomic context; rather than simply measuring one's socioeconomic position in society (as in occupation and income), education also captures the ability to engage in the legitimization of the status quo with more sophisticated language (Jackman and Muha 1984). It is not clear to what extent education measures status or access to resources.

Regardless of measurement issues, it is clear that there is considerable utility in examining the effects of socioeconomic context on racial attitudes, especially at the level of the neighborhood and especially when considering interactions with racial composition. Initial indications that income and education contexts are related to white racial attitudes, independent of individual class attributes, need to be extended and tested with other datasets and measures. In particular, multiple measures of class, including occupation, need to be tested at the contextual level of the census block group.

Situational context

Researchers interested in the study of racial attitudes have long been concerned with race-of-interviewer effects in surveys (e.g., Schuman and Converse 1971). Much of the research in this area treats race-of-interviewer effects as a methodological problem that can be overcome by matching the race of the interviewer to the survey respondent. However, Kinder and Winter (2001) suggest that race-of-interviewer effects deserve to be studied in their own right as contextual effects on the expression of racial and political attitudes. Ethnographic and social-psychological studies of the expression of attitudes confirm that many whites converse differently in interracial settings than in mono-racial contexts (McDermott 2006). An analysis of the patterning of race-of-interviewer effects in a large survey can illustrate which types of opinions are likely to be tailored to the racial composition of the audience.

In this article, differences in the expression of racial attitudes in the Multi-City Survey of Urban Inequality (MCSUI) are the focus. Unlike many large-scale surveys, the MCSUI includes a substantial number of whites who are interviewed by blacks, as well as the more common pattern of blacks interviewed by whites. Typically, small sample sizes have prevented the systematic analysis of white responses to black interviewers (Hatchett and Schuman 1975); consequently, much of the literature on race-of-interviewer effects has focused on black respondents interviewed by whites (Kinder and Sanders [1996], Kinder and Winter [2001], and Hill [2002] are exceptions). Among both blacks and whites, race-of-interviewer effects are evident even after controlling for individual characteristics such as age, income, education, and political ideology (Hatchett and Schuman 1975; Schaeffer 1980; Anderson 1988; Bernick 1994; Kinder and Sanders 1996; Kinder and Winter 2001), with whites giving more liberal or tolerant responses when a black interviewer conducted the survey and blacks giving more conservative responses when a white survey taker conducted the interview.

Such results are often thought to reflect social-desirability effects, whereby respondents are influenced by what they perceive the interviewers want them to say. In an innovative experiment, Krysan (1998) finds that whites give more racially tolerant responses to questions about race when interviewed face-to-face; when filling out an anonymous mail-back survey, whites report more conservative attitudes, especially with regard to policy preferences. The highly educated are especially likely to report conservative attitudes in a more private setting. The types of questions asked proved important in gauging race-of-interviewer effects in a sample of Los Angeles residents, as well (Bobo and Johnson 2000). While the race of the interviewer did not affect the responses of whites or blacks to a number of questions about policy preferences,[2] the effect was evident in some questions about stereotypes, varying in terms of target group.

While the existence of a race-of-interviewer effect on questions that specifically mention race may appear to be self-evident, these effects are not consistent across all types of questions that mention race or discuss racial stereotypes. In fact, the effect of the race of the interviewer is much greater for a question assessing white support for special hiring preferences for women, Hispanics, or Asians than it is for a number of racial stereotype questions (McDermott 2002). In addition, there is an interaction effect between race of the interviewer and education for some of the respondents, as suggested by Krysan's (1998) research.

While a sizable race-of-interviewer effect indicates the importance of racial context in interviews, it is conceivable that an unobserved effect across class lines is occurring as well. While there is no variable that indicates the social class or regional or educational background of interviewers, they are typically chosen because they speak with minimal local accents and have a fairly high level of education. As much as whites may choose to give the socially desirable response to a black interviewer, so might they adapt their responses to that which is thought to be socially desirable to a well-spoken, well-dressed, educated interviewer. This line of thinking follows from the consideration of racial attitudes as partly the reflection of broader cultural norms (Schuman et al. 1997, 2–5). Rather than reflecting a "true" internalized attitude, responses to survey questions reflect the dominant mode of public discourse about race. This hardly renders such survey data useless; as Schuman et al. (1997) note, measuring "socially desirable" attitudes about race is an important activity in and of itself, serving as a barometer of broad societal norms about appropriate speech and beliefs about racial matters.

It is perhaps most helpful to think of attitudes expressed in the survey interview as a type of context or situation, much as the norms governing the appropriateness of ideas about race in less formalized encounters might differ (McDermott 2006). Layered on these situational contexts are broader contexts that localized norms shape.

Data and Methods

In this study, I draw on data from the MCSUI, conducted between 1992 and 1994 in four metropolitan areas: Atlanta, Boston, Detroit, and Los Angeles. The survey consisted of face-to-face interviews in the homes of respondents; multistage area probability sampling[3] of adults took place across the four areas between April 1992 and November 1994, varying by location (Bobo et al. 1998). A battery of questions on racial attitudes and a wealth of data on labor market experience, social networks, and demographic characteristics render these data ideal for the analysis of the effects of social class and neighborhood context on racial attitudes. One of the main virtues of the MCSUI data on racial attitudes is its inclusion of questions addressing not only whites' attitudes toward blacks but also the attitudes of blacks, Hispanics, and Asians toward whites and toward each other. Both blacks and low-income areas were oversampled; in all, there were 8,916 respondents.

To assess the contextual effects of environment on racial attitudes, census data from the 1990 STF3A files are matched to the individual respondents in the MCSUI. Hierarchical linear models are employed to provide reliable estimates of the environmental effects on individual attitudes.[4] Hierarchical linear models provide for the analysis of contextual effects while maintaining robust standard errors (Bryk and Raudenbush 1992). In addition, such models enable one to analyze variation in the slopes of individual-level predictors across different geographic units.

Three basic equations are simultaneously estimated, one at the individual level (level 1), one at the level of the census block group (level 2), and one at the city level (level 3). Several different questions assessing respondents' stereotypes of other racial groups and opinions about policies, such as affirmative action, are the dependent variables. The means of all of the variables used in the analysis are presented in Table 1, and the text of the survey questions for the dependent variables is presented in the appendix. The stereotype scale is an index of four questions: (group) tend to be rich, (group) tend to be intelligent, (group) tend to be self-supporting, and (group) tend to be easy to get along with.[5] Since the slopes of the individual-level predictors vary little across census block groups, the slopes are fixed in the estimation of the multilevel equations.[6] All predictors are uncentered.

Individual-level class is conceptualized in four ways: as educational attainment, as mother's educational attainment, as family income, and as occupation. Occupation is coded as a dummy variable with 1 equal to blue-collar (1990 Census occupation codes 403–905 in Bobo et al. 1998). Race is coded as a dummy variable with "white" as the omitted category. At level 2, the proportion of a neighborhood that is of a given racial composition is matched with the level 1 group, such that "percentage black" is modeled as an effect on blacks, "percentage Hispanic" as an effect on Hispanics, and so forth. Controls in the model include gender, age, and residence in the South at age 16. The South is defined as consisting of the original states of the Confederacy: Alabama, Arkansas, Florida, Georgia, Louisiana, Mississippi, North Carolina, South Carolina, Tennessee, Texas, and Virginia.[7]

In the sections that follow, the results of the models are presented from city-level effects to individual-level effects, with a focus on the influence of the race of the interviewer variable at the individual level. Cross-level interaction effects are discussed at the highest level of the interaction—interactions between percentage black in a neighborhood and black at the individual level are discussed in relation with other direct neighborhood effects.

Results

The individual-level OLS regressions show the importance of race, education, and situational context (interviewer match) on endorsements of stereotypes, beliefs about the amount of discrimination, and support for affirmative action–type programs (see Table 2). Perhaps most notable is the consistently strong effect of

TABLE 1
Means and Standard Deviations for Variables Used in the Analysis

	Mean	SD
Individual-level variables		
Sex	1.59	0.49
Age (*ln*)	3.71	0.36
Lived in South at age 16	0.13	0.34
Years of education	12.28	3.37
Mother's education	9.64	4.14
Family income (20 category)	8.48	5.01
Blue-collar	0.32	0.46
Black	0.37	0.47
Hispanic	0.17	0.36
Asian	0.13	0.33
Interviewer match	0.79	0.39
Black stereotypes scale	11.89	3.21
White stereotypes scale	9.5	3
Hispanic stereotypes scale	11.74	2.88
Asian stereotypes scale	9.82	2.85
No anti-black discrimination	1.85	0.87
No anti-Hispanic discrimination	2.02	0.89
No anti-Asian discrimination	2.5	0.87
Oppose job training for blacks	2.06	1.01
Oppose job training for Hispanics	2.19	0.93
Oppose job training for Asians	2.38	0.93
Oppose hiring preferences for blacks	2.76	1.19
Oppose hiring preferences for Hispanics	2.87	1.03
Oppose hiring preferences for Asians	2.99	0.99
Immigration = less political influence	3.01	1.09
Immigration = less economic influence	3.24	1.04
Block-group-level variables		
Percentage black	32.15	36.15
Percentage Hispanic	18.66	23.33
Percentage Asian	6.42	12.01
Proportion native born	0.75	0.43
Family income (*ln*)	10.3	0.58
Percentage college degree	18.72	16.74
Percentage blue-collar workers	45.13	18.57
MSA-level variables		
Percentage black	24.65	5.13
Percentage Hispanic	8.25	11.03
Percentage Asian	3.25	2.5
Percentage bachelor's degree	24.65	5.13

NOTE: Individual N = 8,905; block group N = 929; city N = 4.

TABLE 2
Level-One Estimates of the Effects of Individual Variables on Racial Attitudes

| | Stereotype Scale | | | | Against Training Programs | | |
Variable	Against Blacks	Against Hispanics	Against Asians	Against Whites	For Blacks	For Hispanics	For Asians
Black	−1.32***	0.00	1.05***	1.76***	−0.85***	−0.46***	−0.27***
	(0.08)	(0.08)	(0.07)	(0.08)	(0.03)	(0.02)	(0.03)
Hispanic	1.18***	−0.93***	0.19	1.02***	−0.36***	−0.54***	−0.28***
	(0.12)	(0.12)	(0.11)	(0.12)	(0.04)	(0.04)	(0.04)
Asian	1.78***	1.37***	−1.20***	1.06***	0.04	0.01	−0.13***
	(0.11)	(0.10)	(0.10)	(0.11)	(0.03)	(0.03)	(0.03)
Education	−0.10***	−0.04***	−0.10***	−0.00	−0.01*	−0.01	−0.00
in years	(0.01)	(0.01)	(0.01)	(0.01)	(0.00)	(0.00)	(0.00)
Mother's	−0.03**	0.00	−0.03**	−0.00	−0.00	0.00	0.01**
education	(0.01)	(0.01)	(0.01)	(0.01)	(0.00)	(0.00)	(0.00)
Blue-collar	0.13	0.20**	0.09	−0.08	0.00	0.01	−0.00
	(0.07)	(0.07)	(0.07)	(0.07)	(0.02)	0.01	0.02
Interviewer	0.82***	0.41***	0.11	0.16*	0.07**	0.15***	0.18***
race match	(0.08)	(0.08)	(0.08)	(0.08)	(0.03)	(0.02)	(0.03)
R-squared	.17	.05	.09	.06	.15	.08	.03

| | No Perceptions of Discrimination | | | | Against Hiring Preferences | | |
	Against Blacks	Against Hispanics	Against Asians		For Blacks	For Hispanics	For Asians
Black	−0.68***	−0.20***	−0.06**		−1.30***	−0.81***	−0.64***
	(0.02)	(0.02)	(0.02)		(0.03)	(0.03)	(0.03)
Hispanic	−0.38***	−0.65***	0.09*		−0.69***	−0.84***	−0.63***
	(0.03)	(0.04)	(0.04)		(0.04)	(0.04)	(0.04)
Asian	0.24***	0.29***	0.06		−.041***	−0.36***	−0.50***
	(0.03)	(0.03)	(0.03)		(0.04)	(0.04)	(0.03)
Education	−0.03***	−0.02***	−0.02***		0.03***	0.02***	0.02***
in years	(0.00)	(0.00)	(0.00)		(0.00)	(0.00)	(0.00)
Mother's	−0.01**	−0.00	−0.01*		−0.01	−0.00	0.00
education	(0.00)	(0.00)	(0.00)		(0.00)	(0.00)	(0.00)
Blue-collar	0.05**	0.02	0.01		0.02	0.00	0.00
	(0.02)	(0.02)	(0.02)		(0.03)	(0.02)	(0.02)
Interviewer	−0.02	−0.01	0.13***		0.05	0.09**	0.14***
race match	(0.02)	(0.02)	(0.02)		(0.03)	(0.03)	(0.03)
R-squared	.16	.08	.02		.21	.15	.10

NOTE: Unstandardized coefficients from the MCSUI. Controls are age, gender, and lived in South at age 16. N = 8,916.
*p < .05. **p < .01. ***p < .001.

being black[8] on giving a racially liberal response, even to questions about support for job training and hiring for Asians and Hispanics; the lone exception is a greater endorsement of anti-Asian and anti-white stereotypes than among whites

(b = 1.05, 1.76). Hispanic respondents are much more likely than whites to endorse negative stereotypes against both blacks and whites; this effect might be expected to lessen as the group consciousness among Hispanics rises (Sanchez 2008). Asians are much more likely than whites to endorse negative stereotypes of any group other than their own.

Among the individual-level class variables, only education has a fairly consistent significant impact on attitudes. However, this effect is different for affirmative action questions than for stereotypes or perceptions of discrimination. The more education one has, the more likely one is to perceive discrimination against blacks, Hispanics, or Asians, and the less likely one is to hold negative stereotypes of these same groups. On the other hand, more education makes one less likely to support hiring programs for blacks (b = 0.03) as well as other non-white groups. The situational context of the interview also matters, as more stereotypes of blacks, Hispanics, and whites are endorsed when respondents are surveyed by a "same-race" interviewer. Situational context also matters for affirmative action–type questions, with nearly all versions of the two questions sensitive to race-of-interviewer matching.

City-level variables

While there is little independent effect at the city level of racial context on stereotypes (Table 3), perceptions of discrimination (Table 4), or affirmative action beliefs (Table 5), there are cross-level interactions between city racial context and neighborhood racial context. As the percentage black of a city increases, adherence to anti-black stereotypes increases, although there is no independent effect of neighborhood racial composition on stereotype adherence. Thus, one might expect majority-black neighborhoods in majority-black cities to be less likely to endorse anti-black stereotypes than majority-black neighborhoods in majority-white cities. The same holds true for the effect of Hispanic racial composition on anti-Hispanic stereotype adherence and for the effect of Asian racial composition on anti-Asian stereotype adherence. However, there is no such effect for adherence to anti-white stereotypes.

Similar cross-level interactions are evident in the models of perceptions of discrimination (see Table 4). As the percentage black of a city increases, the effect of percentage black at the neighborhood level increases: the greater the black population of a city, the more likely an increasingly black neighborhood will result in greater perceptions of discrimination. In the case of Hispanic neighborhoods, the significant independent effect of the Hispanicity of a neighborhood is mitigated by the concentration of Hispanics in the city as a whole. While individuals are less likely to perceive discrimination against Hispanics as the size of the Hispanic population of a neighborhood increases, this effect is lessened as the size of the Hispanic population in the city increases. Hence, a majority-Hispanic neighborhood in a majority-Hispanic city is more likely to positively affect perceptions of discrimination against Hispanics than is a majority-Hispanic neighborhood in a minority-Hispanic city.

TABLE 3
Unstandardized HLM Estimates of the Effects of Individual
and Contextual Variables on Stereotype Scale

	Stereotypes Against			
Variable	Blacks	Hispanics	Asians	Whites
Individual level				
Black	−1.54***	−0.39*	0.84***	1.34***
Impact of neighborhood % black on effect	0.01***	0.00	0.00	0.00
Hispanic	0.49*	−1.11***	0.40*	0.69**
Impact of neighborhood % Hispanic on effect	0.01	0.00	−0.00	−0.01
Asian	1.35***	1.18***	−1.02***	0.64**
Impact of neighborhood % Asian on effect	0.00	0.01	0.02*	−0.01
Education in years	−0.08***	0.00	−0.07***	−0.01
Impact of neighborhood % BA on effect	−0.00	−0.00**	−0.00	0.00
Mother's education	−0.03**	0.00	−0.02*	0.00
Blue-collar	0.26	0.31	0.13	−0.32
Impact of neighborhood % blue-collar on effect	−0.00	−0.00	−0.00	0.00
Interviewer match	0.16**	−0.07	0.10*	0.39***
Neighborhood level				
Percentage black	−0.00			0.00
Impact of city % black on effect	−0.00***			−0.00
Percentage Hispanic		0.00		
Impact of city % Hispanic on effect		−0.00*		
Percentage Asian			0.03	
Impact of city % Asian on effect			−0.01**	
Family income (*ln*)	−0.02	−0.15	0.10	0.25*
Percentage college degree	0.01	0.02	−0.00	−0.02
Percentage blue-collar workers	−0.00	−0.00	−0.00	0.00
Variance component (0.1109; 0.2957)	0.42***	0.34***	0.27***	0.35***
City level				
Percentage black	0.00			−0.02
Percentage Hispanic		0.03		
Percentage Asian			−0.01	
Variance component (0.0823; 0.1063)	0.00	0.04***	0.13***	0.06***

*p < .05. **p < .01. ***p < .001.

These cross-level interactions are much less pronounced with regard to affirmative action beliefs (see Table 5). The only statistically significant interaction effect of city context on attitudes toward affirmative action is the effect of percentage black at the city level on the effect of percentage black at the neighborhood level on attitudes toward training programs for blacks. While respondents are increasingly likely to support affirmative action as the proportion of blacks in the neighborhood increases, this effect is magnified as the proportion of blacks

TABLE 4
Unstandardized HLM Estimates of the Effects of Individual
and Contextual Variables on Perceptions of Discrimination

Variable	No Discrimination Against		
	Blacks	Hispanics	Asians
Individual level			
Black	–0.67***	–0.40***	–0.22***
Impact of neighborhood % black on effect	0.00	0.00**	0.00
Hispanic	–0.34***	–0.44***	–0.16*
Impact of neighborhood % Hispanic on effect	–0.00	–0.00**	0.00
Asian	0.17**	0.21**	0.01
Impact of neighborhood % Asian on effect	0.00	0.00	–0.00
Education in years	–0.02***	–0.01**	–0.02***
Impact of neighborhood % BA on effect	0.00	–0.00	0.00
Mother's education	–0.01*	–0.00	–0.01***
Blue-collar	0.03	0.11	–0.01
Impact of neighborhood % blue-collar on effect	0.00	–0.00	0.00
Interviewer match	0.00	–0.01	–0.01
Neighborhood level			
Percentage black	–0.00		
Impact of city % black on effect	–0.00*		
Percentage Hispanic		0.00*	
Impact of city % Hispanic on effect		–0.00**	
Percentage Asian			–0.00
Impact of city % Asian on effect			–0.00
Family income (*ln*)	0.02	0.05	0.00
Percentage college degree	0.00	0.00	–0.00
Percentage blue-collar workers	–0.00	0.00	0.00
Variance component (0.1109; 0.2957)	0.01***	0.03***	0.02***
City level			
Percentage black	0.01		
Percentage Hispanic		0.01	
Percentage Asian			0.07
Variance component (0.0823; 0.1063)	0.00***	0.00***	0.01***

*p < .05. **p < .01. ***p < .001.

in the city increases, especially in the case of training programs. However, no such effects are evident in the case of opinions about affirmative action programs targeted at Asians or Hispanics.

Neighborhood-level variables

While there are few direct effects of neighborhood-level variables on attitudes, there are a number of cross-level interactions between neighborhood context and individual-level effects. In Table 3, only family income has an independent effect on adherence to anti-white stereotypes, with respondents from higher-income

TABLE 5
Unstandardized HLM Estimates of the Effects of Individual and Contextual Variables on Affirmative Action Beliefs

Variable	Against Training Programs			Against Hiring Programs		
	Blacks	Hispanics	Asians	Blacks	Hispanics	Asians
Individual level						
Black	−0.75***	−0.57***	−0.42***	−1.10***	−0.84***	−0.68***
Impact of neighborhood % black on effect	0.00**	0.00*	0.00***	0.00**	0.00	0.00*
Hispanic	−0.27***	−0.50***	−0.33***	−0.45***	−0.70***	−0.65***
Impact of neighborhood % Hispanic on effect	0.00	0.00*	0.00	−0.00	−0.00	0.00
Asian	0.08	0.05	0.05	−0.23**	−0.22**	−0.25**
Impact of neighborhood % Asian on effect	0.00	0.00	−0.01*	−0.00	−0.00	−0.01**
Education in years	−0.02**	−0.01*	−0.01*	0.02***	0.02***	0.02***
Impact of neighborhood % BA on effect	0.00	0.00	0.00	−0.00	−0.00*	−0.00*
Mother's education	−0.00	−0.00	0.01	−0.01*	−0.00	−0.00
Blue-collar	0.05	0.06	0.05	0.10	0.06	0.09
Impact of neighborhood % blue-collar on effect	−0.00	−0.00	−0.00	−0.00	−0.00	−0.00
Interviewer match	−0.03*	−0.06***	−0.10***	−0.04*	−0.05**	−0.07***
Neighborhood level						
Percentage black	−0.00*			−0.01***		
Impact of city % black on effect	−0.00*			−0.00		
Percentage Hispanic		−0.00			−0.00	
Impact of city % Hispanic on effect		−0.00			0.00	
Percentage Asian			0.01			−0.00
Impact of city % Asian on effect			−0.00			0.00
Family income (*ln*)	0.10*	0.00	0.01	0.13**	0.08*	0.08*
Percentage college degree	−0.01*	−0.00	−0.00	0.00	0.01	0.01
Percentage blue-collar workers	−0.00*	−0.00	−0.00	−0.00	−0.00	−0.00
Variance component (0.1109; 0.2957)	0.05***	0.05***	0.05***	0.08***	0.07***	0.06***
City level						
Percentage black	0.01			0.01		
Percentage Hispanic		0.00			−0.00	
Percentage Asian			0.02			−0.01
Variance component (0.0823; 0.1063)	0.00***	0.03***	0.03***	0.00	0.01***	0.01***

*p < .05. **p < .01. ***p < .001.

neighborhoods increasingly endorsing anti-white stereotypes. However, several cross-level interactions between neighborhood race and class context and individual-level race and class are evident. For example, as the proportion of blacks in a neighborhood increases, the inverse effect on adherence to anti-black stereotypes is mitigated. While blacks are much less likely than whites to endorse anti-black stereotypes, this difference is not as strong as the proportion of blacks in a neighborhood increases. A similar effect is evident for Asians in the case of anti-Asian stereotypes. The effect of being Asian on reducing adherence to anti-Asian stereotypes is significantly stronger in neighborhoods that have smaller proportions of Asian residents.

In the case of anti-Hispanic stereotypes, the educational context of the neighborhood interacts with individual-level educational attainment, such that the likelihood of endorsing anti-Hispanic stereotypes is lessened as the proportion of neighborhood residents with a college degree increases. On the other hand, the positive relationship between median family income in the neighborhood and adherence to anti-white stereotypes suggests that class influences whites as a reference group for stereotypes in a way that it does not for other racial groups.

While socioeconomic variables influence adherence to anti-Hispanic stereotypes, it is the racial composition of the neighborhood that influences perceptions of discrimination against Hispanics in several ways (see Table 4). There is a direct effect of the proportion of a neighborhood that is Hispanic on perceptions of discrimination toward Hispanics, with those in more heavily Hispanic areas less likely to perceive discrimination, net of individual characteristics; however, this effect is mitigated by the size of the Hispanic population at the city level. In addition, neighborhood racial composition also indirectly affects perceptions of discrimination through its influence on individual racial effects. As the proportion of Hispanics in a neighborhood increases, the effect of being Hispanic on perceptions of anti-Hispanic discrimination is intensified, such that Hispanics living in heavily Hispanic neighborhoods are even more likely to perceive discrimination against their group than are Hispanics living in neighborhoods with relatively small Hispanic populations. Notably, neighborhood racial composition on black perceptions of discrimination against Hispanics has the opposite effect, with blacks living in heavily black neighborhoods *less* likely to believe that Hispanics are victims of discrimination. This may be the result of blacks viewing anti-Hispanic discrimination as relative to that of other groups, while Hispanics may have a stronger sense of group identity in majority-Hispanic neighborhoods, which increases the likelihood of perceiving anti-Hispanic discrimination.

Neighborhood effects are much more pronounced in the case of support for affirmative action programs (see Table 5). The proportion of blacks in a neighborhood has a significant impact on support for affirmative action programs targeting blacks; the greater the proportion of the census block group population that is black, the greater the support for affirmative action policies. This suggests that those who live near large black populations are more sensitive to the need for policies to address racial disparities, holding constant individual attributes. Family income is also related to support for affirmative action programs targeting blacks, with residents of more affluent areas more likely to be opposed to programs, echoing earlier findings on the effect of economic self-interest on affirmative action beliefs at the individual level (Kluegel and Smith 1983). This relationship also holds when Hispanics and Asians are the target groups. And after controlling for the income of a neighborhood, the proportion of residents with a college degree is actually positively related to support for training, but not hiring, programs. The proportion blue-collar has a similar pattern on training programs for blacks.

Regarding interactions between neighborhood and individual-level factors, as the proportion of blacks in a neighborhood grows, blacks are less likely to support affirmative action programs, regardless of the target group. In areas where blacks predominate, there is presumably less perceived need for special programs to aid in access to jobs and training, as blacks in the top decile of jobs (such as executives, managers, and so on) are most likely to supervise black employees (Alba 2009). Blacks are less well represented in positions of supervision over whites; presumably, there is some relationship between the racial concentration in a neighborhood and racial concentration in employment, such that blacks see fewer opportunities for non-whites in areas with a greater concentration of whites.

Racial context of interview

The final contextual variable to consider is that of the interview itself. The "interviewer match" variable is dichotomous, with 1 indicating a same-race interviewer and 0 indicating a different-race interviewer. In all but the case with Hispanics as the target group, the context of the interview matters for the expression of stereotypes (see Table 3). If the interviewer and the respondent are the same race, stereotypes against blacks, Asians, and whites are more likely to be expressed. This suggests that there is a perception that expressing stereotypes is socially undesirable, so that such beliefs should be expressed only to co-ethnics.

There is no such social-desirability effect for perceptions of discrimination against any target group (see Table 4). This suggests that such a question is viewed more objectively and less like a question with a perceived "correct" answer. An interesting effect of interview context emerges in response to the questions about affirmative action–type programs (see Table 5); net of neighborhood and city contexts, individuals who are interviewed by same-race interviewers are actually more likely, not less, to support such programs. This effect is likely because blacks are driven to support affirmative action programs when in an all-black interview context.

Discussion and Conclusion

Significant effects are found across all three contexts: city, neighborhood, and the situational context of the interview. These effects, in turn, can be classified into four categories: the racial composition of the city; the racial composition of the neighborhood; the income of the neighborhood; and the effects of a different-race interviewer on stereotype adherence, perceptions of discrimination, and racial policy support. Only the income and interviewer effects are direct; the racial composition effects are (with one exception) cross-level interaction effects. This suggests the importance of modeling cross-level interactions in future studies of the effects of racial composition on attitudes.

The effects of living in a majority-black neighborhood are especially striking in majority-black cities. As the size of the black population in a city increases, the effect of living in a black neighborhood becomes stronger, influencing beliefs in a racially liberal direction. Those in black neighborhoods in largely black cities are more likely to support affirmative action policies, more likely to perceive anti-black discrimination, and less likely to endorse anti-black stereotypes than are those in black neighborhoods in cities with smaller black populations; this mirrors the effect of black concentration at the neighborhood level on black perceptions of discrimination (Hunt et al. 2007). The same effects are seen for stereotypes among Asians and Hispanics; as the proportion Asian and Hispanic grows at the city level, the effects of living in an increasingly Asian or Hispanic neighborhood decrease adherence to anti-Asian or anti-Hispanic stereotypes, respectively (see Dixon and Rosenbaum 2004). Given the relatively high levels of residential segregation in the four cities used in this study, it is likely that majority-black neighborhoods in cities with large black populations are more isolated from white neighborhoods than are majority-black neighborhoods in cities with smaller black populations. Thus, the level of exposure to racially conservative ideologies might be greater in cities with smaller black populations.

At the neighborhood level, those who live in majority-black neighborhoods are more likely to support affirmative action policies for blacks than are those who live in minority-black neighborhoods. This effect holds true for everyone, regardless of race. However, the individual-level race effect is lessened for blacks as the proportion of a neighborhood's black population increases. In other words, blacks living in majority-black neighborhoods are more likely to oppose affirmative action programs than are blacks living in minority-black neighborhoods. Along these same lines, as the proportion of blacks in a neighborhood increases, blacks are more likely to hold anti-black stereotypes. Again, this might reflect an exposure effect, with anti-black attitudes more common in areas with larger black populations and a greater familiarity with stereotypes about blacks. A similar effect is evident for Asians, with Asians living in neighborhoods with a larger proportion of Asians more likely to endorse anti-Asian stereotypes than Asians living in neighborhoods with a smaller proportion of Asians. There is also a marked effect of the proportion of Hispanics in a neighborhood and Hispanics' perceptions of anti-Hispanic discrimination. In neighborhoods with a larger proportion of Hispanics, Hispanics are more likely to perceive discrimination against Hispanics; it may be the case that Hispanics develop a stronger sense of group identity in majority-Hispanic neighborhoods.

In addition, the income of a census block group directly influences adherence to anti-white stereotypes and support for affirmative action programs for blacks.

More affluent neighborhoods are home to residents who are less likely to support affirmative action–type programs for blacks, consistent with the self-interested stance that many whites take against affirmative action policies. In addition, anti-white stereotypes are more likely to be adhered to by those living in more affluent areas. This suggests that stereotypes such as tending to discriminate or tending to be involved with drugs or gangs are associated with lower-class whites—those distant from the neighborhoods of the affluent. These direct effects of income point to the need to consider class effects at the neighborhood level when analyzing racial attitudes.

Finally, there are the effects of the context of the interview. While social-desirability effects have been noted on survey research on racial attitudes, the only types of questions that evidence such effects in the data presented here, after controlling for contextual effects, are the stereotype questions. This difference might emerge as a result of the greater degree of public discourse around racial policy questions than around stereotypes, such that it is perceived as socially acceptable to disagree with affirmative action policies but not anti-black stereotypes.

These findings support Baybeck's (2006, 386) contention that "racial context needs to be considered as a complex system of overlapping spatial units." Each social arena is embedded within a larger context, and there is little reason to believe that symmetry between levels of analysis will prevail; this is especially true with regard to racial context. In particular, the interaction effects of racial composition at the metropolitan area level and racial composition at the census block group suggest that larger contexts can amplify lower-level spatial effects. Thus, what it means to live in a majority-Hispanic neighborhood is quite different in a city with a large Hispanic population than it is in a city with a relatively small Hispanic population. This has implications not only for survey research but also for case studies of race and ethnic relations, as such studies would need to be situated in the larger urban context. For instance, a largely black neighborhood in Chicago is not as likely to be representative of black neighborhoods in Portland (with a small black population) as it is of black neighborhoods in Detroit.

In sum, class and racial and situational contexts influence responses to questions about racial attitudes and stereotypes. These contexts not only function directly, but higher-level contexts often mediate the effects of individual- or neighborhood-level variables. This suggests that we should pay closer attention to interactions between individuals and their contexts rather than focusing only on the direct effects of contexts on attitudes. It also suggests that policy-makers should pay attention to the income and racial compositions of different areas within a city when trying to articulate the need for race-sensitive programs. The racial composition of a neighborhood is especially important when considering support for affirmative action programs; in particular, non-white groups living in neighborhoods with a relatively small proportion of co-ethnics are especially likely to support such programs.

Appendix
List of Variable Questions

Stereotypes

Now I have some questions about different groups in our (U.S.) society. I'm going to show you a seven-point scale on which the characteristics of people in a group can be rated. In the first statement a score of 1 means that you think almost all of the people in that group are "rich." A score of 7 means that you think almost everyone in the group is "poor." A score of 4 means you think that the group is not toward one end or the other, and of course you may choose any number in between that comes closest to where you think people in the group stand.

In addition to "rich" and "poor," respondents were asked to rate according to the following traits: unintelligent or intelligent, prefer to be self-supporting or prefer to live off welfare, easy to get along with or hard to get along with.

Perceptions of discrimination

In general, how much discrimination is there that hurts the chances of blacks to get good paying jobs? Do you think there is a lot, some, only a little, or none at all?

Affirmative action questions

Now I have some questions about what you think about the fairness of certain policies. Some people feel that because of past disadvantages there are some groups in society that should receive special *job training and educational assistance*. Others say that it is unfair to give these groups special job training and educational assistance. What about you? Do you strongly favor, favor, neither favor nor oppose, oppose, or strongly oppose special job training and educational assistance for blacks?

Some people feel that because of past disadvantages there are some groups in society that should be *given preferences in hiring and promotion*. Others say that it is unfair to give these groups special preferences. What about you? Do you strongly favor, favor, neither favor nor oppose, oppose, or strongly oppose giving special preferences in hiring and promotion to blacks?

Competition with immigrants

If immigration to this country continues at the present rate, how much political influence do you believe people like you, that is (respondent's race) people, will have? Much more than you do now, some but not a lot more, no more or less than now, less than now, a lot less influence than now.

Notes

1. Throughout the article, "neighborhood" is used interchangeably with "census block group" and "city" with "metropolitan area."

2. Bobo and Johnson (2000) were interested in whether the interviewer's race matched that of the respondent's; in the Los Angeles Survey of Urban Inequality (LASUI), this typically meant that whites who were not race-matched were interviewed by Asians rather than blacks. There is little evidence of an effect of Asian interviewers on white responses.

3. Blacks are oversampled in all cities, while Hispanics are oversampled in Boston and Los Angeles.

4. While the sample size at level 3 in this case is extremely small ($n = 4$), there is recent evidence based on Monte Carlo simulations that the highest-level estimates are typically unbiased even with very small sample sizes (Bell et al. 2010).

5. Alpha reliability coefficients for target groups are .49 for blacks, .39 for Hispanics, .33 for Asians, and .38 for whites. The higher coefficient for blacks is most likely due to the greater knowledge that groups have about black stereotypes from sources such as the media.

6. Taylor (1998) follows the same procedure in her analysis of 1990 General Social Survey data across metropolitan areas.

7. Full details on model specifications available from the author upon request.

8. The omitted category is white.

References

Adelman, Robert M. 2005. The roles of race, class and residential preferences in the neighborhood racial composition of middle-class blacks and whites. *Social Science Quarterly* 86:209–28.

Alba, Richard. 2009. *Blurring the color line: The new chance for a more integrated America*. Cambridge, MA: Harvard University Press.

Allport, Gordon. 1954. *The nature of prejudice*. New York, NY: Basic Books.

Anderson, Barbara A. 1988. The effects of the race of the interviewer on race-related attitudes of black respondents in SRC/CPS national election studies. *Public Opinion Quarterly* 52:289–324.

Baybeck, Brady. 2006. Sorting out the competing effects of racial context. *Journal of Politics* 68 (2): 386–96.

Bell, Bethany A., Grant B. Morgan, Jason A. Schoeneberger, Brandon L. Loudermilk, Jeffrey Kromrey, and John M. Ferron. 2010. Dancing the sample size limbo with mixed models: How low can you go? Paper 197-2010 presented at the SAS Global Forum, 11–14 April 2010, Seattle, WA.

Bernick, E. Lee. 1994. Race and dissatisfaction with government services: A cautionary note. *Journal of Urban Affairs* 16:385–93.

Blalock, Hubert. 1967. *Toward a theory of minority-group relations*. New York, NY: Wiley.

Blumer, Herbert. 1958. Race prejudice as a sense of group position. *Pacific Sociological Review* 23:3–7.

Bobo, Lawrence. 1999. Prejudice as group position: Microfoundations of a sociological approach to racism and race relations. *Journal of Social Issues* 55:445–72.

Bobo, Lawrence, and Devon Johnson. 2000. Racial attitudes in a prismatic metropolis: Mapping identity, stereotypes, competition, and views on affirmative action. In *Prismatic metropolis: Inequality in Los Angeles*, eds. Lawrence D. Bobo, Melvin L. Oliver, James H. Johnson Jr., and Abel Valenzuela Jr., 81–163. New York, NY: Russell Sage Foundation.

Bobo, Lawrence, James Johnson, Melvin Oliver, Reynolds Farley, Barry Bluestone, Irene Browne, Sheldon Danziger, Gary Green, Harry Holzer, Maria Krysan, et al. 1998. *Multi-city survey of urban inequality, 1992–1994: [Atlanta, Boston, Detroit, and Los Angeles]* [Household Survey data, computer file]. 2nd ICPSR version. Atlanta, GA: Mathematica/Boston: University of Massachusetts, Survey Research Laboratory/Ann Arbor: University of Michigan, Detroit Area Study and Institute for Social Research, Survey Research Center/Los Angeles: University of California, Survey Research Program.

Branton, Regina P., and Bradford S. Jones. 2005. Reexamining racial attitudes: The conditional relationship between diversity and socioeconomic environment. *American Journal of Political Science* 49 (2): 359–72.

Bryk, Anthony S., and Stephen W. Raudenbush. 1992. *Hierarchical linear models: Applications and data analysis methods.* Thousand Oaks, CA: Sage.

Campbell, Andrea Louise, Cara Wong, and Jack Citrin. 2006. "Racial threat," partisan climate, and direct democracy: Contextual effects in three California initiatives. *Political Behavior* 28:129–50.

Cohen, Philip N. 1998. Black concentration effects on black-white and gender inequality: Multilevel analysis for U.S. metropolitan areas. *Social Forces* 77:207–29.

Dixon, Jeffrey C., and Michael S. Rosenbaum. 2004. Nice to know you? Testing contact, cultural and group threat theories of anti-black and anti-Hispanic stereotypes. *Social Science Quarterly* 85:257–80.

Fossett, Mark A., and K. Jill Kiecolt. 1989. The relative size of minority populations and white racial attitudes. *Social Science Quarterly* 70:820–35.

Gay, Claudine. 2006. Seeing difference: The effect of economic disparity on black attitudes toward Latinos. *American Journal of Political Science* 50 (4): 982–87.

Glaser, James M. 1994. Back to the black belt: Racial environment and white racial attitudes in the South. *Journal of Politics* 56:21–41.

Hatchett, Shirley, and Howard Schuman. 1975. White respondents and race-of-interviewer effects. *Public Opinion Quarterly* 39 (4): 523–27.

Hill, Mark E. 2002. Race of the interviewer and perception of skin color: Evidence from the Multi-City Survey of Urban Inequality. *American Sociological Review* 67:99–108.

Hunt, Matthew O., Lauren A. Wise, Marie-Claude Jipguep, Yvette C. Cozier, and Lynn Rosenberg. 2007. Neighborhood racial composition and perceptions of racial discrimination: Evidence from the Black Women's Health Study. *Social Psychology Quarterly* 70:282–89.

Jackman, Mary R., and Michael J. Muha. 1984. Education and intergroup attitudes: Moral enlightenment, superficial democratic commitment, or ideological refinement? *American Sociological Review* 49:751–69.

Key, V. O. 1949. *Southern politics in state and nation.* New York, NY: Knopf.

Kinder, Donald, and Lynn M. Sanders. 1996. *Divided by color.* Chicago, IL: University of Chicago Press.

Kinder, Donald R., and Nicholas Winter. 2001. Exploring the racial divide: Blacks, whites, and opinion on national policy. *American Journal of Political Science* 45:439–56.

Kluegel, James R., and Eliot R. Smith. 1983. Affirmative action attitudes: Effects of self-interest, racial affect, and stratification beliefs on whites' views. *Social Forces* 61:797–824.

Krysan, Maria. 1998. Privacy and the expression of white racial attitudes: A comparison across three contexts. *Public Opinion Quarterly* 62:506–44.

Krysan, Maria, and Mick P. Couper. 2003. Race in the live and virtual interview: Racial deference, social desirability, and activation effects in attitude surveys. *Social Psychology Quarterly* 66:364–83.

McDermott, Monica. 2002. Race of interviewer effects in a survey of Atlanta whites. Paper presented at the annual meetings of the American Association of Public Opinion Research, 15–19 May 2002, St. Petersburg, FL.

McDermott, Monica. 2006. *Working-class white: The making and unmaking of race relations.* Berkeley, CA: University of California Press.

Oliver, J. Eric, and Tali Mendelberg. 2000. Reconsidering the environmental determinants of white racial attitudes. *American Journal of Political Science* 44:574–89.

Oliver, J. Eric, and Janelle Wong. 2003. Intergroup prejudice in multiethnic settings. *American Journal of Political Science* 47:567–82.

Quillian, Lincoln. 1996. Group threat and regional change in attitudes toward African-Americans. *American Journal of Sociology* 102:816–61.

Rocha, Rene R., and Rodolfo Espino. 2009. Racial threat, residential segregation, and the policy attitudes of Anglos. *Political Research Quarterly* 62:415–26.

Sanchez, Gabriel R. 2008. Latino group consciousness and perceptions of commonality with African Americans. *Social Science Quarterly* 89:428–44.

Schaeffer, Nora Cate. 1980. Evaluating race-of-interviewer effects in a national survey. *Sociological Methods and Research* 8:400–419.

Schuman, Howard, and Jean M. Converse. 1971. The effects of black and white interviewers on black responses in 1968. *Public Opinion Quarterly* 35:44–68.

Schuman, Howard, Charlotte Steeh, Lawrence Bobo, and Maria Krysan. 1997. *Racial attitudes in America*. Cambridge, MA: Harvard University Press.

Soss, Joe, Laura Langbein, and Alan R. Metelko. 2008. Why do white Americans support the death penalty? *Journal of Politics* 65:397–421.

Stolle, Dietlind, Stuart Soroka, and Richard Johnston. 2008. When does diversity erode trust? Neighborhood diversity, interpersonal trust, and the mediating effect of social interactions. *Political Studies* 56:57–65.

Taylor, Marylee C. 1998. The effect of racial composition on racial attitudes of whites. *American Sociological Review* 63:512–35.

"Color Coding" and Support for Social Policy Spending: Assessing the Parameters among Whites

By
GEORGE WILSON
and
AMIE L. NIELSEN

This study uses data from the 1996 through 2002 General Social Survey to examine whether one variant of modern racial prejudice—"color coding"—explains support for several ostensibly nonracial government spending policies regarding crime, urban problems, and drug addiction (welfare and race spending are used as baseline measures). Findings indicate that color coding does not extend appreciably beyond its established focus of welfare and race and operates along a continuum with welfare and race at one end (heavily influenced by prejudice), addiction spending and urban spending at the other end (not influenced by prejudice), and crime spending situated in the middle (moderately influenced by prejudice). Possible causes of the continuum, as well as emerging aspects of the color coding phenomenon—specifically, its possible bidirectional effects and its subordination to political party affiliation in explanatory value—are discussed. Directions for future research that would shed additional light on the color coding phenomenon are also discussed.

Keywords: color coding; racial prejudice; spending policy attitudes

In recent decades, social scientists have made advances in identifying the underpinnings of a critical component of whites' support for government spending to redress social problems in American society. These advances, in fact, have tended to take place in the context of identifying the determinants of whites' fiscal support for policies such as welfare and other programs designed to ameliorate socioeconomic and racial

George Wilson is an associate professor of sociology at the University of Miami. His research interests focus on the institutional production of racial and ethnic inequality in the workplace and the social structural determinants of beliefs about the causes and consequences of racial and stratification ideology.

Amie L. Nielsen is an associate professor in the Department of Sociology at the University of Miami. Her research interests concern the relationships between race, ethnicity, immigration, and crime and substance use and abuse.

DOI: 10.1177/0002716210388880

inequality (Gilens 1999, 1996; Hasenfeld and Rafferty 1989), affirmative action (Kluegel and Smith 1983; Bobo 1988; Steeh and Krysan 1995; Bobo and Smith 1994; Hughes and Tuch 2000), and race-targeted versus income-targeted initiatives across various institutional spheres such as education, health care, and jobs along the opportunity-enhancing and outcome-based policy continuum (Bobo and Kluegel 1993; Wilson 2001; Gilliam and Whitby 1989).

In studies comprising this line of research, sociologists have documented the importance of racial prejudice, particularly toward African Americans, as a primary psychological antecedent of whites' levels of spending support. This line of research encompasses a large volume of studies across a variety of disciplines, including sociology, psychology, and political science. This body of empirical work shows that a unique variant of prejudice emerges as significant: a post-1965 civil rights era form that is more benign in its expression and intensity of negative affect, relative to its more overt and hostile earlier incarnation (Schuman, Steeh, and Bobo 1984; Pettigrew 1987; Hughes and Tuch 2000). Overall, this newer, more subtle variant of prejudice has been documented as being manifest in explicit race-based designations as well as ostensibly nonracial and symbolic expressions (Gilens 1999; Wilson 1996).

The potential applicability of this variant of prejudice, however, has not been extended to the entire range of existing government programs for which it may have explanatory value. For example, scant attention has been paid to the extent to which it can explain orientations toward a range of social issues—such as urban problems and drug addiction—that may not be explicitly inequality-based but nonetheless address long-standing concerns of the American public. More attention has been directed to the possible racialization of crime control policies (e.g., Barkan and Cohn 2005; Mears, Mancini, and Stewart 2009; Unnever and Cullen 2007), although such studies tend to focus exclusively on individual control issues (e.g., support for the death penalty) or indexes (Johnson 2001; Peffley and Hurwitz 2002) rather than attempting to determine the scope of the color coding phenomenon. Yet these various social issues have for decades been considered "conventional" (Newport 2006) outlets for government resources and involve a spatial dynamic (urban problems), a legal status (crime control), and a marginalized condition (drug addiction) that may trigger a racial cue. In fact, there have been calls for the testing of the effects of racial prejudice on support across a wider range of polices and issues (see Gilens 1999; Bobo and Kluegel 1993) to determine the extent to which such prejudice constitutes a "fundamental roadmap that guides the policy-based perceptions of whites" (Wilson 1996, 421).

This study examines how far this roadmap can be followed. It extends our understanding of the scope of whites' prejudice in explaining support for spending policies. Specifically, data from the General Social Survey (GSS) are used to examine if and how racial prejudice toward African Americans—particularly in its modern, post-1965 incarnation—explains levels of support for spending policies. We consider first an explicitly racial spending issue, as well as one that has been demonstrated to be color coded (welfare), and then consider the extent to which racial prejudice may be related to three other policies that have received less attention in the literature: urban problems, crime control, and drug addiction.

Modern Racial Prejudice

In the past several decades, sociologists, psychologists, and political scientists have captured the changing nature of whites' racial prejudice toward African Americans in the United States. In this regard, whites have moved from a traditional "Jim Crow" prejudice to a more subtle form of prejudice variously labeled as "aversive racism" (Dovidio 2001), "symbolic racism" (Sears and Henry 2003), "racial resentment" (Sears, Sidanius, and Bobo 2000), and "laissez-faire racism" (Bobo, Kluegel, and Smith 1997). Accordingly, a relatively harsh set of beliefs—characterized, for example, by a reliance on biological or genetic stereotypes; a denial of the ideal of racial equality in principle; as well as support for segregation across institutional spheres such as education, the workplace, and residence—has given way to a relatively more benign and subtle set of prejudicial beliefs. This "new racism" is associated with stereotypes about cultural and motivational deficiencies, an affirmation of support for the ideal of racial equality in principle, and support for integration across major institutional spheres (Schuman, Steeh, and Bobo 1984; Tuch and Martin 1997). In fact, the thrust of modern prejudice is referred to as constituting an "indirect" manifestation of negative racial attitudes: the emphasis on relatively benign stereotypes as well as beliefs in equality in principle are thought to mask a "blame-the-victim" rationale for the socioeconomic inequities experienced by African Americans who continue to be victimized in a labor market inaccurately characterized as operating on principles of fair and equitable treatment for all (Bobo, Kluegel, and Smith 1997; Tuch and Martin 1997).

Sociologists have documented that prejudice in its modern incarnation is manifest in two principal forms. These include attitudes toward explicitly racial phenomena and the form under scrutiny in this study: subtle color coding. In the case of color coding (also referred to here as "racial coding"), exaggerated or wholly erroneous group generalizations, associated with invidious stereotypes regarding the cultural and motivational personal characteristics of African Americans (e.g., laziness or lack of work ethic), are linked to ostensibly nonracial specific statuses and conditions (Gilens 1999, 1996; Federico 2005). Overall, the racial coding phenomenon—similar to the explicit form of prejudice—is rooted in stereotypes that originate from several possible sources, such as social learning, motivational- or interest-based sources, or through cognitive biases (see Bobo and Massagli 2001); and it has alternatively been referred to as constituting a hallmark of modern anti-black prejudice (Schuman, Steeh, and Bobo 1984) as well as a "relatively pure representation of contemporary prejudice" (Wilson 1996, 423) toward African Americans in the United States.

The impact of modern racial stereotypes on policy support, particularly in the inequality domain, has been well documented. In the context of explicit racial designations, studies have found that whites' negative stereotypes toward African Americans reduce support for government spending to address, for example, race-targeted policies but show weaker effects in reducing support for income-targeted policies across a variety of institutional spheres such as education, residence, and labor market inclusion (Bobo and Kluegel 1993; Shelton and Wilson 2006). In the context of nonracial designations, stereotypes may be triggered and thus impact support for seemingly nonracial policies. Finding that prejudice is associated with attitudes toward these ostensibly nonracial policies indicates the presence of the color coding phenomenon.

Application to Social Issues

To date, the effects of racial coding have been found to be potent primarily in the context of policies targeted toward welfare recipients. The association between stereotypes of African Americans and views of welfare recipients has notably served to undermine support for policies that range from providing welfare recipients job training and educational access, to offering guarantees of jobs and minimal amounts of income (Gilens 1999, 1996; Shelton and Wilson 2006). In the sections that follow, we discuss how and why racial coding may apply to the other social issues under consideration in this article—urban problems, crime control, and drug addiction.

Urban problems

Sociologists have paid little attention to exploring the determinants of attitudes toward spending on policies that address urban problems. In fact, we know of no work going beyond the survey research that has continually identified urban problems as a relatively low-priority social problem over the past several decades (Newport 2006). The invocation of racial prejudice among whites regarding support for spending to redress urban problems is predicated on the association of African Americans with urban residence. In fact, there is a basis in sociological research, deriving primarily from qualitative studies, for maintaining that whites make this linkage. Specifically, in several ethnographic and community-based studies, whites express frustration and anger that the urban neighborhoods, communities, and cities in which they live "are being overrun" by Africans Americans (Anderson 1990; Dunier 1992). In addition, objective demographic and sociopolitical developments associated with well-documented dynamics of deindustrialization in recent decades (e.g., the growing preponderance and concentration of African Americans in cities coupled with the out-migration of whites from cities [Polen 2002; Teaford 1986]) are matched by subjective perceptions of whites who view cities as increasingly populated by minorities, including, most notably, African Americans.

Crime control

Social scientists have devoted more attention to documenting the role of prejudice in explaining perceptions related to crime control among whites than they have to either urban problems or drug addiction. Overall, this sociological research establishes a solid basis for positing that there should be a spillover of prejudicial attitudes into the spending issue. Most relevant is the study by Barkan and Cohn (2005), who use GSS data from 2000 to examine how racial prejudice affects whites' support for spending to address crime control. Their key finding is that more prejudiced whites support greater spending for crime control. However, their operationalization of prejudice is based on a single item, namely, whites' belief that African Americans are prone to violence.

Additional support for the notion that the prejudicial association between African Americans and crime should affect attitudes about spending comes from related lines of inquiry. In particular, whites' negative stereotyping of African Americans as prone to criminality and violence has been found to predict greater fear of criminal victimization by African American strangers than by white strangers (Dorfman and Schiraldi 2001; Barkan and Cohn 1998) and greater support for the more punitive treatment of criminals (Entman and Rojecki 2001; Johnson 2001, 2008). This is manifested, for example, in support for harsher criminal sentencing (Barkan and Cohn 1998), the death penalty (Soss, Langbein, and Metelko 2003; Aguirre and Baker 1993; Bobo and Johnson 2004), and the use of force by police (Barkan and Cohn 1998). Furthermore, two other lines of research document the "racial typification of crime" (Chiricos, Welsh, and Gertz 2004). Documenting the assimilation of media depictions of street criminals as African Americans into "real life," whites, when victimized, tend to believe it was at the hands of African Americans (Taylor and Covington 1993; St. John and Heald-Moore 1996) and adhere to the notion that one of the key background characteristics of criminals is their race—they tend to be black (St. John and Heald-Moore 1996; Gilliam and Iyengar 2000).

Drug addiction

The relatively small sociological literature on whites' prejudicial attitudes toward drug control issues offers a basis for theorizing that prejudice and attitudes relating to drug control are connected. First, survey-based findings indicate that whites view drug addiction at all class and occupation levels as involving a choice by individuals rather than as reflecting social structural factors (Beckett 1997). Second, several scholars have also noted the use of race as a key factor in drug-related media coverage at the national and local levels (Beckett 1997; Reinarman and Levine 1989; Reeves and Campbell 1994), and they and others speculate that drug abuse has become racialized in the public imagination (Beckett et al. 2005; Beckett and Sasson 2004; Reeves and Campbell 1994; Reinarman and Levine 1989).

Third, a handful of empirical examinations of stereotypes suggest their potentially important role with drug-related issues (see, however, Hurwitz and Peffley 1997). For example, Peffley, Hurwitz, and Sniderman (1997) found in their analyses of vignette data from the Race and Politics Survey that racial stereotypes in their modern incarnation—namely, that blacks have tendencies to be violent—predicted an increase in whites' belief that police searches of people walking near a known drug location were reasonable. Using GSS data, Timberlake, Rasinski, and Lock (2001) examined factors associated with attitudes toward drug-related spending. Their results revealed that net other predictors, whites opposed to "race targeting" (e.g., spending targeted toward blacks and the idea that the government is obligated to improve blacks' living standards) were less supportive of greater spending than those who were proponents of race targeting, although "traditional" prejudice (e.g., whites have the right to segregated neighborhoods and the idea that there should be laws prohibiting miscegenation) was not related to views about drug-related issues. Bobo and Johnson (2004) also examined the relationship between racial attitudes and drug-related views. Using data from a nationally representative sample, collected through an Internet-based survey, they examined whether respondents supported more severe sentencing for crack relative to powder cocaine. In some surveys, a "racial bias cue" was included to indicate that there are racial disparities in convictions for these drugs. Whites with less education and who harbored greater racial resentment, along with those who were not given the racial bias cue and did not believe the criminal justice system is biased against blacks, were more supportive of the differential sentencing.

Data and Measurement

To assess the color coding phenomenon, data from the GSS are used in this study. The GSS is a repeated cross-sectional survey that has been conducted annually or biannually since 1972. The GSS uses multistage area probability sampling, and the samples are nationally representative of the English-speaking U.S. adult population, ages 18 and older, living in noninstitutionalized settings (Davis, Smith, and Marsden 2007). Consistent with the theoretical aims of seeking to establish the range of social problems subject to color coding, we focus exclusively on the racial attitudes of whites in this study.

Core questions, such as those pertaining to demographics, are repeated in all surveys. However, due to random question rotations, not all items of interest appear on all GSS questionnaires during each survey year (Davis, Smith, and Marsden 2007). The measures of our key independent variables—racial attitudes—and our dependent variables were asked in 1996, 1998, 2000, and 2002; thus, those four waves of data are used. Missing data are also a consideration, especially for the family income measure. Overall, approximately 70 percent of eligible cases had complete data across all independent measures for each of the outcomes (ranging from 69.9 percent for welfare spending to 71.3 percent for urban spending). To address missing data, we used multiple imputation methods in Stata to impute missing data for the independent variables (Allison 2002; StataCorp 2005; Royston 2005).[1] However, the results were substantively similar to those obtained using listwise deletion of cases with missing data.[2]

Dependent variables

Five dependent variables are examined in this article. The three core variables (i.e., largely unexamined outcomes in prior research) relate to crime, urban problems, and drug addiction. Measurement of each of these outcomes is based on the following question: "We are faced with many problems in this country, none of which can be solved easily or inexpensively. I am going to name some of these problems, and for each one I would like you to tell me whether you think we are spending too much money on it, too little money, or about the right amount: 1) solving the problems of the big cities (urban spending); 2) halting the rising crime rate (crime spending); and 3) dealing with drug addiction (drug spending)."[3] For each of these items, "too little" money is coded as 1 and "too much" and "about right" are combined and coded as 0. Thus, higher values indicate greater support for social spending.

Two additional variables—support for policies targeting blacks and welfare—are analyzed as baseline measures (i.e., those that have been examined in prior research). One is explicitly race-based and the other has been demonstrated to be subject to the color coding phenomenon. Inclusion of these baseline measures thus provides a racialized reference point for contextualizing the impact of prejudice-induced color coding on the three core variables. These two baseline variables are measured in response to the question above and consist of (1) "improving the conditions of blacks" (race spending) and (2) "welfare" (welfare spending).

Independent variables

Several variables represent racial attitudes. The first, race push, is measured by responses to the question, "Here are some opinions other people have expressed in connection with (negro/black)-white relations. (Negroes/blacks/African Americans) should not push themselves where they are not wanted." Responses range from *agree strongly* (1) to *disagree strongly* (4); thus, higher values indicate the more liberal responses.

The second item, black stereotypes, is an additive index made up of hardworking and intelligence measures. The index is based on responses to the following: "I am going to show you a seven-point scale on which the characteristics of people in a group can be rated . . . if people in the group tend to be hardworking or lazy. Where would you rate [blacks] on this scale?" and "Do people in these groups tend to be unintelligent or tend to be intelligent? Where would you rate [blacks] in general on this scale?" For each item, responses range from 1 to 7, where 1 is *hardworking or intelligent* and 7 is *lazy or unintelligent*, with higher scores indicating more prejudiced views.

The third set of items assesses whether inequality between whites and blacks is attributed to individualistic and social structural factors. These are based on responses to the following: "On average (negroes/blacks/African Americans) have worse jobs, income, and housing than white people. Do you think these differences are . . . mainly due to discrimination? Because most (negroes/blacks/African Americans) have less in-born ability to learn? Because most (negroes/blacks/African Americans) do not have the chance for education that it takes to rise out of poverty? Because most (negroes/blacks/African Americans) just do not have the motivation or will power to pull themselves up out of poverty?" For these items, yes is coded 1 and no is coded 0. The number of yes responses to the first and third items (discrimination and educational opportunity) are summed to create the race differences–structural index (range 0–2), while the number of yes responses to the second and fourth items (inborn ability and motivation or willpower) are summed to create the race differences–individual factors index (range 0–2).[4]

Following past research, a number of sociodemographic control variables are also included in our analyses (see Barkan and Cohn 2005; Timberlake, Rasinski, and Lock 2001; Mears, Mancini, and Stewart 2009). Age is measured as a continuous variable. Gender is coded as male (1) and female (0). A continuous variable indicates the number of years of education completed. Total family income is continuous (based on 1986 U.S. dollars divided by 1,000). One dummy variable (yes = 1) for Republicans represents political party. Two dummy variables (yes = 1) represent residence in the South and urban areas (within a Standard Metropolitan Statistical Area and in a medium or large central city), respectively. To control for period effects we include three dummy variable for GSS years 1996, 1998, and 2000 (yes = 1); the year 2002 is the comparison category.

Analysis

We first present descriptive statistics and then consider the bivariate relationships between the racial prejudice variables and each of the outcome measures. Then, to examine whether prejudice and racial attitudes are related to the outcomes, net other predictors, multivariate logistic regression is utilized. For each dependent variable, both the racial attitudes and prejudice variables along with the control measures are included in the model. The results presented for all multivariate analyses are logistic regression coefficients and their accompanying standard errors. For all analyses, we checked for collinearity because of the possible overlap in the racial prejudice predictors. Across the analyses (based on varying sample sizes), the highest obtained Variance Inflation Factor (VIF) was 2.09, indicating no collinearity problems (Chatterjee and Price 1991).

Results

Table 1 reports descriptive statistics for all variables included in the analyses. These figures indicate that views about spending vary across social issues. While approximately 30 percent of respondents said too little is spent on improving the conditions of blacks, about 16 percent indicated that too little is spent on welfare. In contrast, about one-half (49 percent) indicated that too little is spent to

TABLE 1
Descriptive Statistics for Dependent Variables and for Independent Variables

Dependent Variables	% Too Little	% About Right/Too Much	N
Race spending	29.66	70.34	934
Welfare spending	15.66	84.34	1,009
Urban spending	48.96	51.04	917
Drug addiction spending	58.55	41.45	1,006
Crime spending	61.34	38.66	1,014

Independent Variables[a]	Mean	Standard Deviation
Racial attitudes variables		
Race push	2.722	1.070
Black stereotypes index	8.149	1.735
Race differences: individual	0.601	0.648
Race differences: structural	0.780	0.786
Sociodemographic controls		
Age	46.355	17.204
Male (yes = 1)	0.468	—
Republican (yes = 1)	0.419	—
Education	13.541	2.948
Income ($/1,000)	34.110	31.905
South (yes = 1)	0.330	—
Urban (yes = 1)	0.358	—
1996 (yes = 1)	0.180	—
1998 (yes = 1)	0.342	—
2000 (yes = 1)	0.314	—
2002 (yes = 1)[b]	0.165	—

a. Descriptive statistics for independent variables based on sample included in crime spending analyses ($n = 1,014$).
b. Comparison category for year variables.

solve the problems of big cities, and approximately six in ten respondents said too little is spent both on dealing with drug addiction (59 percent) and on halting the rising crime rate (61 percent). For the prejudice measures, the mean view about blacks "pushing themselves where they are not wanted" fell between "slightly agree" and "slightly disagree." The stereotypes index mean suggests respondents tend to view blacks as slightly more lazy than hardworking and as slightly less intelligent than intelligent. For the race differences indexes, on average respondents tended to agree with one of the two items composing both the individual factors and structural factors indexes.

Table 2 shows zero-order correlations between each of the racial attitude predictors and each of the spending outcomes, enabling initial consideration of the extent to which these social issues may be "color coded." All four of the predictors are, not surprisingly, significantly related to the explicitly racial item—spending to improve the conditions of blacks. All four of the predictors are also correlated with

TABLE 2
Zero-Order Correlations between Racial Prejudice Attitudes and Spending Outcomes

Racial Attitudes Variables	Race Spending	Welfare Spending	Urban Spending	Addiction Spending	Crime Spending
Race push	.177**	.123**	.067*	−.051	−.096**
Black stereotypes index	−.087**	−.073*	−.058	.017	−.008
Race differences: individual	−.203**	−.113**	−.059	.028	.084**
Race differences: structural	.392**	.193**	.090**	−.027	−.013
N	934	1,009	917	1,006	1,014

NOTE: Too little = 1; too much, about right = 0.
*p < .05. **p < .01.

spending on welfare, the ostensibly nonracial but established color coded outcome. These bivariate results indicate that those who disagree with the statement that blacks "should not push themselves where they are not wanted" are more likely to say that too little is spent to improve the conditions of blacks and on welfare. Respondents who view blacks as lazier and less intelligent are more likely to believe spending is adequate, as are those that attribute black-white inequality to individual characteristics. On the other hand, those who view such inequality as stemming from structural factors (discrimination and lack of educational opportunities) are more likely to believe that too little is spent to improve the conditions of blacks and on welfare. For the other three outcomes, the bivariate results are less consistent. Those who disagree with the statement that blacks "should not push themselves where they are not wanted" tend to believe that too little is spent on solving the problems of big cities, and they are less likely to believe that too little money is spent to halt the rising crime rate. Respondents who attribute black-white inequality to individual-level factors (lack of willpower and less inborn ability) are more likely to believe spending on crime is inadequate. Those who view inequality between blacks and whites as due to structural factors are more likely to believe that too little is spent on big cities. Spending to address addiction is not correlated with any of the prejudice variables.

The bivariate results thus indicate that, consistent with the color coding phenomenon, racial prejudice and prejudicial views are related to the social issues' spending measures (except for drug addiction). Whether such findings will persist in the face of controls for the other prejudice items and sociodemographic controls is assessed through the logistic regression analyses presented in Table 3.

As Table 3 shows, the prejudice variables are related to some, but not all, of the outcomes. In particular, net the other predictors in the analysis, those who attribute black-white inequality to individual-level factors are less likely to believe spending to improve the conditions of blacks is inadequate, while respondents

TABLE 3
Logistic Regression Results for Spending Outcomes

	Race Spending	Welfare Spending	Urban Spending	Addiction Spending	Crime Spending
Racial attitudes variables					
Race push	.185	.212*	.063	−.057	−.150*
	(.098)	(.105)	(.077)	(.074)	(.074)
Black stereotypes index	.009	−.039	−.038	.005	−.056
	(.052)	(.057)	(.043)	(.041)	(.042)
Race differences: individual	−.432**	−.206	−.025	−.012	.221
	(.152)	(.176)	(.126)	(.121)	(.128)
Race differences: structural	1.073**	.519**	.171	−.090	.064
	(.115)	(.127)	(.098)	(.092)	(.094)
Sociodemographic controls					
Age	−.007	−.001	−.008	.002	−.007
	(.005)	(.006)	(.004)	(.004)	(.004)
Male (yes =1)	.345*	.186	.042	.094	−.175
	(.173)	(.191)	(.143)	(.135)	(.138)
Republican (yes = 1)	−.709**	−.979**	−.583**	−.372**	−.247
	(.176)	(.212)	(.143)	(.136)	(.141)
Education	−.055	.008	.013	−.032	−.060*
	(.033)	(.038)	(.028)	(.028)	(.027)
Income ($/1,000)	−.002	−.008*	−.003	−.001	−.001
	(.003)	(.004)	(.002)	(.002)	(.003)
South (yes = 1)	.175	.017	−.088	−.286*	.043
	(.185)	(.209)	(.152)	(.143)	(.148)
Urban (yes = 1)	.250	.186	.121	.006	.229
	(.167)	(.188)	(.143)	(.137)	(.141)
Year 1996 (yes = 1)[a]	.036	−.532	1.010**	.084	.886**
	(.278)	(.327)	(.237)	(.220)	(.231)
Year 1998 (yes = 1)[a]	.248	−.096	.645**	.180	.520**
	(.245)	(.268)	(.208)	(.197)	(.197)
Year 2000 (yes = 1)[a]	.210	.046	.486*	.036	.287
	(.248)	(.269)	(.210)	(.199)	(.198)
Constant	−1.281	−1.891*	−0.085	1.066	1.988**
χ^2, df =14	196.814**	85.631**	57.647**	21.350	52.962**
N	934	1,009	917	1,006	1,014

NOTE: Too little = 1; too much, about right = 0. Coefficients with standard errors are in parentheses.
a. 2002 is the reference category.
*$p < .05$. **$p < .01$.

who attribute these differences to structural factors are more likely to believe that too little is spent. For welfare spending, those who disagree with the statement that blacks "should not push themselves where they are not wanted" are more likely to say too little is spent addressing this issue. In addition, those who attribute black-white inequality to structural factors are more likely to believe that welfare spending is inadequate. Those who disagree with the statement that blacks "should not push themselves where they are not wanted" are less likely to believe that spending on crime is inadequate. None of the racial prejudice variables are related to either spending to solve the problems of big cities or to spending to address drug addiction.

Of the sociodemographic variables, few are consistently associated with the spending items net the other predictors. One notable exception is political party affiliation; Republicans are less likely than non-Republicans to say that spending is inadequate for all outcomes except crime. Some differences in views are also evident across GSS years, with support for spending on urban areas and crime control appearing to decline over time.

Conclusion

This study advances our understanding of the parameters of whites' color coding of spending to address social issues in America. Findings indicate that the color coding phenomenon does not extend appreciably beyond welfare and race to the issues considered in this study, especially to support for urban spending and addiction spending. However, racial attitudes do impact one of the three core issues considered, support for increasing spending on crime-related issues, as whites believe that African Americans are "pushing themselves where they are not wanted" in American society. In accordance, emerging from these findings, color coding—at least in the context of spending support—operates along a continuum with the already-established welfare and race at one end (heavily influenced by prejudice), addiction spending and urban spending at the other end (apparently not influenced by prejudice net other predictors), and crime spending situated in the middle (moderately influenced by prejudice).

It is crucial to speculate about the factors driving this continuum. In this regard, we suspect that crime, similar to welfare and race, triggers prejudice because of powerful socialization agents, including racialized depictions of criminals (Gilliam and Iyengar 2000) as well as peer- and family-driven influences (Allport 1954; Bobo and Massagli 2001). Also, a factor unique to the domain of crime—its "daily relevance" or its perceived generalized or specific threat—may trigger a racialized interpretation (see Allport 1954). Urban issues, in contrast, may be too diffuse and too broad a construct to have been media packaged and, at a time when whites increasingly live outside urban areas, may not pose a perceived threat. Finally, drug addiction appears to be subject to an interpretation that is analogous to that of urban problems concerning, specifically, the influence of recent media depictions, and drug addiction may be too remote an issue for most whites to pose any kind of direct perceived threat.

It is also crucial to highlight additional dynamics between prejudice-induced color coding and spending support for social policies that emerge from the findings. First, color coding may influence spending attitudes in diametrically opposed ways across social policies. Specifically, color coding reduces support for welfare spending while increasing support for crime spending. Indeed, in accord with a distillation of recent social psychological research on stereotypes' fluid nature, stereotypes may be the basis of calls for proactive governmental intervention if, for example, there is a perception of a generalized or specific threat (e.g., crime victimization) as a result of those stereotypes. They may, alternatively, be a basis for reduction or cessation in government spending if, for example, minority groups are perceived as gaining an unfair or undeserved windfall in the distribution of socioeconomic resources (Allport 1954; Bobo and Massagli 2001). Second, in the context of spending support, attitudes appear to be driven more by traditional political philosophy or affiliation than by racial attitudes. Why this is the case remains unclear to us: we suspect that when the issue of spending is broached, it triggers attitudes associated with long-standing political affiliation.

It is premature to conclude that the scope of the color coding phenomenon is narrow along lines enunciated in this study. First, each of the core domains considered here—crime, urban problems, and drugs—needs to be explored in greater detail, focusing especially on their "constituent grounded issues" (Allport 1954) that encompass both spending and nonspending bases. For example, within the domain of crime, attitudes across a variety of issues, ranging from criminal sentencing, to the death penalty, to specific types of crime (e.g., drug dealing and white-collar offenses), need to be explored to more fully understand the range of racialization of crime. Furthermore, within the domain of urban problems, it is important to assess the impact of prejudice on, for example, tax incentives to induce businesses to relocate and to improve schools in urban areas. Second, it is necessary to explore domains that have already been explored (e.g., the labor market) that are fluid and generate new issues that may be affected by prejudice. Issues of job displacement, as well as the outsourcing of jobs and opportunities pursuant to the rapidly accelerating global economy, merit attention. Finally, it is important to examine a wider range of marginalized populations, including, for example, specific subgroups of the poor such as the homeless and the "new" working poor, immigrants, and other ethno-racial groups such as Latinos. Examinations of these populations will determine if color coding operates to differentiate the generic poor into more concrete referents that likely are related to varying levels of sympathy for their respective plights and whether ethnic coding also occurs. In short, when these recommendations for research are implemented, we will have a more solid basis for assessing the breadth of an attitudinal phenomenon— color coding—that, at least to a moderate extent, constitutes a subtle form of prejudice in contemporary American society.

Notes

1. The results presented were obtained using random draws from the posterior predictive distribution from regression models, and five data sets were imputed for each model. The five data sets were then combined and logistic regression parameter estimates were obtained (the Li-Raghunathan-Rubin robust estimate of the variance-covariance matrix of coefficients was used).

2. Results for this are not shown here but are available upon request.

3. Crime rates in the United States actually dropped during the period under examination (FBI 2002). Despite this, and similar to Barkan and Cohn (2005), we nonetheless examine this as a proxy for views toward crime and to assess whether crime is a color coded phenomenon.

4. The Cronbach's alpha for race differences–individual index was approximately .37 (ranging from .36 to .37 across the subsets of respondents) and was approximately .48 (ranging from .48 to .49) for the race differences–structural index. For black stereotypes, the alpha was approximately .42 (and ranged from .42 to .46 across the subsets of respondents). Because the reliability levels for the three indexes were lower than ideal, we also replaced the indexes in the analyses with the individual items composing them. The results with the individual items in place of the indexes produced very similar results to those shown. Results for individual items are available upon request.

References

Aguirre, Adalberto, and David Baker. 1993. Racial prejudice and the death penalty: A research note. *Social Justice* 20:150–55.

Allison, Paul D. 2002. *Missing data*. Thousand Oaks, CA: Sage.

Allport, Gordon. 1954. *The nature of prejudice*. New York, NY: Basic Books.

Anderson, Elijah. 1990. *Code of the streets*. Chicago, IL: University of Chicago Press.

Barkan, Steven, and Steven Cohn. 1998. Racial prejudice and support by whites for police use of force. *Justice Quarterly* 15:743–53.

Barkan, Steven, and Steven Cohn. 2005. Why whites favor spending more money to fight crime: The role of racial prejudice. *Social Problems* 52:300–14.

Beckett, Katherine. 1997. *Making crime pay: Law and order in contemporary American politics*. Oxford: Oxford University Press.

Beckett, Katherine, Kris Nyrop, Lori Pfingst, and Melissa Bowen. 2005. Drug use, drug possession arrests and the question of race: Lessons from Seattle. *Social Problems* 52 (3): 419–41.

Beckett, Katherine, and Theodore Sasson. 2004. *The politics of injustice: Crime and punishment in America*. 2nd ed. Thousand Oaks, CA: Sage.

Bobo, Lawrence. 1988. Race and beliefs about affirmative action. In *Racialized politics: The debate about racism in America*, eds. David Sears, James Sidanius, and Lawrence Bobo, 137–64. Chicago, IL: University of Chicago Press.

Bobo, Lawrence, and Devon Johnson. 2004. A taste for punishment: Black and white Americans' views on the death penalty and the war on drugs. *Du Bois Review* 1:151–80.

Bobo, Lawrence, and James Kluegel. 1993. Opposition to race-targeting: Self-interest, stratification ideology, or racial attitudes *American Sociological Review* 58:443–64.

Bobo, Lawrence, James Kluegel, and Ryan Smith. 1997. Laissez-faire racism: The crystallization of a kinder, gentler, anti-black ideology. In *Racial attitudes in the 1990s*, eds. Steven Tuch and Jack Martin, 15–44. Westport, CT: Praeger.

Bobo, Lawrence, and Michael Massagli. 2001. Stereotyping and urban inequality. In *Urban inequality: Evidence from four cities*, 89–162. New York, NY: Russell Sage Foundation.

Bobo, Lawrence, and Ryan Smith. 1994. Antipoverty policy, affirmative action, and racial attitudes. In *Confronting poverty: Prescriptions for change*, eds. Sheldon Danziger, Gary Sandefur, and Daniel Weinberg. Cambridge, MA: Harvard University Press.

Chatterjee, Samprit, and Bertram Price. 1991. *Regression analysis by example*. 2nd ed. New York, NY: John Wiley.

Chiricos, Ted, Kelly Welsh, and Marc Gertz. 2004. Racial typification of crime and support for punitive measures. *Criminology* 42:359–89.

Davis, James A., Tom W. Smith, and Peter V. Marsden. 2007. *General Social Surveys, 1972–2006*. Chicago, IL: National Opinion Research Center.

Dorfman, Lori, and Vincent Schiraldi. 2001. *Off balance: Youth, race, and crime in the news*. Washington, DC: Building Blocks for Youth.

Dovidio, John F. 2001. On the nature of contemporary prejudice: The third wave. *Journal of Social Issues* 57 (4): 829–49.

Dunier, Mitchell. 1992. *Slim's table*. Chicago, IL: University of Chicago Press.

Entman, Robert, and Andrew Rojecki. 2001. *The black image in the white mind*. Chicago, IL: University of Chicago Press.

FBI. 2002. *Crime in the U.S., 2001*. Washington, DC: Department of Justice.

Federico, Christopher. 2005. *The political psychology of race*. Chicago, IL: University of Chicago Press.

Gilens, Martin. 1996. Race coding and white opposition to welfare. *American Political Science Review* 90:593–604.

Gilens, Martin. 1999. *Why Americans hate welfare*. Chicago, IL: University of Chicago Press.

Gilliam, Franklin, and Snato Iyengar. 2000. Prime suspects: The influence of local television news on the viewing public. *American Journal of Political Science* 44:560–73.

Gilliam, Franklin, and Kenny Whitby. 1989. Race, class, and attitudes toward social welfare spending: An ethclass interpretation. *Social Science Quarterly* 70:88–100.

Hasenfeld, Yeheskel, and Jane Rafferty. 1989. The determinants of public attitudes toward the welfare state. *Social Forces* 67:1028–48.

Hughes, Michael, and Steven Tuch. 2000. How beliefs about poverty influence racial policy attitudes. In *Racialized politics: The debate about racism in America*, eds. David Sears, James Sidanius, and Lawrence Bobo, 165–90. Chicago, IL: University of Chicago Press.

Hurwitz, Jon, and Mark Peffley. 1997. Public perceptions of race and crime: The role of racial stereotypes. *American Journal of Political Science* 41:375–401.

Johnson, Devon. 2001. Punitive attitudes on crime: Economic insecurity, racial prejudice, or both? *Sociological Focus* 34:33–54.

Johnson, Devon. 2008. Racial prejudice, perceived injustice, and the black-white gap in punitive attitudes. *Journal of Criminal Justice* 36:198–206.

Kluegel, James, and Eliot Smith. 1983. Affirmative action attitudes: Effects of self-interest, racial affect, and stratification beliefs on whites' views. *Social Forces* 61:797–824.

Mears, Daniel P., Christina Mancini, and Eric A. Stewart. 2009. Whites' concern about crime: The effects of interracial contact. *Journal of Research in Crime and Delinquency* 46:524–52.

Newport, Frank. 2006. *Polling matters*. New York, NY: Gallup Polling Organization.

Peffley, Mark, and Jon Hurwitz. 2002. The racial components of "race-neutral" crime policy attitudes. *Political Psychology* 23:59–75.

Peffley, Mark, Jon Hurwitz, and Paul Sniderman. 1997. Racial stereotypes and whites' political views of blacks in the context of welfare and crime. *American Journal of Political Science* 41:30–60.

Pettigrew, Thomas. 1987. Shaping the organizational context for African American inclusion. *Journal of Social Issues* 43:41–78.

Polen, John. 2002. *The urban world*. New York, NY: McGraw-Hill.

Reeves, Jimmie, and Richard Campbell. 1994. *Cracked coverage: Television news, the anti-cocaine crusade, and the Reagan legacy*. Durham, NC: Duke University Press.

Reinarman, Craig, and Harry Levine. 1989. The crack attack: Politics and media in America's latest drug scare. In *Images of issues: Typifying contemporary social problems*, ed. Joel Best, 115–37. New York, NY: Aldine de Gruytor.

Royston, Patrick. 2005. Multiple imputation of missing values: Update. *Stata Journal* 5:188–201.

Schuman, Howard, Charlotte Steeh, and Lawrence Bobo. 1984. *Racial attitudes in America*. Cambridge, MA: Harvard University Press.

Sears, David, and Paul Henry. 2003. The origins of symbolic racism. *Journal of Personality and Social Psychology* 85:259–75.

Sears, David, James Sidanius, and Lawrence Bobo, eds. 2000. *Racialized politics: The debate about racism in America*. Chicago, IL: University of Chicago Press.

Shelton, Jason, and George Wilson. 2006. Race, socioeconomic standing and attitudes toward inequality. *Sociological Spectrum* 26:51–70.

Soss, Joe, Laura Langbein, and Alan Metelko. 2003. Why do white Americans support the death penalty? *Journal of Politics* 65:397–421.

StataCorp. 2005. Stata statistical software: Release 9.0. College Station, TX: StataCorp.

Steeh, Charlotte, and Maria Krysan. 1995. Trends: Affirmative action and the public, 1970–1995. *Public Opinion Quarterly* 60:128–58.

St. John, Craig, and Tamara Heald-Moore. 1996. Racial prejudice and fear of criminal victimization by strangers in public settings. *Sociological Inquiry* 66:267–84.

Taylor, Ralph, and Jeanette Covington. 1993. Community structural change and fear of crime. *Social Problems* 40:374–97.

Teaford, John. 1986. *The twentieth century American city*. Baltimore, MD: Johns Hopkins University Press.

Timberlake, Jeffrey M., Kenneth A. Rasinski, and Eric D. Lock. 2001. Effects of conservative sociopolitical attitudes on public support for drug rehabilitation spending. *Social Science Quarterly* 82:184–96.

Tuch, Steven, and Jack Martin. 1997. *Racial attitudes in the 1990s*. Westport, CT: Praeger.

Unnever, James D., and Francis T. Cullen. 2007. The racial divide in support for the death penalty: Does white racism matter? *Social Forces* 85:1281–1301.

Wilson, George. 1996. Toward a revised framework for analyzing beliefs about the causes of poverty. *Sociological Quarterly* 37:413–28.

Wilson, George. 2001. Support for redistributive policy among the African American middle class: Race and class effects. *Research in Social Stratification and Mobility* 18:97–118.

The Sweet Enchantment of Color-Blind Racism in Obamerica

By
EDUARDO BONILLA-SILVA
and
DAVID DIETRICH

It has become accepted dogma among whites in the United States that race is no longer a central factor determining the life chances of Americans. In this article, the authors counter this myth by describing how the ideology of color-blind racism works to defend and justify the contemporary racial order. The authors illustrate three basic frames of this ideology, namely, abstract liberalism, cultural racism, and minimization of racism. The authors then examine research that has empirically shown the effects of color-blind racism on whites' reactions to Hurricane Katrina, among whites who have adopted children of color, and in America's elite law schools. Finally, the authors examine how the election of Barack Obama is not an example of America becoming a "post-racial" country but reflects color-blind racism. The authors argue that the Obama phenomenon as a cultural symbol and his political stance and persona on race are compatible with color-blind racism. The authors conclude with the prognosis that, under the Obama administration, the tentacles of color-blind racism will reach even deeper into the crevices of the American polity.

Keywords: racism; color-blind racism; Obama; post-racial; ideology

To see what is in front of one's nose needs constant struggle.

—George Orwell, *In Front of Your Nose* (1946/1968)

Eduardo Bonilla-Silva is a professor of sociology at Duke. To date he has published four books, White Supremacy and Racism in the Post–Civil Rights Era, Racism without Racists, White Out *(with Woody Doane), and* White Logic, White Methods *(with Tukufu Zuberi). He is working on a book titled* The Invisible Weight of Whiteness: The Racial Grammar of Everyday Life in America. *He is the 2007 recipient of the Lewis A. Coser Award for theoretical agenda setting in sociology.*

David Dietrich is a PhD candidate in sociology at Duke University. His areas of interest are racial and ethnic relations, social movements, immigration, social stratification, sociological theory, and sociology of law. His recent research includes examinations of racism in the popular debate over illegal immigration, race in online virtual worlds, and an examination of anti–affirmative action protests on college campuses. His dissertation is titled "Rebellious Conservatives: A Study of Conservative Social Movements."

DOI: 10.1177/0002716210389702

ANNALS, *AAPSS*, 634, March 2011

Amythology that emerged in post–civil rights America has become accepted dogma among whites with the election of Barack Obama: the idea that race is no longer a central factor determining the life chances of Americans (D'Souza 1995).[1] Journalists (Dowd 2009; B. Shapiro 2009), political advisors (Ifill 2009), some people of color (W. Reed and Louis 2009), and most whites (CBS 2009) have deemed the election of our first black president proof positive that we have entered a "post-racial" era. However, whites and people of color remain mostly separate and disturbingly unequal (Daniels 2008; Sampson and Sharkey 2008; Massey 2007; Western 2006). Since whites believe race has "declined in significance" (Wilson 1978), they account for this seeming contradiction—America as post-racial yet minorities lagging well behind whites—as the result of the cultural deficiencies of people of color (Bobo and Charles 2009; Hunt 2007). Many conservative people of color (e.g., Steele 2006; Patterson 2004, 2006; McWhorter 2001) as well as many liberals such as comedian Bill Cosby (Cosby and Poussaint 2007) and actor Will Smith also embrace this view (W. Smith 2008).

In contrast, Bonilla-Silva (2001), among others (R. C. Smith 1995; Brooks 1996), argues that the existing racial inequality in the United States is the product of a new racial regime, which he has labeled the "new racism." We agree with Feagin (2006) that racial oppression is still systemic in America, affecting all people, networks, and institutions. However, the main racial practices of this regime are quite different from those typical of Jim Crow. Today, discrimination is mostly subtle, apparently nonracial, and institutionalized (see also R. C. Smith 1995). Not surprisingly, the ideological anchor of this new regime, which Bonilla-Silva has labeled "color-blind racism," is as slippery as the practices it supports (see Caditz 1976 for an early work that captured this ideological transition). Whereas Jim Crow racism explained minorities' social standing as the outcome of their imputed biological and moral inferiority, color-blind racism avoids such facile arguments. Instead, the ideology rationalizes the status of minorities as the product of market dynamics, naturally occurring phenomena, and their alleged cultural deficiencies (Berry and Bonilla-Silva 2008; Lipsitz 2006). Much as Jim Crow racism served as the glue for defending racial oppression in the past, color-blind racism provides the ideological armor for the "new racism" regime (Sullivan 2006).

Although survey research shows a decline in overt or Jim Crow–style prejudice among whites since the 1960s, there is broad consensus in the academic community that racial prejudice continues to plague America (Yancy 2008; Picca and Feagin 2007). Nevertheless, unlike the prejudice of yesteryear, it is expressed in covert, subtle, or symbolic fashion (Hill 2008; Myers 2005; Bush 2004). Various terms have been used to refer to this new kind of prejudice, such as "laissez-faire racism" (Bobo, Kluegel, and Smith 1997), "symbolic racism" (Tarman and Sears 2005), and "aversive racism" (Dovidio and Gaertner 2004). The concept of color-blind racism is related to these concepts but differs substantively and theoretically from them. Substantively, the examination of the ideology has uncovered the existence of frames, stylistic components, and racial stories that, given their reliance on surveys, most survey researchers have not addressed. Theoretically, color-blind racism is not regarded as "prejudice" grounded in individual-level or affective dispositions but rather as the collective expression of whites' racial dominance (Bonilla-Silva 1997). Thus, in our view, actors' attitudes are fundamentally connected to their location in the racial order (Prager 1982; Bonilla-Silva 2001), whether they are expressed with animosity or not. Our main concern is examining the various ways color-blind racism composes an ideology whites use to explain, rationalize, and defend their racial interests.

In this article, we first outline and illustrate the basic frames of color-blind racism. Second, we examine recent research that substantiates and expands knowledge about this racial ideology. Third, we argue that in many ways the Obama phenomenon reflects and enhances color-blind racism. We conclude with a discussion of the future implications of this ideology for the well-being of our nation.

The Ideology of Color-Blind Racism

In this section we discuss one of the three[2] component parts of color-blind racism: frames. We use systematic interview data to illustrate how the frames function to create apparently nonracial explanations of race events. The data come from two similarly structured projects. The first is the 1997 Survey of Social Attitudes of College Students, based on a convenience sample of 627 college students (including 451 white students) surveyed at a large midwestern university (MU henceforth), a large southern university, and a medium-size West Coast university. The second data source is the 1998 Detroit Area Study (DAS), a probabilistic survey of 323 white and 67 black Detroit metropolitan area residents.

Color-blind frames

The frames of any dominant racial ideology are set paths for interpreting information and operate as cognitive culs-de-sac because, after people invoke them, they explain racial phenomena in a predictable manner—as if they were getting on a one-way street without exits. Dominant racial frames are not "false consciousness" but rather unacknowledged, contextual standpoints that provide the intellectual (and moral) building blocks whites use to explain racial matters. The central frames of color-blind racism are abstract liberalism, cultural racism, minimization of racism, and naturalization; we illustrate the first three here (Bonilla-Silva 2006).

Abstract liberalism. This frame incorporates tenets associated with political and economic liberalism in an abstract and de-contextualized manner. By framing race-related issues in the language of liberalism, whites can appear "reasonable" and even "moral" while opposing all practical approaches to deal with de facto racial inequality. For instance, by using the tenets of the free market ideology in the abstract, they can oppose affirmative action as a violation of the norm of equal opportunity. The following example illustrates how whites use this frame. Jim, a 30-year-old computer software salesman from a privileged background, explained his opposition to affirmative action:

> I think it's unfair top to bottom on everybody and the whole process. Often, you know, discrimination itself is a bad word, right? But you discriminate every day. You wanna buy a beer at the store and there are six kinds [of] beers you can get from Natural Light to Sam Adams, right? And you look at the price and you look at the kind of beer, and you . . . *it's a choice*. . . . And it's the same thing about getting into school or getting into some place. . . . I don't think [MU] has a lot of racism in the admissions process. . . . So why not just pick people that are going to do well at [MU], pick people by their merit? I think we should stop the whole idea of choosing people based on their color.

Since Jim assumes that hiring decisions are like market choices (choosing between competing brands of beer), he embraces a laissez-faire position on hiring. The problem with Jim's view is that labor market discrimination is alive and well (Holtzer 2009), and most jobs are obtained through informal networks (Royster 2003). Jim's abstract position is further cushioned by his belief that although blacks "perceive or feel" that there is a lot of discrimination, he does not see much out there. Therefore, by upholding a strict laissez-faire view on hiring and, at the same time, ignoring the significant impact of discrimination in the labor market, Jim can safely voice his opposition to affirmative action in an apparently race-neutral way. This frame allows whites to be unconcerned about school and residential segregation, oppose almost any kind of government intervention to ameliorate the effects of past and contemporary discrimination, and prefer whites as partners/friends.

Cultural racism. Pierre Andre Taguieff (2001) has argued that modern racial ideology does not portray minorities as inferior biological beings. Instead, it biologizes their presumed cultural practices (i.e., presents them as fixed features) and uses that as the rationale for justifying racial inequality. The newness of this frame resides in the centrality it has acquired in whites' contemporary justifications of minorities' standing. The essence of the frame, as William Ryan (1976) pointed out a long time ago, is "blaming the victim"—arguing that minorities' standing is the product of their lack of effort, loose family organization, and inappropriate values. An example of how whites use this frame comes from Kim, a student at MU. In response to the question, "Many whites explain the status of blacks in this country as a result of blacks lacking motivation, not having the proper work ethic, or being lazy. . . . What do you think?" Kim said,

> Yeah, I totally agree with that. I don't think, you know, they're all like that, but, I mean, it's just that if it wasn't that way, why would there be so many blacks living in the projects? . . . If they worked hard, they could make it just as high as anyone else could. You know, I just think that's just, you know, they're raised that way and they see that their parents are so they assume that's the way it should be.

Although not all whites were as crude as this student, most subscribed to this belief either by overt racist comments or in a so-called "compassionate conservative" manner.

Minimization of racism. Whites do not believe that minorities' social standing today is the product of discrimination. Instead, they believe it is due to "their culture," "class," "legacies from slavery," "the culture of segregation," "lack of social capital," "poverty," and so forth. In other words, it is anything but racism. Sandra, a retail saleswoman in her early 40s, provides an example of how whites use this frame when she explained her view on discrimination:

> I think if you are looking for discrimination, I think it's there to be *found*. But if you make the best of any situation, and if *you don't use it as an excuse*. I think sometimes it's an excuse because people felt they deserved a job, whatever! I think if things didn't go their way I know a lot of people have a tendency to use prejudice or racism as whatever, as an *excuse*. I think in some ways, *yes*, there is [*sic*] people who are prejudiced. It's not only blacks, it's about Spanish, or women. In a lot of ways there [is] a lot of *reverse* discrimination. It's just what you wanna make of it.

Since most whites, such as Sandra, believe discrimination has all but disappeared, they regard minorities' claims of discrimination as excuses or as minorities playing the infamous "race card."

Research on Color-Blind Racism

Current research substantiates Bonilla-Silva's claims (2003, 2006) about color-blind racism's centrality to racial stratification in the United States. It demonstrates its broad impact in the population as well as in institutions. In this section, we discuss efforts to quantify color-blind racism, examine color-blind racism among individuals and institutions, and change color-blind racist attitudes.

Quantitative measures of color-blind racism

In addition to qualitative studies, recent research on color-blind racism has employed quantitative measures. These range from simple questions about beliefs in equal opportunity to a multidimensional scale, the Color-Blind Racial Attitudes Scale (CoBRAS), which Neville et al. (2000) developed. Using more than eleven hundred observations in five studies, Neville et al. (2000) identified several major cognitive dimensions of color-blind racism, including denial of white privilege, lack of awareness of the implications of institutional racism, rejection of social policies such as affirmative action, and denial of pervasive racial discrimination in the United States. Neville et al. (2000) also distinguished color-blind racism, a distorted view of race relations, from racial prejudice, negative stereotypes of racial minorities. Although conceptually different, the CoBRAS measure of color-blind racism was positively correlated with many measures of racial prejudice. Other studies have found that the CoBRAS measure of color-blind racism was positively correlated with white fear of other races (Spanierman and Heppner 2004).

Individual-level analyses

Evidence of color-blind racism was found in several sociological analyses of individuals' reactions to the Hurricane Katrina disaster. Sweeney (2006) studied responses to an article in the *Atlanta Journal-Constitution* that expressed black rapper Kanye West's contention that the media coverage of New Orleans after Katrina was racially biased. Sweeney found that most of the comments blamed the disproportionately black hurricane victims for making the "choice" not to heed warnings and leave the city. Many also blamed the victims as "whiners" who expected government handouts instead of helping themselves. Their answers implied that racism was not an issue. Another study analyzed the attitudes of Houstonians to the influx of black evacuees following Katrina. Using data from the 2006 and 2008 Houston Area Surveys, Shelton and Coleman (2009) found that antagonistic attitudes toward black Katrina migrants to Houston were greater among respondents who professed a belief that America had attained "equal opportunity for all" and adhered to individualistic explanations for existing racial inequalities, both central to the abstract liberal frame of color-blind racism.

Research also suggests that color-blind racism is evident even among whites most likely to have transcended race: white parents who have adopted children of color. This is the major finding of Carla Goar (2009) in her study of parents in interracial adoptive families who participated in three "adoption camps." The purpose of the camps was to provide support for the interracial families and to "celebrate race" to positively influence the racial identity of the children. Goar found, however, that many of the adoptive parents evinced a color-blind ideology by de-emphasizing the importance of race and emphasizing instead their unique individual characteristics ("We are special parents") and those of their children and minimizing the challenges of raising children of different races in a racially stratified country.

Other work also suggests that the ideology of color-blindness is increasingly affecting even those who are at or near the bottom of the economic and social hierarchies in the United States: blacks and Latinos.[3] Using data from a telephone survey of 1,005 respondents, Public Opinion on the Courts in the United States, 2000, Kalscheur (2009) studied differences between whites, blacks, and Latinos in their assessments of equal opportunity in the United States and perceptions of equality in the U.S. justice system. Kalscheur found that Latinos were as likely as non-Hispanic whites to profess a color-blind view, regardless of social class and gender. More than three-fourths of Latinos in the survey agreed with the statement that the United States provides equal opportunity to blacks. This evidence lends credence to the notion that Latinos have adopted anti-black beliefs to distance themselves from blacks in the U.S. racial hierarchy (McClain et al. 2006). What is more, more than three-fourths of Latinos in the survey also agreed that Latinos had equal opportunity to get ahead in life. This may reflect Twine and Gallagher's (2008) contention that many Latinos identify as "white" as well as Bonilla-Silva's (2004) claim about some Latinos becoming white and others "honorary whites."

Other research reveals that many blacks subscribe to color-blind racism, although fewer blacks than whites endorse its major frames (Kalscheur 2009). Neville et al. (2005) studied 211 self-identified black American college students in the Midwest and West Coast. The black students who exhibited color-blind attitudes were more likely to blame blacks for racial inequalities, believe in a hierarchical system of inferior and superior social groups, have internalized racial stereotypes about blacks, and prefer to associate with white rather than black friends. This evidence substantiates Bonilla-Silva's (2006, 2009) suggestions that the elite segments of the black community are more likely to subscribe to color-blind racism and exhibit anti-black views. Neville et al. (2005) contend that these color-blind racist perspectives of blacks represent a "false consciousness" that contributes to their own oppression by preventing them from supporting structural change.

Institutional analyses

Other research shows increasing evidence that color-blind racism permeates American social institutions. Below we describe studies that highlight this development in two arenas: professional education and sports.

Educational institutions have significant power to maintain racial hierarchies by limiting individual social mobility. Akom (2004) documents color-blind racism in the educational system of one of America's most politically liberal communities, Berkeley, California. Akom argues that the students of Berkeley High School are conspicuously racially stratified and attributes this racial inequality to abstract liberalism, particularly the prevailing ideology of meritocracy, which assigns pejorative stereotypes to black and Latino students, blaming these students for their own failures. This appears to create a self-fulfilling prophecy whereby the students conform to a spoiled or stigmatized identity (Goffman 1963; Lewis 2003).

In addition to limiting social mobility, color-blind racism in higher education, especially professional schools, influences the attitudes and, hence, the services provided by the professionals who graduate from these schools. Wendy Moore (2008) demonstrates this phenomenon in her study of color-blind racism at two elite American law schools. In these law schools, the frame of abstract liberalism—ignoring America's racial history and contemporary discrimination—dominated the discourse, including law school curricula, professorial and textbook interpretations of the law, and advocacy of race-blind admissions. Consistent with color-blind racism, white students used a narrative of cultural deficiency when referring to students of color and attributed their imagined underperformance (they speculate on this without data) to a pathological background. School administrators also minimized incidents of explicit racism. Furthermore, professors used sarcastic humor when addressing race matters, thereby diminishing the seriousness of the subject and the potential empathy of white students. This evidence of color-blind racism has disturbing implications given that elite American law schools are the wellspring of our federal judiciary (Schleef 2006).

Color-blind racism also operates in another of America's most powerful institutions: sports. Upon superficial examination, sports would seem to be the most racially inclusive arena of American society. White fans have embraced black athletes as celebrities, wearing their sports jerseys and purchasing their sports memorabilia. On the surface, this hero worship would seem to suggest a breakdown of racial prejudice. However, close inspection of the celebrity-media-audience dynamic reveals the undeniable, covert presence of racism behind these seemingly benign behaviors. For example, whites attribute the outstanding athletic performance of black athletes to their "superior" natural physical skills (Rada and Wulfemeyer 2005). While whites may consider this as evidence of their own race neutrality, this stand renders invisible the actual work of black athletes and contrasts with the attributions of mental acumen, leadership ability, moral character, and hard work they attribute to white athletes (Coakley 2006; Collins 2005). Buffington and Fraley (2008) found evidence of this brawn-versus-brain racial dichotomy in their study of media coverage and college students' racial attributions to participants in the 2000 NCAA men's basketball championships. The researchers found that physical skills were much more likely to be assigned to blacks than to whites. Even though blacks were also more likely to be mentioned as leaders, interestingly, their leadership skills were attributed to their superior physical skills, not intelligence or leadership skills per se. These findings fit quite well with the naturalization frame of color-blind racism (see Bonilla-Silva [2006] for a full discussion of the naturalization frame).

Implications for change

What can change racial attitudes in this age of new racism? Richeson and Nussbaum (2003) explored whether color-blind (ignoring race and ethnic differences) or multicultural (celebrating racial and ethnic differences) ideologies were more likely to change pro-white bias. In a controlled experimental design, fifty-two white undergraduates at Dartmouth were exposed to messages advocating color-blind or multicultural ideological approaches to reducing interethnic tensions. The researchers employed as their dependent variable the IAT assessment of automatic racial attitudes (see Greenwald et al. [1998] for more information regarding the IAT assessment). Richeson and Nussbaum found that pro-white bias was greater for participants exposed to color-blind ideology than for those exposed to multicultural ideology.

McClelland and Linnander (2006) used longitudinal data to assess the role of contact and information in producing change in color-blind racism. Survey data were collected in five waves from 1990 to 2002 for a panel of white students from two small, private, predominantly liberal arts colleges on the East Coast. The researchers found both contact and exposure to information about race to predict reappraisals of the discrimination that blacks face and the values of affirmative action. White students who had black friends on campus, attended extracurricular race-related programming, took courses in Africana studies, and engaged in informal discussions in racially diverse groups were more likely to reappraise their notions of color-blindness. They also found that parental education was positively related to reappraisals of racial group structures. McClelland and Linnander speculate that the privileged class positions of these students obviated any threat they might have otherwise felt from the potential "redistributive" effects of affirmative action. Many of these findings fit quite well with Bonilla-Silva's characterizations of "racial progressives" (see 2006, 131–49).

The work on color-blind racism taken together reveals how pervasive this ideology has become in America. But how can color-blind racism be central in a nation that just elected a black man as its president?

Color-Blind Racism and Obamerica

There are two central ways in which the election of Barack Obama as president relates to color-blind racism. First, Obama has become a cultural symbol compatible with color-blind racism. Second, Obama's own political stand on race and the way he has positioned himself are in line with color-blind racism.

Obama's color-blind success

The secret to Obama's rise to the nation's highest office lies in his symbolic appeal to both racial minorities and whites. Symbols are, in the words of Geertz (1973, 45), "sources of illumination" that orient people to their cultural systems of meanings. Hence, as Geertz (1973) and Turner (1967) have demonstrated, cultural symbols can have immense power to instigate and guide action. But as Turner (1974) points out, cultural symbols can be "multivocal" and thus interpreted quite differently by different people. Obama reveals his awareness of his multivocal appeal in *The Audacity of Hope* (2006, 11): "I am new enough on the national political scene that I serve as a blank screen on which people of vastly different political stripes project their own views."

Obama has become a symbol with especially different meanings for people of color and whites. For non-whites, Obama became a symbol of their possibilities in what they hoped would become a more egalitarian America (Hunt and Wilson 2009). For blacks, the possibility of having a black president became a symbol of their historical aspirations as a people, of "a dream deferred, now realized" (Howell 2008, 187). For older generations of blacks desperate to see racial equality before they die, and for many post–Reagan generation blacks and minorities who have seen very little racial progress in their lifetimes, Obama became the new messiah of the civil rights movement (Bonilla-Silva and Ray 2009). In contrast, the symbolic meaning of Obama to whites was compatible with their belief that America was indeed a color-blind nation. Obama quickly became for whites an Oprah- or Tiger Woods–like figure, a black person who has "transcended" his blackness to become a national hero. Thus, for whites and other supporters around the globe, Obama also represented "possibilities," the American promise of the Horatio Alger myth that "no matter how humble the beginnings, or how tattered the overcoat, once washed up on America's shores anyone can attain anything" (Howell 2008, 187).

Obama, the consummate politician, fostered these multivocal interpretations with his "own American story":

> I am the son of a black man from Kenya and a white woman from Kansas. . . . I am married to a black American who carries within her the blood of slaves and slave owners—an inheritance we pass on to our two precious daughters. I have brothers, sisters, nieces, nephews, uncles and cousins, of every race and every hue, scattered across three continents, and for as long as I live, I will never forget that in no other country on Earth is my story even possible. (Obama 2008b)

Similarly, he said in his election-night victory speech,

> If there is anyone out there who still doubts that America is a place where all things are possible, who still wonders if the dream of our founders is alive in our time, who still questions the power of our democracy, tonight is your answer. (Obama 2008a)

Obama's popularity also lies in his adoption of a post-racial (racially transcendent) persona and politics (Kamiya 2009; see Bonilla-Silva forthcoming). He has distanced himself from most leaders of the civil rights movement, from his reverend, from his church, and from anything or anyone who made him look "too black" or "too political." Obama's campaign even retooled Michelle Obama to make her seem less black, less strong, and more white-lady-like for the white electorate. For his white supporters, Obama was the first "black" leader they felt comfortable supporting because he did not talk about racism; because he kept reminding them he is half-white; because he was so "articulate" or—in Senator Biden's words, later echoed by Karl Rove—Obama was "the first mainstream African American who is articulate and bright and clean and a nice-looking guy" (CNN 2007). Furthermore, unlike black leaders such as Jesse Jackson and Al Sharpton, he did not make them feel guilty about the state of racial affairs in the country. Instead, Obama preached unity. As he said in the speech that catapulted him into the national spotlight, his keynote address to the Democratic National Convention in 2004, "There's not a black America and white America and Latino America and Asian America; there's the United States of America" (Obama 2004).

Finally, and most important, having a black man "in charge" symbolizes to both blacks and whites monumental change. For blacks, the symbolism of a black man's election has generated unprecedented optimism about the future of race relations in the United States. In a Pew survey shortly after the election, 75 percent of blacks expressed the belief that Obama's election would make race relations in the United States better (Pew 2008). And a more recent CBS/*New York Times* poll found, for the first time in CBS polling history, that the majority of blacks (59 percent) and 65 percent of whites characterized the relationship between blacks and whites in the United States as "good" (CBS 2009). Nevertheless, evidence of racial prejudice in preelection and postelection surveys (Associated Press 2008; Campus Compare 2008) reveals that Obama's appeal to whites is not indicative of post-racialism. Noted survey researchers Tom Pettigrew (2009) and Vincent

Hutchings (2009) found that Obama's white voters were just slightly less prejudiced than McCain's white voters. The problem is that with the misconstrued symbolism of Obama's election, racism recedes even deeper beneath our individual as well as national consciousness. After all, now many whites can state proudly, "I voted for Obama, so I cannot be racist."

Obama's color-blind racist ideology

On March 4, 2007, at a commemoration of the Selma Voting Rights March, then-senator and presidential candidate Barack Obama (2007) likened the civil rights marchers to Moses, who challenged the "powers who said that some are atop and others are at the bottom." He credited this "Moses generation" with taking us "90 percent of the way" to equality. Acknowledging a still-existing "health care gap," "achievement gap" in the face of unequal school resources, "empathy gap" as reflected by the government's lack of response to New Orleans after Katrina, and "hope gap" as reflected in disproportionately black low-wage jobs, he challenged the present "Joshua generation" to take us the remaining 10 percent of the way. Said Obama, "Take off your bedroom slippers. Put on your marching shoes. Go do some politics. Change this country." But Obama was not calling for the Joshua generation to socially protest for their rights. Rather, he beseeched them to elect a responsible government and, in the same breath, "to ask what we can do for ourselves." "The civil rights movement wasn't just a fight against the oppressor; it was also a fight against the oppressor in each of us."

Obama's Selma speech was spiced with color-blind racist ideology, and this color-blind spiciness becomes more apparent when Obama addresses wider (and whiter) audiences. Obama minimized contemporary racism in his tribute to the sacrifices of Selma's civil rights marchers. The depth of racial inequalities of health, achievement, and justice in this country clearly indicates that we have much further to go than 10 percent. In addition, Obama framed the problems of the black poor in the speech as cultural pathology—"black blame" (Price 2009).

These frames of color-blind racism were also evident in Obama's (2006) book *The Audacity of Hope.* He claimed that although race still matters, "prejudice" is declining. As proof he heralded the growth of the black elite whose members do not "use race as a crutch or point to discrimination as an excuse for failure" (p. 241). He explicitly blamed poor blacks for their own failures, stating that they watch "too much television," consume "too much . . . poisons," lack an "emphasis on educational achievement," and do not have two-parent households (pp. 244–45). He chastised those unwilling to acknowledge how their "values" contributed to their predicament (p. 254). And his structural solution to racial inequalities was an "emphasis on universal, as opposed to race-specific, programs," which he stated "isn't just good policy; it's also good politics" (p. 247).[4]

Obama's color-blind racist ideology was also evident in his so-called "race speech" in March 2008 to quiet the uproar over his association with the Reverend Jeremiah Wright. Obama characterized Wright as divisive and condemned his perspective as "a profoundly distorted view of this country—a view that sees white racism as endemic" (Obama 2008b). Obama admitted that race was still an issue that the "nation cannot afford to ignore" and acknowledged America's segregated schools, legalized discrimination, lack of economic opportunity, and the anger these issues foster in the black community. However, he implied that racism is a two-way street in his conciliatory reference to a similar anger among working- and middle-class white Americans who "don't feel they have been particularly privileged by their race. . . . So when they are told to bus their children to a school across town, when they hear that an African American is getting an advantage in landing a good job or a spot in a good college because of an injustice that they themselves never committed . . . resentment builds up over time." Therefore, Obama eschewed the need for structural solutions to racial problems. Instead, he proposed an abstract liberal resolution to racial inequality: "to bind our particular grievances—for better health care, and better schools, and better jobs—to the larger aspirations of all Americans—the white woman struggling to break the glass ceiling, the white man who's been laid off, the immigrant trying to feed his family." He also challenged blacks to step up morally: "It means taking responsibility for our own lives by demanding more from our fathers and spending more time with our children."

When pressed more specifically about affirmative action as a solution to current racial inequality and the effects of discrimination, Obama hinted at a class-based rather than racially based program. In an April 2008 interview with ABC's George Stephanopoulos, he stated,

> I still believe in affirmative action as a means of overcoming both historic and potentially current discrimination, but I think that it can't be a quota system and it can't be something that is simply applied without looking at the whole person, whether that person is black, or white, or Hispanic, male or female. What we want to do is make sure that people who've been locked out of opportunity are going to be able to walk through those doors of opportunity in the future. (Quoted in Canellos 2008)

Obama's minimization of racism and his refusal to tackle solutions to racial inequalities carried over into his presidential press conferences. For example, in Obama's one-hundred-days press conference, Andre Showell, a black journalist, asked what specific policies Obama had enacted to benefit specifically minority communities. Obama answered,

> Well, keep in mind that every step we're taking is designed to help all people. But folks who are most vulnerable are most likely to be helped because they need the most help. . . . So my general approach is that if the economy is strong, that will lift all boats as long as it is also supported by, for example, strategies around college affordability and job training, tax cuts for working families as opposed to the wealthiest that level the playing field and ensure bottom-up economic growth. And I'm confident that that will help the African American community live out the American dream at the same time that it's helping communities all across the country. (Quoted in *Huffington Post* 2009b)

Obama even projected the minimization of racism onto the global stage when he decided not to attend the 2009 UN-sponsored World Conference on Racism in Geneva. Obama's reasons for not attending were quite similar to those of his predecessor—he did not want to contend with the dicey issue of reparations for racial injustice or attendees who would accuse Israel of being a racist state (*Huffington Post* 2009a). He also used the cultural racism frame in his second trip to Africa (specifically, in his visit to Ghana), where he focused on issues of local governance rather than the negative effects of Western imperialism in the region (Karenga 2009).

Conclusion: Prognosis for Obamerica

Although Jim Crow is all but dead and most Americans vociferously denounce overt acts of racism, people of color remain economically and socially disadvantaged compared with whites (Pager and Shepherd 2008; Oliver and Shapiro 2006; Shapiro 2004). Whites have explained this inequality over the past 30 years by resorting to color-blind racism. This ideology, we argue, is central to understanding the Obama phenomenon. It was the cornerstone of the 43 percent white support he received in the election (Noah 2008) and of how whites explained their support for *this* black politician. What is more significant, color-blind racism is in many ways central to Obama's stand on race, his post-racial politics, and his own persona. Accordingly, the blessing of having a black president may become a curse as he can legitimate whites' color-blind views. The American public has interpreted Barack Obama's election as president as all but the fulfillment of Martin Luther King Jr.'s dream. But for whites, Obama's blackness is more about style than political substance (Wise 2009); "Obama is the 'cool' exceptional black man not likely to rock the American racial boat" (Bonilla-Silva 2009, 1076). He advocates "universal" (class-based) policies in lieu of race-based social policy—a policy stand that will not sufficiently ameliorate racial inequality. He talks about inequality and discrimination but always mentions the need for blacks to be personally accountable. Consequently, Obama's blackness is becoming whites' new weapon of choice for singing their color-blind lullaby.

Since whites have the upper hand discursively, the space for challenging racial inequality may be reduced and even diluted. By de-racializing his presidency and sponsoring color-blindness, Obama has maneuvered himself into this narrow "white space" (Street 2009, 120). Even as he has strategically claimed a black insider standing (to attract the black electorate), he has simultaneously distanced himself from the black community by interjecting the cultural frame of blaming poor blacks for their own problems (A. Reed 2008). Blacks are reluctant to challenge Obama's repudiation of race-based policies out of their strong desire to protect his image and "preserve the historic moment" (Price 2009, 178). And the few blacks who have criticized Obama's race-neutral policies have incited outrage among other blacks (Holmes 2008). Hence, the unity message of Obama (and white America) goes unchallenged (R. M. Smith and King 2009), and we all, like Pangloss, believe we live in the "best of all possible worlds" (Voltaire 1759/1929).

One clear indication of how the space for talking about race has been diminished is the recent national controversy over the arrest of Harvard professor Henry Louis Gates. After President Obama made a seemingly "racial" (that is, supportive of blacks' narrative on this event) comment in a press conference where he said the Cambridge police department "acted stupidly" (ABC News 2009), he was condemned by friends and foes (Political Bulletin 2009; Inside Cover 2009). This forced Obama to recant, claiming that all parties misread and overreacted to the situation (Baker and Cooper 2009). But this was not enough, and he was forced to, in the interest of "unity," invite all parties to the White House for a "beer summit" to temper the political fallout from his comment (Associated Press 2009). Obama's resolution to this incident of racial profiling reinforces whites' views on racism: that it is no longer central; that most racial incidents are misunderstandings with "two sides"; and that if we talk things out, we can settle matters and create "racial harmony."

Therefore, our prognosis is that, under the Obama administration, the tentacles of color-blind racism will reach deeper into all the crevices of the American polity. Unless people of color awake from the nationalist moment engendered by the election of a black man as president (Bonilla-Silva forthcoming) and return to militant social movements to advance racial justice in this country (Jeffries 2009), the color-blind racist drama will monopolize America. If this happens, Obama's naive belief in a "United" States of America will simply reinforce the racial order of white privilege. In the words of William Faulkner (misquoted by Obama in his speech "A More Perfect Union," 2008b), "The past is never dead. In fact, it isn't even past" (Faulkner 1951).

Notes

1. Bonilla-Silva has used the term "Obamerica" to capture the fact that Obama was elected president without the backing of a social movement. This, he has argued, severely limits the possibility for meaningful change during his presidency.

2. Besides frames, the ideology includes styles and racial stories. Because of space limitations we do not discuss the latter two here. Interested readers should see Bonilla-Silva (2006).

3. This evidence confirms Bonilla-Silva's claim that, as color-blind racism becomes cemented as the dominant ideology, it dictates the terrain of ideological contestation for all Americans. See Chapters 7 and 8 in Bonilla-Silva (2006).

4. This "cultural racism" was part of his campaign's appeal to whites. He used it in his criticism of black fathers and in his relentless insistence on "personal responsibility." Most recently, he used the frame again in his speech commemorating the 100th anniversary of the NAACP.

References

ABC News. 22 July 2009. Obama: Police acted "stupidly" in Gates case. Available from abcnews.go.com.

Akom, Antwi. 2004. Ameritocracy. PhD diss., University of Pennsylvania, Philadelphia.

Associated Press. 2008. Election 2008 political pulse. Available from news.yahoo.com.

Associated Press. 29 July 2009. Obama's "beer summit" with policeman, professor. Available from www.nytimes.com.

Baker, Peter, and Helene Cooper. 24 July 2009. Obama shifts tone on Gates after mulling debate. *New York Times*. Available from www.nytimes.com.

Berry, Brent, and Eduardo Bonilla-Silva. 2008. They should hire the one with the best score. *Ethnic and Racial Studies* 31:215–42.

Bobo, Lawrence D., and Camille Z. Charles. 2009. Race in the American mind. *The Annals of the American Academy of Political and Social Science* 621:243–59.

Bobo, Lawrence D., James R. Kluegel, and Ryan A. Smith. 1997. Laissez-faire racism. In *Racial attitudes in the 1990s*, eds. Steven Tuch and Jack K. Martin, 15–42. Westport, CT: Praeger.

Bonilla-Silva, Eduardo. 1997. Rethinking racism: Toward a structural interpretation. *American Sociological Review* 62:465–80.

Bonilla-Silva, Eduardo. 2001. *White supremacy and racism in the post–civil rights era*. Boulder, CO: Lynne Rienner.

Bonilla-Silva, Eduardo. 2003. *Racism without racists*. Lanham, MD: Rowman & Littlefield.

Bonilla-Silva, Eduardo. 2004. From bi-racial to tri-racial. *Ethnic and Racial Studies* 27:931–50.

Bonilla-Silva, Eduardo. 2006. *Racism without racists*. 2nd ed. Lanham, MD: Rowman & Littlefield.

Bonilla-Silva, Eduardo. 2009. Are the Americas "sick with racism" or is it a problem at the poles? *Ethnic and Racial Studies* 32:1071–82.

Bonilla-Silva, Eduardo. Forthcoming. *Racism without racists*. 3rd ed. Lanham, MD: Rowman & Littlefield.

Bonilla-Silva, Eduardo, and Victor Ray. 2009. When whites love a black leader. *Journal of African American Studies* 13:176–83.

Brooks, Roy. 1996. *Integration or separation?* Cambridge, MA: Harvard University Press.

Buffington, Daniel, and Todd Fraley. 2008. Skill in black and white. *Journal of Communication Inquiry* 32:292–310.

Bush, Melanie E. L. 2004. *Breaking the code of good intentions*. Lanham, MD: Rowman & Littlefield.

Caditz, Judith. 1976. *White liberals in transition*. New York, NY: Spectrum.

Campus Compare. 2008. Survey says . . . whites and non-whites unified on the prevalence of prejudice on U.S. campuses. Available at www.campuscompare.com.

Canellos, Peter. 29 April 2008. On affirmative action, Obama intriguing but vague. Available from www.boston.com.

CBS. 27 April 2009. Poll: Blacks see improved race relations. Available from www.cbsnews.com.

CNN News Bureau. 9 February 2007. Biden's description of Obama draws scrutiny. Available from www.cnn.com.

Coakley, Jay. 2006. *Sports in society*. New York, NY: McGraw-Hill.

Collins, Patricia Hill. 2005. *Black sexual politics*. New York, NY: Routledge.

Cosby, Bill, and Alvin F. Poussaint. 2007. *Come on, people*. Nashville, TN: Thomas Nelson.

Daniels, Lee A. 2008. *Last chance*. New York, NY: Public Affairs.

Dovidio, John F., and Samuel L. Gaertner. 2004. Aversive racism. *Advances in Experimental Social Psychology* 36:1–51.

Dowd, Maureen. 22 February 2009. Dark, dark, dark. *New York Times*.

D'Souza, Dinesh. 1995. *The end of racism*. New York, NY: Free Press.

Faulkner, William. 1951. *Requiem for a nun*. New York, NY: Garland.

Feagin, Joe R. 2006. *Systemic racism*. New York, NY: Routledge.

Geertz, Clifford. 1973. *The interpretation of cultures*. New York, NY: Basic Books.

Goar, Carla. 2009. Race camps. Paper presented at the Spring Colloquium, University of North Carolina-Charlotte.

Goffman, Erving. 1963. *Stigma*. Upper Saddle River, NJ: Prentice Hall.

Greenwald, Anthony G., Debbie E. McGhee, Jordan Schwartz, and L. K. Pages. 1998. Measuring individual differences in implicit cognition. *Journal of Personality and Social Psychology* 74:1464–80.

Hill, Jane H. 2008. *The everyday language of white racism*. Hoboken, NJ: Wiley-Blackwell.

Holmes, Steven. 1 October 2008. Blacks forming a rock-solid bloc behind Obama. *The Washington Post*, A7.

Holtzer, Harry J. 2009. The labor market and young black men: Updating Moynihan's perspective. *The Annals of the American Academy of Political and Social Science* 621:47–69.

Howell, Angela McMillan. 2008. President-elect Obama: His symbolic importance in his own words. *Journal of African American Studies* 13:187–9.

Huffington Post. 15 April 2009a. Obama team tells Jewish leaders: UN Durban text crosses "Red Line." Available from www.huffingtonpost.com.

Huffington Post. 29 April 2009b. Obama's 100 days press conference: Full transcript. Available from www .huffingtonpost.com.

Hunt, Matthew O. 2007. African American, Hispanic, and white beliefs about black/white inequality, 1977–2004. *American Sociological Review* 72:390–415.

Hunt, Matthew O., and David C. Wilson. 2009. Race/ethnicity, perceived discrimination, and beliefs about the meaning of an Obama presidency. *Du Bois Review* 6:173–99.

Hutchings, Vincent. 2009. Paper presented at the conference "Still Two Nations?" 20–21 March, Duke University, Durham, NC.

Ifill, Gwen. 2009. *The breakthrough*. New York, NY: Doubleday.

Inside Cover. 23 July 2009. Limbaugh blasts Obama's reaction to Gates arrest. Available from newsmax.com.

Jeffries, Hasan Kwame. 2009. *Bloody Lowndes*. New York, NY: New York University Press.

Kalscheur, Ben. 2009. Courting color-blind racism: Using perceptions of equal opportunity and the U.S. court system to measure the prevalence of color-blind ideology. MA thesis, University of Wisconsin-Milwaukee.

Kamiya, Gary. 2009. Obama and race: Silence is golden. Available at www.salon.com.

Karenga, Maulana. 20 July 2009. Obama in Africa: Rethinking reality and responsibility. Humanities Net Online. Available from h-net.msu.edu.

Lewis, Amanda E. 2003. *Race in the schoolyard*. Newark, NJ: Rutgers University Press.

Lipsitz, George. 2006. *The possessive investment in whiteness*. Philadelphia, PA: Temple University Press.

Massey, Douglas S. 2007. *Categorically unequal*. New York, NY: Russell Sage Foundation.

McClain, Paula D., Niambi M. Carter, Victoria M. DeFrancesco Soto, Monique L. Lyle, Jeffrey D. Grynaviski, Shayla C. Nunnally, Thomas J. Scotto, J. A. Kendrick, Gerald F. Lackey, and Kendra Davenport Cotton. 2006. Racial distancing in a southern city: Latino immigrants' views of black Americans. *Journal of Politics* 68:571–84.

McClelland, Katherine, and Erika Linnander. 2006. The role of contact and information in racial attitude change among white college students. *Sociological Inquiry* 76:81–115.

McWhorter, John H. 2001. *Losing the race*. New York, NY: Free Press.

Moore, Wendy Leo. 2008. *Reproducing racism*. Lanham, MD: Rowman & Littlefield.

Myers, Kristen. 2005. *Racetalk*. Lanham, MD: Rowman & Littlefield.

Neville, Helen A., M. Nikki Coleman, Jameca Woody Falconer, and Deadre Holmes. 2005. Color-blind racial ideology and psychological false consciousness among African Americans. *Journal of Black Psychology* 31:27–45.

Neville, Helen A., Roderick L. Lilly, Richard M. Lee, Georgia Duran, and LaVonne Browne. 2000. Construction and initial validation of the color-blind racial attitudes scale (CoBRAS). *Journal of Counseling Psychology* 47:59–70.

Noah, Timothy. 10 November 2008. What we didn't overcome. Available from www.slate.com.

Obama, Barack. 27 July 2004. Keynote address, Democratic National Convention. Available from www .obamaspeeches.com.

Obama, Barack. 2006. *The audacity of hope*. New York, NY: Crown.

Obama, Barack. 4 March 2007. Speech at voting rights march commemoration, Selma, AL. Available from www.suntimes.com.

Obama, Barack. 4 November 2008a. Election night victory speech. Grant Park, IL. Available from obamaspeeches.com.

Obama, Barack. 18 March 2008b. A more perfect union. Speech given in Philadelphia, PA. Available from www.obamaspeeches.com.

Oliver, Melvin L., and Thomas M. Shapiro. 2006. *Black wealth/white wealth*. New York, NY: Routledge.

Orwell, George. 1946/1968. In front of your nose. In *The collected essays, journalism, and letters of George Orwell*. New York, NY: Harcourt, Brace & World.

Pager, Devah, and Hannah Shepherd. 2008. The sociology of discrimination. *Annual Review of Sociology* 34:181–209.

Patterson, Orlando. 2004. Culture and continuity. In *Matters of culture: Cultural sociology in practice*, 71–109. New York, NY: Cambridge University Press.

Patterson, Orlando. 26 March 2006. A poverty of the mind. *New York Times*. Available from www.nytimes.com.

Pettigrew, Thomas F. 2009. Paper presented at the conference "Still Two Nations?" March, Duke University, Durham, NC.

Pew Research Center for the People and the Press. 2008. High marks for the campaign, a high bar for Obama. Available from people-press.org.

Picca, Leslie Houts, and Joe R. Feagin. 2007. *Two-faced racism*. New York, NY: Routledge.

Political Bulletin. 24 July 2009. *U.S. News and World Report*. Available from www.usnews.com.

Prager, Jeffrey. 1982. American racial ideology as collective representation. *Ethnic and Racial Studies* 5:99–119.

Price, Melanye T. 2009. *Dreaming blackness*. New York, NY: New York University Press.

Rada, James A., and Tim K. Wulfemeyer. 2005. Color coded. *Journal of Broadcasting and Electronic Media* 49:65–85.

Reed, Adolph. 2008. Obama: Vacuous opportunist. *The Progressive* 72 (5): 14–15.

Reed, Wornie L., and Bertin M. Louis Jr. 2009. No more excuses. *Journal of African American Studies* 13:97–109.

Richeson, Jennifer A., and Richard J. Nussbaum. 2003. The impact of multiculturalism versus color-blindness on racial bias. *Journal of Experimental Social Psychology* 40:417–23.

Royster, Deidre A. 2003. *Race and the invisible hand*. Berkeley, CA: University of California Press.

Ryan, William A. 1976. *Blaming the victim*. New York, NY: Random House.

Sampson, Robert J., and Patrick Sharkey. 2008. Neighborhood selection and the social reproduction of concentrated racial inequality. *Demography* 45:1–29.

Schleef, Debra J. 2006. *Managing elites*. Lanham, MD: Rowman & Littlefield.

Shapiro, Ben. 14 January 2009. Liberals. Available at www.townhall.com.

Shapiro, Thomas. 2004. *The hidden cost of being African American*. New York, NY: Oxford University Press.

Shelton, Jason E., and M. Nicole Coleman. 2009. After the storm. *Social Science Quarterly* 90:480–96.

Smith, Robert C. 1995. *Racism in the post–civil rights era*. Albany, NY: State University of New York Press.

Smith, Rogers M., and Desmond S. King. 2009. Barack Obama and the future of American racial politics. *Du Bois Review* 6:25–35.

Smith, Will. 2008. Appearance on *The Oprah Winfrey Show*. Available from www.oprah.com.

Spanierman, L. B., and M. J. Heppner. 2004. Psychosocial costs of racism to whites scale (PCRW). *Journal of Counseling Psychology* 51:249–62.

Steele, Shelby. 2006. *White guilt*. New York, NY: HarperCollins.

Street, Paul. 2009. *Barack Obama and the future of American politics*. Boulder, CO: Paradigm.

Sullivan, Shannon. 2006. *Revealing whiteness*. Bloomington: Indiana University Press.

Sweeney, Kathryn. 2006. The blame game. *Du Bois Review* 3:161–74.

Taguieff, Pierre-André. 2001. *Force of prejudice*. Minneapolis, MN: University of Minnesota Press.

Tarman, Christopher, and David O. Sears. 2005. The conceptualization and measurement of symbolic racism. *Journal of Politics* 67:731–61.

Turner, Victor. 1967. *The forest of symbols*. Ithaca, NY: Cornell University Press.

Turner, Victor. 1974. *The ritual process*. Ithaca, NY: Cornell University Press.

Twine, Frances Winddance, and Charles Gallagher. 2008. The future of whiteness. *Ethnic and Racial Studies* 31:4–24.

Voltaire. 1759/1929. *Candide*. New York, NY: Literary Guild.

Western, Bruce. 2006. *Punishment and inequality in America*. New York, NY: Russell Sage Foundation.

Wilson, William Julius. 1978. *The declining significance of race*. Chicago, IL: University of Chicago Press.

Wise, Tim J. 2009. *Between Barack and a hard place*. San Francisco, CA: City Lights Books.

Yancy, George. 2008. *Black bodies, white gazes*. Lanham, MD: Rowman & Littlefield.

The "Obama Effect" and White Racial Attitudes

To what extent did the presidential candidacy and election of Barack Obama affect whites' more general perceptions of African Americans? Responses to survey questions in which respondents were asked to place blacks on scales running from "stupid" to "intelligent" and from "lazy" to "hardworking" revealed that whites' views of blacks' intelligence and work ethic have become somewhat more positive, though whites continued to be rated higher on these attributes than were blacks. The fact that negative stereotypes of blacks were least pronounced among younger whites implies that these stereotypes will continue to fade in the future. These data do not constitute proof positive of an "Obama effect" on whites' racial attitudes, but they are largely consistent with that idea.

Keywords: Obama; opinion change; racial attitudes; stereotypes

By
SUSAN WELCH
and
LEE SIGELMAN

Martin Luther King Jr. once asserted that the civil rights movement would change not only the lives of black people, but the very soul of America. Change has been slow, but on election night in 2008, it was evident in the tears of joy shed by African Americans and other Americans who were moved by the election of Barack Obama. The idea that within a few decades an African American would be elected president with the support of millions of whites would probably have seemed just as far-fetched to King as to George Wallace.

Susan Welch is dean of the College of the Liberal Arts and professor of political science at Pennsylvania State University. She is the coauthor, with Lee Sigelman, of Black Americans' Views of Racial Inequality: The Dream Deferred *(Cambridge University Press 1991) and, with Timothy Bledsoe, Lee Sigelman, and Michael Combs, of* Race and Place: Residence and Race Relations in an American City *(Cambridge University Press 2001).*

Lee Sigelman was Columbian College Distinguished Professor of Political Science at George Washington University. He wrote extensively on a wide range of topics in the social sciences. Lee Sigelman died on December 21, 2009, a few months after this article was completed.

DOI: 10.1177/0002716210386302

The election of Barack Obama raises the possibility that the candidacy of an African American for the nation's most powerful office, and of course his subsequent election, might have continued or even accelerated changes that have been occurring in recent decades in white Americans' racial attitudes. The most visible African American political activists and leaders of the past half century—King, Jesse Jackson, Louis Farrakhan, Colin Powell, and now, of course, Obama—have been a diverse lot, but Obama stands out as the most successful member of a new generation of black leaders who have taken an electoral route to national visibility rather than rising through the ranks of the civil rights movement, religious institutions, or, in Powell's case, the military. Has the sudden emergence of Obama—obviously intelligent, extremely articulate, and unostentatiously charismatic—on the national scene prompted whites nationwide to view blacks in a new light or at least accelerated attitudinal changes that were already under way?

Changing Racial Attitudes

The onrush of media attention surrounding Obama's candidacy and election highlighted the changes he seemed to have wrought on public attitudes. Headlines on November 5, 2008, resplendent with phrases such as "Barriers Fall," "Obama Overcomes," "Historic," "Obama Seizes Historic Win," "In Our Lifetime," "Obama in Historic Win," "Face of Change," and "Historic Change," trumpeted a breakthrough in race relations.[1] In a survey conducted immediately after the election, Gallup reported that 71 percent of Americans considered Obama's victory the most important advancement for black Americans in the past century or at least one of the most important (Gallup 2008). A few months later, pollsters reported that the number of both black and white Americans describing race relations as good had increased significantly over the previous year (Stolberg and Connelly 2009).

Aside from media pronouncements that Obama had produced a change in whites' views of blacks, are there other reasons to think that even as prominent a political figure as Obama could have caused much change in whites' attitudes toward blacks in such a short time? Social scientists have offered some reasons for thinking that he could have, but along the way they have also revealed an incomplete understanding of what moves racial attitudes.

Why Do Mass Opinions Change?

The most comprehensive examinations of changes in white Americans' racial attitudes are a series of studies of attitudes toward racial integration that Sheatsley and colleagues have undertaken and those by Schuman and colleagues (Greeley and Sheatsley 1971; Hyman and Sheatsley 1956, 1964; Taylor, Sheatsley, and Greeley 1978; Schuman, Steeh, and Bobo 1985; Schuman et al. 1997). According to these studies, tolerance and support for racial equality rose rapidly among whites from the early 1940s through the early 1970s, at which point the pace of change began to slow. Those who had grown up in the early Jim Crow era of the late nineteenth and early twentieth centuries constituted a substantial part of the American public in the 1940s and 1950s, but by the 1960s, they had begun to pass from the scene. By the mid-1970s, they had dwindled to a minority; and the baby boomers, who came of age politically during the years of the civil rights movement, were replacing them. Because the younger cohorts were replacing the older ones, even if no one moderated his or her attitudes on racial issues, the racial attitudes of white Americans as a group would have become significantly more open. Even the generation that grew up in the era of the supposed "white backlash" and had many of its formative political experiences during the conservative Reagan-Bush years was more liberal on racial issues than the generation that had preceded it. This is not to say that opinions moved uniformly in the direction of liberalization; some did not. For example, whites' opposition to federal intervention in school segregation cases hardened, and whites clung to explanations of persisting black-white socioeconomic inequalities that emphasized blacks' shortcomings rather than the continuing legacy of racism and discrimination.

Influences in addition to cohort replacement were also at work. Many whites reconsidered their previous attitudes toward blacks, though such individual-level change was the secondary dynamic that had distinguished whites' attitudes in more recent years from the attitudes that prevailed in earlier eras. The occurrence of a major event or series of events, the initiation of new policies, or the emergence of new personalities might be covered in the media and become the focus of social movements, interest groups, and political parties, any or all of which seized upon these new opportunities to influence public opinion. For example, during World War II, the fight against Nazism, coupled with appeals by pro-integration groups, led many whites to reconsider their views about equality at home. The brutal treatment of civil rights demonstrators in the South during the 1950s, which the media displayed for the nation and the world to see, produced a further shift toward pro-integration sentiments. Such changes are consistent with theoretical arguments and experimental indications that some racial attitudes, especially those formed on the basis of incomplete or incorrect information, can change when new information is brought into play (Allport 1954; Katz 1991; Sniderman and Piazza 1993).[2] Sheatsley and his colleagues (Hyman and Sheatsley 1956, 1964) found that such attitude changes emerged first among young people, the more highly educated, and northerners. Later, after the Civil Rights Act of 1964 and the civil rights movement, other portions of the white public began to hold more tolerant positions.

Less sudden or dramatic changes than war, protest, policy shifts, and riots have also contributed to the shift toward more tolerant racial attitudes. For example, the gradual growth of the black middle class (Oliver and Shapiro 1995; Pattillo-McCoy 1999), the increase in the number of elected black officials at all levels of government, the growing presence of African Americans in prominent positions in business and the arts (McDermott 2002), and the rise in the political and economic prominence of members of other ethnic groups along with women of various races and ethnicities all have presumably propelled and reinforced the growth of more favorable attitudes toward African Americans.

At the same time, in some ways, attitudes toward black Americans have not changed much in recent decades or have even become marginally less favorable. For example, from 1964 to 1992, despite all the changes in the status of black Americans, whites' mean score on the generic 0 to 100 degree "feeling thermometer" scale of affect toward blacks hovered only 3 points on either side of 60 (Schuman et al. 1997, 184–85). Moreover, whites' agreement with the statement that blacks are not getting ahead because they do not try hard enough increased slightly, and their willingness to pin the blame on generations of slavery and discrimination as causes of persisting racial inequalities decreased slightly (Schuman et al. 1997, 222–24). These attitudes might have been expected to fade with the appearance of more successful African Americans in whites' daily lives, as teachers and business and political leaders, and in the news.

In sum, the experience of the past six decades demonstrates that changes in Americans' racial attitudes have been driven by both demographic changes and specific events and trends. In most cases, these events and trends have moved opinions rather gradually in a more positive direction, but in some arenas, the shift has been minimal or even retrograde.

Prominent Blacks' and Whites' Opinion Changes

Given that many aspects of whites' racial attitudes have been changing slowly but steadily over a lengthy time span, should Obama's candidacy and election be regarded as the kind of dramatic event that could have changed the trajectory of whites' attitudes toward blacks? There can be no doubt that the 2008 election was an extremely salient event or that its outcome was widely regarded as an occasion for celebration (and, for millions of blacks and whites alike, self-congratulation).[3] On one hand, the Obama campaign enhanced the salience of race in general. On the other, his own characteristics in particular—his obvious intelligence, discipline, and interpersonal appeal—were made salient topics for media and public discussion. Daily tracking polls revealed that white prejudice toward blacks did decline during several weeks of the final stages of the campaign (Goldman 2009). As one analyst put it, "Obama is successful, well educated, and cosmopolitan. He seems free of the counterproductive rage, alienation, and self-doubt that are often a toxic by-product of the American Black experience" (Ford 2009, 42). Obama is the type of black political leader who has been historically most popular among whites—one who was not part of the civil rights movement, who accommodates rather than confronts, and who maintains close personal and political ties to whites.

Whereas the most visible black leaders of the 1960s and 1970s were insurgents dedicated to the sweeping reform or, in some cases, even the overthrow, of "the system," the new breed of black leaders sought to advance within—or even to gain control of—the system. . . . This new breed, eschewing the characteristic styles and appeals of black leaders of the 1960s and 1970s, emphasized pragmatism and skills, articulating means and ends that sounded racially and culturally inclusive rather than pitched specifically toward African Americans. (Sigelman 1997, 181)

Of course, no other black elected official in the United States has been nearly as visible or salient as Obama has become. Viewed more broadly, though, Obama is not merely a uniquely prominent black elected official; he is an extraordinarily successful African American with significant white approbation. Precisely because of their conspicuous success, such individuals have all the attributes that are required for the high levels of admiration they evoke among whites to carry over to whites' attitudes toward blacks more generally. However, the situation is not as simple as that, as a sizable body of social psychological research has established.

On one hand, when members of an "in-group" are exposed to positive (high-achieving, well-liked) members of a stigmatized "out-group," their negative stereotypes of the out-group can be moderated or at least become less salient. For example, in a classic study, Bodenhausen et al. (1995) referred to Oprah Winfrey and Michael Jordan in some versions of a questionnaire. In an ostensibly unrelated questionnaire, they queried the same respondents about the sources of racial discrimination in American society. Those to whom these two supersuccessful African Americans had been mentioned expressed greater support for blacks on the second questionnaire. This response pattern "suggests that Obama could indeed lead to more favorable evaluations of blacks overall, to the extent that he represents a successful and well-liked black exemplar" (Peery and Bodenhausen 2009, 78).

On the other hand, the very attributes that distinguish positively viewed out-group members from the rest of their negatively stereotyped out-group may undermine any tendency by the in-group to project their positive attributes onto out-group members in general. The problem is that of subtyping: the tendency to see members of a group who contradict the group stereotype and thus to place them in a separate category (Richards and Hewstone 2001; Dasgupta and Greenwald 2001; Richeson and Trawalter 2005). Thus, while Ford (2009, 42) concedes that "perhaps whites will associate the black race with the elite characteristics of Obama," he considers it more likely "that whites will learn—as Obama's election proves that they are already learning—to distinguish between elite, Obama-like blacks, whom they will treat like an American ethnic group, and the underclass, whom they will continue to treat as a despised and inferior race." The "exceptional" black person (or before that, the "exceptional Negro") has been a staple stereotype in race relations since the slavery era (Phillips 1918), exemplified by the tendency of whites to refer to high-achieving blacks as "a credit to their race"—a term they ostensibly intended as a compliment. By classifying Obama as an exception, prejudiced individuals can rationalize and recognize his obvious intelligence, leadership skills, and work ethic while still clinging to broader negative stereotypes of African Americans.

Finally, the emergence and successes of a highly visible leader such as Obama might have triggered offsetting changes in the attitudes that different subgroups expressed. For example, Obama's candidacy and election might have had a positive impact on racial attitudes among those who were already predisposed to racial equalitarianism but a negative impact on those who were already hostile. To the latter group, Obama's ascension might be seen as threatening, further provoking negative racial attitudes.

Our Analysis

To assess the potential Obama effect on whites' racial attitudes, we searched for appropriate survey items that have been used for many years and were repeated during the 2008 election cycle. The best data source for our purposes was the quadrennial series of American National Election Studies (ANES), which in every presidential election year since 1992 have asked respondents to rate blacks, along with members of several other groups, on a pair of seven-point scales with endpoints labeled "lazy" or "hardworking" and "stupid" or "intelligent."[4] Based on these responses, we examined the attitudes that non-Hispanic whites expressed in the 1992 through 2008 surveys.

Before we turn to the results, let us briefly provide some context from prior research. From the Hunt (2007) study, we know that from 1977 to the 2000 to 2004 period the proportion of whites attributing the black-white socioeconomic gap to blacks' lack of "motivation or willpower to pull themselves out of poverty" decreased from 66 to 50 percent (see also Schuman et al. 1997, 156–57). The trend was encouraging, but when viewed from a different perspective, those responses point toward the tendency, among whites, to feel that blacks as a group are neither amply endowed with, nor severely lacking in, a work ethic. As for whites' perceptions of blacks' intelligence, from the early 1940s through the early 1950s, the percentage of whites who responded that blacks were just as intelligent and "educable" as whites increased from slightly more than 40 to about 70 percent. From there, the trend line rose to 80 percent and remained on that plateau through the mid-1960s (Hyman and Sheatsley 1964, 20).[5] Schuman et al. (1997, 156–57) examined a variant of that question, which asked whether the black-white gap in "jobs, income, and housing" reflected "less in-born ability to learn" among blacks. There was no change in responses to that question in 2004 (see Hunt 2007, especially Table 2). On that item, too, negative stereotypes of blacks lessened over the years, from 1977, when 27 percent of whites saw deficient learning ability as a partial cause of blacks' unequal status, through 2004, when only 10 percent thought this.

The Obama Effect

According to the ANES survey results shown in Figure 1, from 1992 through 2004, white Americans, on average, gave blacks ratings that clustered close to the

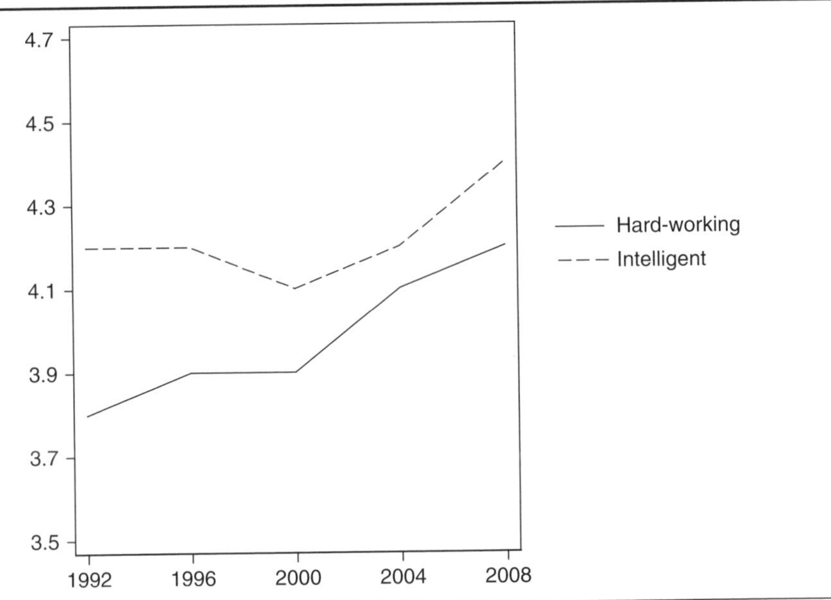

FIGURE 1
Whites' Perceptions of Blacks as Hardworking and Intelligent

NOTE: The means for 2004 and 2008 are significantly different at $p < .05$, one-tailed.

midpoint on the 1 to 7 "lazy" to "hardworking" scale. Before 2004, whites' mean assessment of blacks' work ethic was slightly on the "lazy" side of the neutral point. In 2004, it crossed the midpoint to the "hardworking" side of the scale. Overall, these mean ratings rose slowly from 3.8 in 1992 to 4.1 in 2004. Whites' appraisals of blacks' intelligence were more positive, topping 4.0 in every survey from 1992 through 2004 but never exceeding 4.2. Although these results are not strictly comparable to those summarized in the immediately preceding paragraph, in combination, they portray whites' attitudes as (1) falling close to the midpoint on both scales, (2) rising somewhat in recent years to points slightly above the scale midpoints, and (3) changing relatively little from one quadrennial survey to the next.

This brings us to 2008. Whites' responses to the "hardworking" item rose slightly from 4.1 to 4.2, and, after a period of little change from 1992 to 2004, their mean assessment of blacks' intelligence increased from 4.2 in 2004 to 4.4 in 2008.

If we were to leave the analysis at this point, we would conclude that Obama's emergence, candidacy, and election appear to have had modest effects on whites' assessments of blacks' work ethic and intelligence. Obviously, we must provide a caveat that we cannot "prove" that Obama alone, or even Obama in conjunction with other factors, caused this modest change. His emergence is the logical and most likely reason, but our analysis is not definitive. The overall data do not adequately convey the dynamics of the changes in whites' attitudes that Obama seems to have wrought—dynamics that lie beneath the surface of the aggregate trends

FIGURE 2
Whites' Perceptions of Blacks as Hardworking and Intelligent, by Cohort

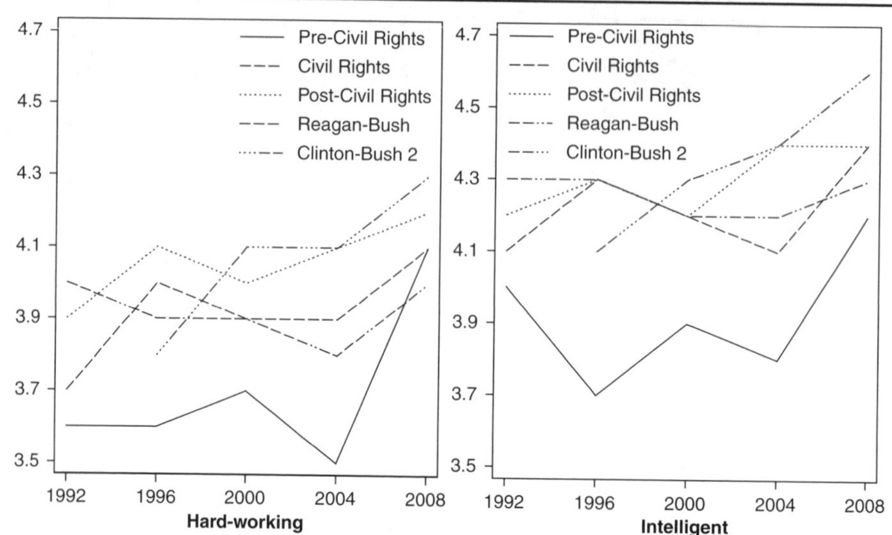

NOTE: The means for 2004 and 2008 are significantly different at $p < .05$, one-tailed, except for the civil rights and post–civil rights cohorts on the "hardworking" and item and the post–civil rights and Reagan-Bush cohorts on the "intelligent" item.

shown in Figure 1. However, further examination of the patterns of change underlying the overall data does provide support for our preliminary conclusion.

What were these dynamics? As a starting point, we expected young whites to be especially susceptible to the Obama effect. Just as it was the youngest generation that first began to accept the idea of legalized racial equality in the 1940s and led the way toward liberalization of racial attitudes thereafter, it seemed likely that the first black president's greatest attitudinal impact would fall on younger whites.

Figure 2 indicates that favorable assessments of blacks' work ethic increased in all five of the cohorts analyzed here,[6] but these increases stood out in certain cohorts. Among these was the youngest cohort, which consisted of those who had come of age during the presidency of Bill Clinton or George W. Bush. Having fewer deeply ingrained negative racial stereotypes than their older counterparts and confronted by a dynamic young candidate who promised to change the established political order, young people flocked to Obama. Their views of African Americans in general were open to being shaped by the first "new" national political leader that they encountered—just as, nearly 80 years ago, young people's political views were shaped by their first vote for Franklin Roosevelt.

Not as easy to explain, though, is the even more marked positive change among members of the pre–civil rights movement cohort, all of whom were at least 73 years old in 2008. Among members of this cohort, the mean score on the "hardworking"

FIGURE 3

Whites' Perceptions of Blacks as Hardworking and Intelligent, by Party

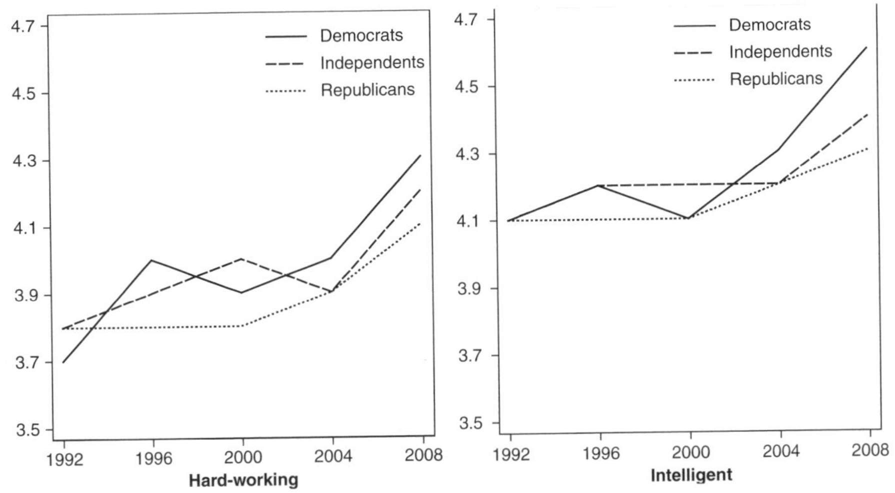

NOTE: The means for 2004 and 2008 are significantly different at $p < .05$, one-tailed, except for Independents on the "intelligent" item.

scale rose from 3.5 in 2004 to 4.1 in 2008. Perhaps because Obama so clearly defied the racial stereotypes that had prevailed when older whites were growing up, he directly challenged their prejudices and caused many of them to rethink their image of blacks in general.

In 2004, members of the pre–civil rights cohort had expressed the least favorable views of blacks' intelligence, but in 2008, their views moved in line with those of the other cohorts. Notable once again was the continuation of the change in the youngest cohort to the extent that by 2008, the mean score for the Clinton–Bush 2 cohort on the intelligence scale was 4.6—the highest that any cohort has recorded on either scale. To a considerable degree, then, the aggregate positive changes we glimpsed in Figure 1 were driven largely by the youngest and oldest white cohorts.

One possible explanation for the change in the oldest cohort is that the cohort is shrinking. Although older people do not change their attitudes individually, an involuntary self-selection may have been operating, for it is possible that individuals who are more tolerant live longer. Mortality is selective on education and cognitive functioning as well as on health. Thus, it may be selective on intolerance, directly or indirectly, because tolerance is related to education and cognitive functioning. If that were so, the older generation would become more tolerant as the number of its members shrinks.[7]

In Figure 3, we show the trends for Democrats, Independents, and Republicans. From 1992 through 2004, these three groups closely tracked one another in their perceptions of blacks' work ethic and intelligence. That continued to hold true in

FIGURE 4

Whites' Perceptions of Blacks as Hardworking and Intelligent, by Region

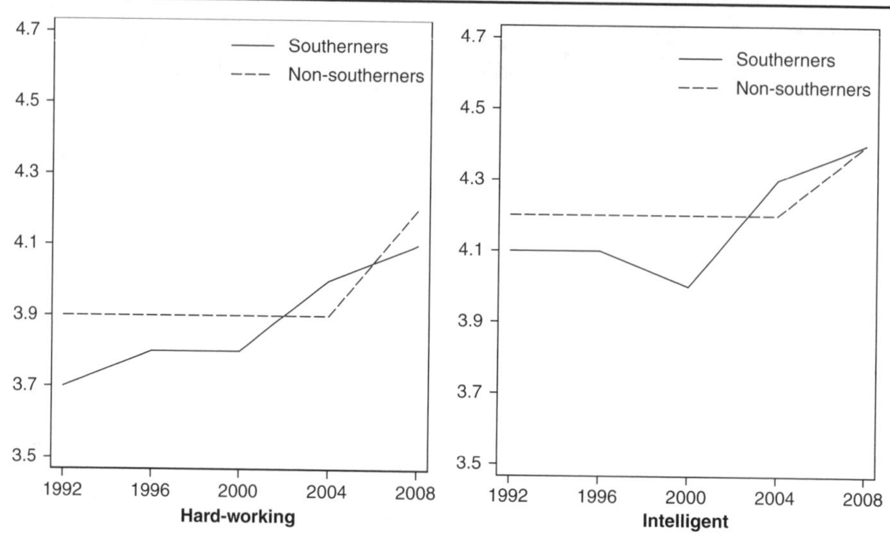

NOTE: The "hardworking" means for 2004 and 2008 are significantly different at $p < .05$, one-tailed, for southerners; and the means for 2004 and 2008 are significantly different at $p < .05$, one-tailed, for nonsoutherners.

2008 for scores on the "hardworking" scale, which turned upward for all three groups alike; consequently, the partisan gap in these perceptions was only 0.2, about the same as it had been in earlier ANES surveys. Perceptions of blacks' intelligence also increased in all three groups in 2008 but did so most rapidly among Democrats, who already held the most favorable images of blacks. The implication of these 2004 to 2008 comparisons is that Obama's candidacy and election enhanced whites' perceptions of blacks—especially white Democrats' perceptions.

The long-term trends for both southerners and those from other parts of the country were positive, but what stands out in Figure 4 is that for whites living outside the South, this change was driven entirely by the 2004 to 2008 jump. We also decomposed the ANES samples according to levels of educational attainment. Of course, those with more education have traditionally expressed more egalitarian racial attitudes (see Glaser 2001), but the trend lines shown in Figure 5 reveal similar patterns of change among those with a high school degree or less education, those who attended college, and college graduates. Predictably, whites whose formal education ended with or was short of high school graduation were less likely than more highly educated whites to view blacks favorably on either scale. But again, what stands out is the marked positive change from 2004 to 2008.

FIGURE 5

Whites' Perceptions of Blacks as Hardworking and Intelligent, by Education

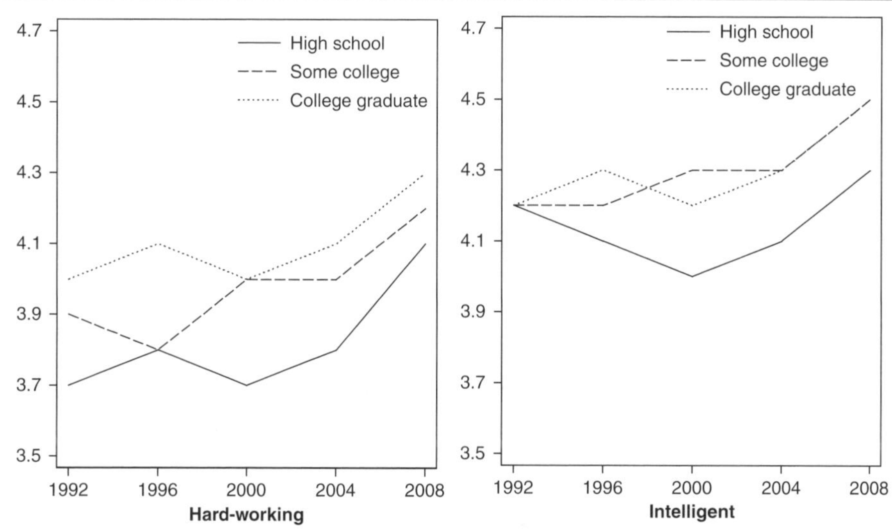

NOTE: The means for 2004 and 2008 are significantly different at $p < .05$, one-tailed, except for those with some college education. "High school" includes those who did not graduate from high school.

Conclusions

We began with the expectation that the candidacy, nomination, and election of Obama might have affected white Americans' attitudes toward black Americans—presumably not a truly fundamental effect, given all that has come before in the history of race relations in this country but a perceptible effect nonetheless. That expectation has largely been borne out. Between 2004 and 2008, whites' views of blacks' work ethic and intelligence did become somewhat more positive. Because whites' racial attitudes, as measured by the two indicators employed here, had been growing more positive since 1992, the Obama effect did not change the direction in which whites' attitudes had been heading. Nevertheless, Obama's emergence as an important figure in American politics, his candidacy, and his election did seem to accelerate that trend (as well as reflect it). Thus, Obama's pursuit of and election to the nation's highest office can be seen as one of those historical events—such as World War II, the civil rights movement, and the passage of the Civil Rights Act of 1964—that move mass public opinion in a more equalitarian direction.

Of course, we have no data that definitively establish that the attitudinal changes we have observed were products of an Obama effect rather than some other factor or combination of factors. Our evidence is indirect, and our causal interpretation of these results is an inference that we have drawn rather than a result that we have firmly established.

The positive trajectory of whites' attitudes toward black people—and especially certain subgroups' attitudes toward black people—does not mean that whites now equate blacks to whites on intelligence and work ethic. Whites' increasingly positive reactions to blacks on the two dimensions considered here should not obscure the fact that they rated blacks 0.7 to 0.9 percent lower than whites on the 1 to 7 "hardworking" and "intelligent" scales. Thus, whites still perceive blacks less favorably than whites. However, the gaps between whites' views of blacks and whites on these attributes have been narrowing somewhat over time, just as they have for other views about black and white characteristics (Hunt 2007). Fiske et al. (2009, 89) noted that "negative racial stereotypes do not readily reverse, although they may fade from prominence," and fading is generally a long-drawn-out process.

Our subgroup analysis suggests that cohort replacement will continue to be a major force propelling liberalization of whites' racial attitudes. Younger whites have the most equalitarian attitudes in assessing traits of intelligence and work ethic, views that should continue to shape their overall stance toward African Americans. The other generations lag behind, most notably, the pre–civil rights movement generation.

Whether the Obama effect will prove transitory or permanent is impossible to foresee. After all, the ANES survey was conducted at the height of Obama's popularity, after the intraparty rift had healed, in the midst of a period of good feeling, and before the real world of presidential decision-making had imposed casualties among those who had supported Obama or among those at least willing to give him an initial benefit of the doubt. If Obama proves to be a successful president, one might reasonably expect his impact to persist beyond the presidential honeymoon. But given the difficulties of his presidency, at least in the first two years, the halo effect he appears to have cast on whites' perceptions of blacks in general might well fade.

Notes

1. See www.diversityinc.com/article/4730/Obamas-Victory-Headlines-From-Around-the-Nation/ for a display of election headlines.

2. Another possible source of attitudinal shifts is age—individuals might change their views as they get older. However, there is little evidence that this occurs in any social or political realm (Krosnick and Alwin 1989; Schuman et al. 1997).

3. Analyzing some nine million first-person sentences that contained the word "feel" and appeared in blogs from midsummer 2005 through midsummer 2009, Dodds and Danforth (2009) found that the happiest day in that four-year period was election day 2008—a result driven to a considerable degree by the elevated usage of "proud."

4. The items were as follows: "Now I have some questions about different groups in our society. I'm going to show you a seven-point scale on which the characteristics of the people in a group can be rated. In the first statement a score of 1 means that you think almost all of the people in that group tend to be 'hardworking.' A score of 7 means that almost all of the people in the group are 'lazy.' A score of 4 means that you think that most people in the group are not closer to one end or the other, and of course you may

choose any number in between. . . . Where would R[espondent] rate the group's work ethic: Blacks?" "The next set asks if people in each group tend to be unintelligent or tend to be intelligent. . . . Where would you rate the group's intelligence: Blacks?" To avoid confusion, we flipped the scoring of responses on the "hardworking" item so that on both it and the "intelligence" item, a higher score would indicate a more positive assessment of blacks. According to Fiske et al. (2009), the two fundamental dimensions of social cognition are warmth and competence. Unfortunately, hardworking or lazy and intelligent or unintelligent do not mesh neatly with the warmth and competence dimensions. Whites' 0 to 100 "feeling thermometer" ratings of blacks are also available for the entire 1992 to 2008 period. However, we chose not to use those responses because we considered the 2004 scores suspect. They were much higher than in any other year, and that difference held for whites' ratings not only of blacks but of other groups as well, such as Jews.

5. Southern whites' responses rose from 20 to 50 percent and then to slightly less than 60 percent during this time; nonsouthern whites went from 50 to 80 percent and then 85 percent.

6. Following the lead of Schuman et al. (1997, 196–237), we grouped respondents into four cohorts: pre–civil rights movement (those who turned 18 before 1953); civil rights movement (those who turned 18 between 1954 and 1965); post–civil rights movement (those who turned 18 between 1966 and 1980); and Reagan-Bush (those who turned 18 between 1981 and 1992). We added a fifth cohort, Clinton–Bush 2, composed of those who turned 18 between 1993 and 2008.

7. To our knowledge, this possibility has not been systematically examined, though there has been considerable research on the stability of attitudes into old age; see, for example, Alwin and Krosnick (1991). Conversations with Duane Alwin stimulated our thinking on this point.

References

Allport, Gordon W. 1954. *The nature of prejudice*. Cambridge, MA: Addison-Wesley.

Alwin, Duane, and Jon Krosnick. 1991. Aging, cohorts, and the stability of sociopolitical attitudes over the life span. *American Journal of Sociology* 97 (1): 169–95.

Bodenhausen, Galen V., Norbert Schwarz, Herbert Bless, and Michaela Wänke. 1995. Effects of atypical exemplars on racial beliefs: Enlightened racism or generalized appraisals? *Journal of Experimental Social Psychology* 31 (1): 48–63.

Dasgupta, Nilianjana, and Anthony G. Greenwald. 2001. On the malleability of automatic attitudes: Combating automatic prejudice with images of admired and disliked individuals. *Journal of Personality and Social Psychology* 81 (5): 800–814.

Dodds, Peter S., and Christopher M. Danforth. 2009. Measuring the happiness of large-scale written expression: Songs, blogs, and presidents. *Journal of Happiness Studies* 11:441–56. Available from www.springerlink.com/content/g4223k018g44/ (accessed 30 August 2010).

Fiske, Susan T., Hilary B. Bergsieker, Ann Marie Russell, and Lyle Williams. 2009. Images of black Americans: Then, "them," and now, "Obama!" *Du Bois Review* 6 (1): 83–101.

Ford, Richard T. 2009. Barack is the new black: Obama and the promise/threat of the post–civil rights era. *Du Bois Review* 6 (1): 37–48.

Gallup. 2008. Available from www.gallup.com/poll/111817/americans-see-obama-election-race-relations-milestone.aspx.

Glaser, James. 2001. The preference puzzle: Educational differences in racial-political attitudes. *Political Behavior* 23 (4): 313–34.

Goldman, Seth K. 2009. Effects of television coverage of the 2008 presidential campaign on white racial prejudice. PhD diss. proposal, Annenberg School for Communication, University of Pennsylvania, Philadelphia.

Greeley, Andrew, and Paul B. Sheatsley. 1971. Attitudes toward racial integration. *Scientific American* 225:12–19.

Hunt, Matthew O. 2007. African American, Hispanic, and white beliefs about black/white inequality, 1977–2004. *American Sociological Review* 72 (3): 390–415.

Hyman, Herbert, and Paul B. Sheatsley. 1956. Attitudes toward desegregation. *Scientific American* 195:35–39.

Hyman, Herbert, and Paul B. Sheatsley. 1964. Attitudes toward desegregation. *Scientific American* 211:16–23.

Katz, Irwin. 1991. Gordon Allport's "The nature of prejudice." *Political Psychology* 12 (1): 125–57.

Krosnick, Jon, and Duane Alwin. 1989. Aging and susceptibility to attitude change. *Journal of Personality and Psychology* 57 (3): 416–25.

McDermott, Monica. 2002. Trends in the race and ethnicity of eminent Americans. *Sociological Forum* 17 (1): 137–60.

Oliver, Melvin, and Thomas Shapiro. 1995. *Black wealth/white wealth: A new perspective on racial inequality*. New York, NY: Routledge.

Pattillo-McCoy, Mary. 1999. *Black picket fences: Privilege and peril among the black middle class*. Chicago, IL: University of Chicago Press.

Peery, Destiny, and Galen V. Bodenhausen. 2009. Ambiguity and ambivalence in the voting booth and beyond: A social-psychological perspective on racial attitudes and behavior in the Obama era. *Du Bois Review* 6 (1): 71–82.

Phillips, Ulrich Bonnell. 1918. *American Negro slavery: A survey of the supply, employment, and control of Negro labor as determined by the plantation régime*. New York, NY: D. Appleton and Company.

Richards, Zoeë, and Miles Hewstone. 2001. Subtyping and subgrouping: Processes for the prevention and promotion of stereotype change. *Personality and Social Psychology Review* 5 (1): 52–73.

Richeson, Jennifer A., and Sophie Trawalter. 2005. On the categorization of admired and disliked exemplars of admired and disliked racial groups. *Journal of Personality and Social Psychology* 89 (4): 517–30.

Schuman, Howard, Charlotte Steeh, and Lawrence Bobo. 1985. *Racial trends in America*. Cambridge, MA: Harvard University Press.

Schuman, Howard, Charlotte Steeh, Lawrence Bobo, and Maria Krysan. 1997. *Racial attitudes in America*. Cambridge, MA: Harvard University Press.

Sigelman, Lee. 1997. Blacks, whites, and the changing of the guard in black political leadership. In *Racial attitudes in the 1990s*, eds. Steven Tuch and Jack Martin, 177–200. Westport, CT: Praeger.

Sniderman, Paul, and Thomas Piazza. 1993. *The scar of race*. Cambridge, MA: Belknap Press.

Stolberg, Sheryl, and Marjorie Connelly. 27 April 2009. Obama is nudging views on race, a survey finds. *New York Times*.

Taylor, Garth, Paul Sheatsley, and Andrew Greeley. 1978. Attitudes toward racial integration. *Scientific American* 238:42–49.

In Remembrance

The American Academy of Political and Social Science notes with great sadness the untimely passing of its Executive Director, Phyllis Kaniss, on December 17, 2010, after a long struggle with cancer. Phyllis was admired and loved by all who knew her, both inside and outside the Academy. In many ways, she was the heart and soul of the Academy, the person with whom fellows and board members interacted most frequently. She was always full of enthusiasm and energy and was instrumental in repositioning the Academy for the digital age. She was the person who shepherded the Daniel Patrick Moynihan Prize into existence. She oversaw the redesign of the Academy's Web site and personally launched its blog and innovated podcasts of important Academy events. She combined warmth, ebullience, and a wry sense of humor with superb judgment, incisive organizational skills, and a creative intelligence that envisioned a pathway to the future for all things related to the Academy. She was the glue that held the whole operation together and it is difficult to contemplate moving forward without her. Through her vision and effort, the Academy grew in stature and visibility and her personal touch will be deeply missed by everyone associated with the Academy. The officers, staff, board, and fellows of the American Academy of Political and Social Science offer sincere condolences to her husband Paul Wheeling and sons Josh and Max. We join you in sorrow at her passing but celebrate the joy she brought to everyone in life.

DOI: 10.1177/0002716211398767

Stay up-to-date with the latest research

Sign up for FREE Journal Email Alerts
http://online.sagepub.com/cgi/alerts

Register on **SAGE Journals Online** and start receiving…

Content Alerts

Receive table of contents alerts when a new issue is published.

OnlineFirst Alerts

Receive notification when forthcoming articles are published online before they are scheduled to appear in print.

Announcements

Receive need-to-know information about a journal such as calls for papers, special issue notices, and events.

CiteTrack Alerts

Receive notification for citations and corrections to selected articles.

Search Alerts

Create custom fielded boolean search alerts across one or more journals.

Also available

RSS Feeds

RSS Feeds are also available on each journal's homepage and will be sent directly to your web page or RSS Reader. Available for the following content:

- Current issue
- Recent issues
- Most Frequently Read Articles
- Most Frequently Cited Articles

SAGE journals online
http://online.sagepub.com

Award-winning & authoritative reference at your fingertips...

JOURNAL AUTHORS
Help your work be discovered, read, used and cited

The search engine is now the first port of call for many researchers. Today, Google and Google Scholar are the top ways in which researchers find your article online. Taking some simple steps will help optimize your article for search engines.

Search engines use secret, complex mathematical algorithms that change every month to keep their search results as accurate as possible. They take into account more than 100 factors and do not disclose the weighting or importance of each.

FIVE SIMPLE STEPS TO HELP INCREASE DISCOVERABILITY

Write naturally but repeat key phrases in the abstract
Imagine the words and phrases that you would search for if you wanted to find your paper online and use them repeatedly but keep it natural. Google may un-index your article if you go overboard on the repetition.

Get the title right
The main key phrase for your topic should be in your article title. Make sure your title is descriptive, unambiguous, accurate and reads well. People search on key phrases not just single words (e.g. 'women's health' not 'health').

Choose your key words carefully
Include your main three or four key phrases and add in another three or four key words.

Pay extra attention to writing your abstract
The better written your abstract, the better chance your article will appear high in the search results rankings. Researchers will rarely investigate beyond the first 20 results from a search so getting in the top results is vital to your work being discovered.

Visit SAGE for more tips
For more information on how to make your article more discoverable, visit
www.sagepub.com/authorgateway and click Maximizing Readership.